Skye and North West Highlands Sea Kayaking

Doug Cooper

PESDA PRESS
WWW.PESDAPRESS.COM

First published in Great Britain by Pesda Press 2017

Tan y Coed Canol

Ceunant

Caernarfon

LL55 4RN

Wales

Copyright © 2017 Doug Cooper

ISBN 9781906095574

The Author asserts the moral right to be identified as the author of this work.

All rights reserved. No part of this publication may be reproduced or transmitted, in any form or by any means, electronic or mechanical, including photocopying, recording or otherwise, without the prior written permission of the Publisher.

Contains Ordnance Survey data © Crown copyright and database right 2017

Maps by Bute Cartographic

Printed in Poland, www.lfbookservices.co.uk

Foreword

Being a West Coast Boy, I am biased. The North West of Scotland is quite simply the best place to paddle a sea kayak in the world. I know that this is a big statement, but I can speak with reasonable authority having lived here, on the Isle of Skye, for over sixteen years, paddling almost every day and guiding people to many of the places featured in this guidebook. I've also paddled extensively around the world in the northern and southern hemispheres; nowhere else offers such variety. From gently rolling fields to monster cliffs, from sea stacks to fishing villages, and from historic ruins to exposed headlands, it has all of this and more, much more.

As a youngster, our family holidays were always in the out-of-the-way places you'll find within this guidebook, mostly by the water in order that my brother and I could kayak. I have kayaked on the sea, in these waters, for well over forty years and still find new things to keep my interest.

Ardnamurchan Point to Cape Wrath, the names of the headlands at either end of the area contained within these pages, even have their own section in the weather forecast. There are islands galore, hidden beaches, tide races, great places to enjoy the local seafood and amazing people to meet. All of this set within a fantastic, variable culture of Norse and Gaelic influence that go to make this an area you, the reader, will return to time and again. If you like traditional music keep a look out, or an ear tuned, for the many small ceilidhs that happen throughout the year in almost every village you will visit.

Of course there are some places described here that are not for everyone, but such is the beauty of our sport that there is something for everyone, no matter their level of skill or commitment. The wildlife is varied and abundant as is the weather, which can be very changeable in a short timescale.

Enjoy Doug's writing, enjoy the paddling and enjoy the North West of Scotland.

Gordon Brown
Isle of Skye

Contents

Foreword 3
Contents 4
How to Use the Guide 6
About the Author 8
Acknowledgments 9
Scottish Outdoor Access Code 10
Important Notice 11

FAR NORTH WEST 13

1 Cape Wrath 15
2 Loch Laxford 21
3 Handa Island 25
4 Scourie to Kylesku 29
5 Loch Glendhu & Loch Glencoul 33
6 Eddrachillis Bay & Oldany Island 39
7 Point of Stoer 45
8 Loch Inver & Achmelvich 49
9 Rubha Coigeach 53
10 Summer Isles – North 57
11 Summer Isles – South 61
12 Isle Martin & Loch Broom 65

WESTER ROSS 69

13 Cailleach Head 71
14 Gruinard Island 75
15 Greenstone Point & Loch Ewe 79
16 Rubha Rèidh 85
17 Loch Gairloch & Longa Island 89
18 Shieldaig & Torridon 93
19 Applecross Peninsula 97
20 Crowlin Islands 103
21 Plockton & The Black Islands 107

SKYE AND RAASAY 111

22 Inside Passage 113
23 Raasay and Rona 119
24 Kilt Rock 123
25 Rubha Hunish 127

26	Little Minch & the Shiant Islands	133
27	Fladda-chùain	139
28	Waternish Point & the Ascrib Islands	145
29	Loch Dunvegan	149
30	Dunvegan Head	153
31	Neist Point	157
32	Loch Bracadale	161
33	Talisker	165
34	Loch Scavaig & Soay – 'Cuillin Magic'	169
35	Strathaird Peninsula & Spar Cave	173
36	Loch Eishort	177
37	Point of Sleat	181
38	Kyle Rhea	185

SOUND OF SLEAT TO ARDNAMURCHAN ... 191

39	Loch Duich & Eilean Donan Castle	193
40	Loch Hourn	197
41	Loch Nevis	201
42	Sound of Sleat	205
43	Morar & Arisaig	209
44	Sound of Arisaig	213
45	Loch Ailort	217
46	Eilean Shona & Castle Tioram	221
47	Ardnamurchan Point	225

THE SMALL ISLES ... 229

48	Eigg & Muck	231
49	Rum	237
50	Canna & Sanday	243

APPENDICES ... 249

A	HM Coastguard and Emergency Services	249
B	Weather Information	249
C	Mean Tide Ranges	250
D	Glossary of Gaelic Words	250
E	Trip Planning Route Card – User's Guide	253
	Index of Place Names	257

How to Use the Guide

To use the guide you will need an up-to-date tide table for the relevant area, the appropriate Ordnance Survey maps and the knowledge to use them. For some of the open crossings the appropriate admiralty chart can be useful.

Each of the trip chapters is set out into seven sections:

Tidal & route information – A quick reference for all the 'must know' information with which to plan the trip.

Introduction – This is designed to give a brief overview of what to expect from the trip and to whet the appetite.

Description – This provides further detail and information on the trip including the coastline, launching/landing points, the wildlife and environment, historical information and places of interest to visit.

Tides & weather – Further information on how best to plan the trip, which takes the tides, weather and local knowledge into consideration.

Map of route – This provides a visual outline of the route's start/finish points, landing places, points of interest, alternative start/finish points or paddling route and tidal information.

Additional information – This section provides further information (including admiralty charts and other useful resources) that will complement the trip, or be of interest in the local area.

Variations – This final section provides ideas for adapting the suggested route to work better in certain conditions, or so it can be extended or shortened to meet a group's needs.

Using the Tidal & route information

Each route begins with an overview of pertinent details with the following information: grade of difficulty, trip name, route symbols, distance, required Ordnance Survey map number, and trip number.

Grade A | Relatively easy landings with escape routes easily available. Offering relative shelter from extreme conditions and ocean swell. Some tidal movement may be found, but easy to predict with no major tidal races or overfalls.

Grade B | Some awkward landings, and sections of coastline with no escape routes, should be expected. Tidal movement, tidal races, overfalls, crossings, ocean swell and surf may be found on these trips. They will also be exposed to the weather and associated conditions.

Grade C | These trips will have difficult landings and will have no escape routes for long sections of the trip. Fast tidal movement, tidal races, overfalls, extended crossings, ocean swell and surf may be found on all of these trips. They will be very exposed to the weather and sea state, therefore require detailed planning and paddlers competent in rough water conditions. The journey may require good conditions for the trip to be viable.

Distance	Total distance for the trip.
OS Sheet	Number of Ordnance Survey 1:50,000 Landranger map required.
Tidal Port	The port for which tide timetables will be required to work out the tidal streams.
Start	△ map symbol, name and six-figure grid reference of starting point.
Finish	◯ map symbol, name and six-figure grid reference of finishing point.
HW/LW	The high and/or low water time difference between local ports nearest to the trip and the tidal port.
Tidal Times	Location or area of tidal stream movement, the direction to which the tidal stream flows and the time it starts flowing in relation to the tidal port high water.
Max Rate Sp	The areas in which the tidal streams are fastest and the maximum speed in knots attained on the average spring tide.
Coastguard	Name of relevant Coastguard Station, their telephone number and when they announce the inshore weather forecast over the VHF radio on channel 16.

MAP SYMBOLS

About the Author
Doug Cooper

Doug works at Scotland's National Outdoor Training Centre, Glenmore Lodge, where he works as a Level 5 Coach in Sea and White Water. He has the fantastic job of taking people to remote and spectacular coastlines and rivers, then helping them improve their paddling skills and understanding. Many of these days on the sea at work are based in the North West Highlands of Scotland, which provide a great office on work days and an even better playground on days off. When not out on the water, Doug can be found in the mountains at work as a Mountain and Ski Instructor or at play in search of new crags or fresh powder tracks.

As much as Doug loves introducing people to new environments and challenging their skills, it is his days off, personal adventures and expeditions that he lives for. He has sea kayaked extensively around the world including Greenland, Alaska, Iceland, Norway, Ireland, Corsica, Croatia, Sardinia and Greece, and has always got a new destination and adventure planned.

Doug is also co-author of *Scottish Sea Kayaking* and author of *North and East Coasts of Scotland Sea Kayaking*, *Sea Kayak Handling* and *Rough Water Handling*; all published by Pesda Press.

So if it involves discovering new remote parts of the world, having an adventure or helping friends and clients; Doug will have a smile on his face and most definitely be having fun.

Doug Cooper

Acknowledgments

I would like to thank all those who have contributed photographs, shared local knowledge, accompanied me on paddling trips or just been part of my sea kayaking journey over the years. It is the time spent with many friends and clients out on the sea in the North West Highlands and Skye over many years that has evolved my love for and knowledge of this very special area.

Particular thanks need to go to my wife, Lara, who never falters in her support, is always there on the journeys and is always prepared to be in front of, or behind, the camera lens.

Thanks need to go to Pete Astles at Peak UK who has supported me for many years in ensuring I have the best equipment to wear while enjoying my sea kayaking and other paddling. I would also like to thank P&H Sea Kayaks who have made sure I have the world's best sea kayaks to take me on my journeys around the Scottish coastlines and beyond.

Finally, thanks are due to Franco Ferrero and his team at Pesda Press. Yet again, great support and a great book!

Photographs

A special thanks to those who helped with any of the photographs, whether that was in front of or behind the lens. Without these the book would not be what it is. All photographs are by Doug and Lara Cooper unless otherwise acknowledged in the accompanying captions.

Scottish Outdoor Access Code

Access to the outdoors in Scotland is encouraged; visitors and locals have a right of responsible access. Scottish Natural Heritage (SNH) is responsible for promoting and publicising the Scottish Outdoor Access Code (SOAC).

Areas to where you have the right of access are not shown on Ordnance Survey maps, or any other map in Scotland. The Scottish Outdoor Access Code deals with land and freshwater access. This is pertinent to the sea kayaker, as you have to gain access to the sea over land or down a river and then again land to camp, walk or rest. You are completely free to kayak on the sea.

The Scottish Outdoor Access Code is based on three principles, and these apply to the public and to land managers.

RESPECT THE INTERESTS OF OTHER PEOPLE

Acting with courtesy, consideration and awareness is very important. If you are exercising access rights, make sure that you respect the privacy, safety and livelihoods of those living or working in the outdoors, and the needs of other people enjoying the outdoors. If you are a land manager, respect people's use of the outdoors, and their need for a safe and enjoyable visit.

CARE FOR THE ENVIRONMENT

If you are exercising access rights, look after the places you visit and enjoy, and leave the land as you find it. If you are a land manager, help maintain the natural and cultural features which make the outdoors attractive to visit and enjoy.

TAKE RESPONSIBILITY FOR YOUR OWN ACTIONS

If you are exercising access rights, remember that the outdoors cannot be made risk-free and act with care at all times for people's safety.

GETTING MORE ADVICE AND INFORMATION

The Scottish Outdoor Access Code cannot cover every possible situation, setting or activity. Free information and advice on access rights and responsibilities, and on who to contact in your local authority, is available online at:

www.outdooraccess-scotland.com

In addition to this, further information about responsible use of the environment while sea kayaking can be found on the Scottish Canoe Association's website (www.canoescotland.org/where-go/protecting-environment) and Scottish Natural Heritage's website (www.snh.gov.uk).

Important Notice

As with many outdoor activities that take place in remote and potentially hostile environments, technical ability, experience and good planning are essential. The sea is one of the most committing and unforgiving environments; it should be treated with the constant respect that it deserves.

This guide is designed to provide information that will inspire the sea kayaker to venture into this amazing environment; however it cannot provide the essential ingredients of ability, experience and good planning. Before venturing out on any of the trips described in this book, ensure that your knowledge and ability are appropriate to the seriousness of the trip. The book is purely a guide to provide information about sea kayaking trips. For the additional essential knowledge of safety at sea, personal paddling skills, environmental considerations and tidal planning, the author recommends gaining appropriate training and advice from experienced and qualified individuals.

WARNING

Sea kayaking is inherently a potentially dangerous sport. Users of this guide should take the appropriate precautions before undertaking any of the trips. The information supplied in this book has been thoroughly researched; however the author can take no responsibility if tidal times differ or if the information supplied is not sufficient for the conditions on the day. Conditions can change quickly and dramatically on the sea, and there is no substitute for good judgment and personal risk assessment during the planning stages of a sea trip, or out on the water. This guide cannot replace or diminish the need for these essential skills. The decision on whether to go out sea kayaking or not, and of the consequences arising from that decision, remain yours and yours alone.

Enjoying Handa Island, the jewel in the crown of the Far North West

Far North West

Introduction

The sea kayaking in the far North West is about as remote as you can get in mainland Britain, and in this it makes it a very special place to visit. The effort to get there is more than paid off by its unique and rugged beauty, and once visited it will often lead to a lifelong love affair! The coastline boasts some of Scotland's most iconic headlands, Cape Wrath and the Point of Stoer being the classics. Tucked away amongst the rugged cliffs are some of Scotland's most renowned beaches. Sandwood Bay is the best known but Achmelvich and Clachtoll are not to be missed. The sea stacks of this area are equally famous, Stoer, Handa and Am Buachaille being the highlights.

In addition to this fabulous coastline, the islands of the North West offer an incredible playground for the sea kayaker and are home to a wealth of wildlife. Handa with its cliffs, caves and sea stacks is a must and the Summer Isles, with the more sheltered environment they can offer, are many a sea kayaker's favourite. The lochs of Laxford, Glencoul and Glendhu also provide shelter and an opportunity to paddle in amongst some of the area's majestic mountains.

Inland from the sea, the mountains of the North West Highlands are unlike any in the British Isles. They rise dramatically out of the surrounding rugged low-lying landscape, their shapes providing the sea kayaker with an amazing view. Nestled between the sea and these impressive mountains lie a number of welcoming towns and villages where food and refreshments can be enjoyed while exploring the area. Ullapool is the unofficial capital of the North West Highlands and always a great place to visit, but Lochinver and Achiltibuie also provide plenty of choice for those wishing to eat, drink or stay for a while.

Tides and weather

The far North West sits beyond the natural shelter that the Outer Hebrides offers much of the west coast of Scotland. The swell will require greater consideration when planning than in many other areas on the west coast of Scotland. Much of the coastline is remote and access is limited, with exposure to any wind from most directions. For many of the trips the combination of exposure to wind and swell will make them challenging to complete; however the area also offers plenty of sheltered alternatives.

The tidal streams in the area are generally confined to the major headlands, along with a couple of narrow loch entrances. It is therefore easy to choose trips to suit the level of tidal planning required, with plenty of tidal as well as non-tidal options.

Stack Clò Kearvaig, Cape Wrath

Cape Wrath

No. 1 | Grade C | 41km | OS Sheet 9

Tidal Port	Ullapool
Start	△ Kinlochbervie (NC 217 564)
Finish	◯ Balnakeil Bay (NC 391 687)
HW/LW	HW/LW at Kinlochbervie is around 15 minutes after Ullapool.
Tidal Times	From Cape Wrath down to Eilean an Ròin Beag (NC 172 583): The NE going stream starts at about 1 hour and 20 minutes before HW Ullapool. The SW going stream starts at about 4 hours and 55 minutes after HW Ullapool.
	From Cape Wrath to Stack Clò Kearvaig (NC 294 736): The E going stream starts at about 3 hours and 50 minutes before HW Ullapool. The W going stream starts at about 2 hours and 35 minutes after HW Ullapool.
	From Stack Cló Kearvaig eastwards: The E going stream starts at about 2 hours and 20 minutes before HW Ullapool. The W going stream starts at about 3 hours and 50 minutes after HW Ullapool.
Max Rate Sp	At Cape Wrath 5 knots. Between Cape Wrath and Stack Clò Kearvaig 3 knots. Between An Garbh-eilean and Clèit Dhubh 3 knots. Off Eilean an Ròin Beag and between it and the mainland 2–3 knots. South of Cape Wrath 1.5 knots.
Coastguard	South of Cape Wrath: Stornoway, tel. 01851 702013, VHF weather every 3 hours from 0710. East of Cape Wrath: Shetland, tel. 01595 692976, VHF weather every 3 hours from 0710.

© Sandwood Bay and Am Buachaille

Cape Wrath

Introduction

Cape Wrath, the furthest NW point on the Scottish mainland, is a wild place. A lighthouse stands on the headland above the caves and arches where the sea swirls and boils as it forces its way around the headland on its journey from the west coast of Scotland to the north coast and back again. The highest cliffs on the mainland are here at Clò Mòr, 180 metres of towering vertical rock. In amongst this rugged coastline are two beautiful sandy beaches, Kearvaig on the north coast, and the much photographed Sandwood Bay on the west coast.

Description

Kinlochbervie is one of the most important white fish ports in Scotland and provides an industrial, yet remotely beautiful, starting point to the trip. Launching at the head of Loch Clash to the west of the town, as opposed to the slipway within the harbour, provides a peaceful launch site. On leaving Loch Clash you will quickly arrive at the stunning beaches of Oldshoremore and Oldshore Beg, which certainly rival the more famous Sandwood Bay for beauty.

On leaving the beaches, head through the narrow gap that separates Eilean an Ròin Mòr from the mainland; here you may feel the first of the tidal flows experienced along most of this trip. Just beyond the island is the small pier at Droman that marks the last easy escape route until the trip finishes on the north coast.

After the first section of steep coastline with the cliffs towering overhead, you will soon reach the spectacular sea stack of Am Buachaille. The famous Scottish climber Tom Patey first climbed this impressive 65m-tall sea stack in 1968; in Gaelic it translates into 'the herdsman' or 'the shepherd'. Just beyond Am Buachaille the beach at Sandwood Bay stretches for three kilometres. The beach has to rate as one of the most stunning in Britain; superlatives could not even start to do it justice. Getting ashore here is highly recommended; however it has the potential to be a bit exciting if any swell is running. This bay also provides a great place to camp for the night and will certainly provide a view to die for. Having negotiated any surf on leaving the beach, dramatic cliffs continue to another couple of sea stacks, A'Chailleach and Am Bodach. These stand guard over the southern approach to Cape Wrath just 2km away. A'Chailleach translates as 'the old woman' and Am Bodach 'the old man'.

Cape Wrath is as 'out there' as it gets on mainland Britain, and with a lively ocean under you and soaring impregnable cliffs above you, it will feel like it! Underneath the headland are two large arches that you hopefully will be able to paddle through if conditions are favourable. The tidal streams can run fast through these arches, so be prepared to deploy some whitewater

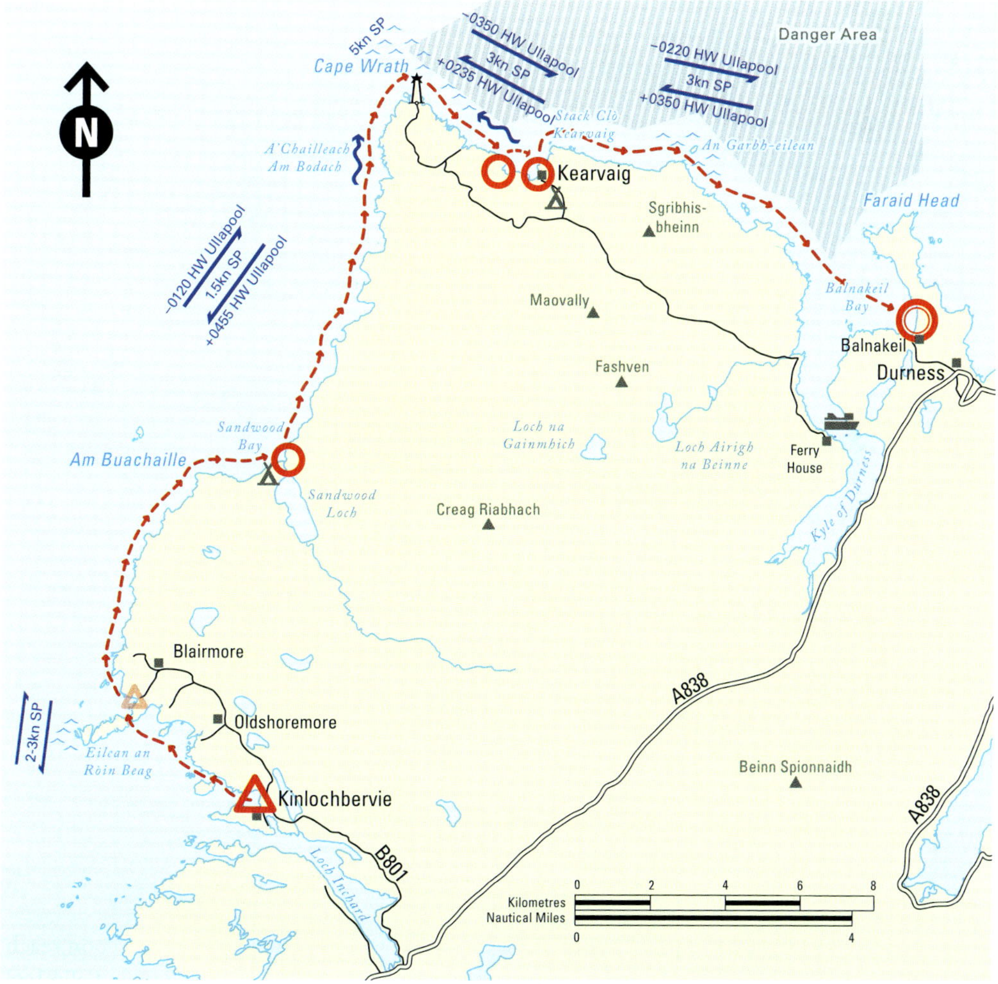

Sunset over Balnakeil Bay and An Garbh-eilean

Cape Wrath

paddling skills. Standing 121 metres above on top of the headland is the Cape Wrath lighthouse, facing out to the expanse of the Atlantic Ocean. First lit on Christmas Day 1828, this light was built by Robert Stevenson and clearly marks this remote corner of Britain. The name Cape Wrath is derived from Old Norse 'hvarf' which means turning point; this is possible due to the fact the Vikings often used to turn around here and return back home.

On leaving Cape Wrath another stunning sandy beach is not far away at Kearvaig Bay. On the way look out for the old lighthouse jetty that can provide a possible landing. This was used by the lighthouse tender MV *Pharos* that brought supplies on an annual basis for the lighthouse keepers. There will always be a certain amount of surf at Kearvaig Bay; a small beach at Geodha na Seamraig offers a possible landing alternative. At Kearvaig there is good camping, as well as Kearvaig House which the Mountain Bothies Association has converted into a bothy. This provides a perfect place to spend the night if you want to take more time to savour this amazing location.

Clearly seen from the beach is the sea stack of Stack Clò Kearvaig, also commonly known as the 'The Cathedral' due to it having two spires and a natural window created by the fierce north coast weather. This stack marks the start of 2km of immense cliffs rising 180 metres straight out of the ocean, these cliffs being the highest in mainland Britain and known as Clò Mòr. The location is truly breath-taking and paddling underneath these cliffs is an unbelievable experience; you will feel very insignificant in this 'on the edge of the world' environment. An Garbh-eilean lies at the end of the cliffs, and the narrow gap between it and the mainland provide the last of the trip's fast flowing tidal streams. If paddling close to the island look out for the remnants of bombs

Looking along Clò Mòr, Cape Wrath in the distance

embedded in the rock, as it is used for target practice when NATO use this area for combined land, air and sea training manoeuvres.

All too soon the cliffs recede and the entrance to the Kyle of Durness is reached. The calm waters this will offer may well be a welcome respite to what has been before. The wonderfully clean, sandy beach of Balnakeil Bay that stretches for 2km is easy to see, and crystal clear azure waters guide you to the finishing point on the magnificent beach.

Tides and weather

This is not a section of coastline to get caught out on. There are few landing spots, all with the potential of big surf and challenging walk-outs. The headland of Cape Wrath is fully exposed to the Atlantic and rarely will there be a day without much swell. Whichever direction the swell comes from it will have an effect on how the trip goes. Ideal conditions are required, light winds and minimum swell.

The trip needs to be planned to make use of the strong tidal movement in this area. Timing the trip so that Cape Wrath is reached at slacker water towards the start of the east going stream works well. This will allow the north going eddy on the west coast to be used to arrive at the headland, and then make use of the faster flow rates with the easterly stream on the north coast. The few kilometres to the east of Cape Wrath will most probably have a continual westerly flow due to the eddy; this can be paddled against at slacker water particularly if on a neap tide. Slack water at the start of the easterly flow is at 3 hours and 50 minutes before HW Ullapool.

The North coast: Clò Mòr, Faraid Head, Whiten Head and beyond

Additional information

Cape Wrath is a live firing exercise area for the military. Check with the coastguard, look out in local papers, check at the shop in Durness and look to see if any red flags are flying before you set off. It is also possible to phone the range control on 0800 317071 to ask about the live firing. At Kinlochbervie there is a shop and toilets are available. At Balnakeil there is a craft village that is worth a look and provides a café, Cocoa Mountain, which is highly recommended for a chocolate fix on completing the trip.

Variations

A great short day out from Kinlochbervie is to circumnavigate Eilean an Ròin Beag and Eilean an Ròin Mòr, including enjoying the incredible beaches at Oldshoremore and Oldshore Beg. On this trip the tide runs up to 3 knots off Eilean an Ròin Beag and needs to be considered in the planning.

If you wish to paddle out and back to Cape Wrath in a day this is best done starting at Balnakeil. Further details of this trip can be found in *North & East Coasts of Scotland Sea Kayaking* by Doug Cooper. From Kinlochbervie it is possible to paddle out and back to Sandwood Bay, this making another great day trip.

Loch Laxford with Ben Stack

Loch Laxford

No. 2 | Grade B | 15km | OS Sheet 9

Tidal Port	Ullapool
Start	△ Kinlochbervie (NC 217 564)
Finish	◯ Laxford Bay (NC 227 477)
HW/LW	HW/LW at Kinlochbervie is around 15 minutes after Ullapool.
Tidal Times	Between Loch Laxford and Kinlochbervie: The NE going stream starts at about 1 hour and 20 minutes before HW Ullapool. The SW going stream starts at about 4 hours and 55 minutes after HW Ullapool.
Max Rate Sp	Between Loch Laxford and Kinlochbervie 1 knot.
Coastguard	Stornoway, tel. 01851 702013, VHF weather every 3 hours from 0710.

Introduction

This journey offers a remote and rarely-paddled section of coastline, exposed to the Atlantic Ocean, with hidden lochs, an abundance of skerries and some great rock formations. Following this, intricately beautiful Loch Laxford provides shelter with stunning mountain scenery. A great paddle with two very contrasting sections of coastline.

◎ Landing/launching spot at Loch Laxford

Description

Launching from the small sheltered beach on the west side of the busy fishing port of Kinlochbervie provides instant access to the remote coastline of the far North West. As you leave Loch Clash and cross the entrance to Loch Inchard it will become apparent how exposed this coastline is to the Atlantic. Small islands and skerries litter this section of coastline, any swell crashing up against them throwing up plumes of white spray. Keep a watchful eye out for any fishing boats leaving or entering Loch Inchard.

Immediately after crossing Loch Inchard there is a choice of narrow passages to paddle between the small islands of Glas Leac and Eilean Dubh. These hide the narrow hidden entrance to Loch Ceann na Sàile which is home, at its head, to what must be one of the remotest houses in the far North West. If time allows it is well worth exploring as it takes you into the heart of this rock, heather and lochan-covered wilderness. Continuing from here, feast your eyes on the sculptured folds and swirls in the colourful Lewisian Gneiss rock that forms the impregnable barrier between ocean and land.

Be sure not to miss the entrance to the next hidden loch, Loch an Ròin. It is narrow and shallow, guarded on one side by an overhanging rock face; depending on the tide there may well be fast-flowing water rushing in or out of the loch providing eddies and rocks to negotiate if you wish to enter. If successful in entering the loch's inner sanctum you are treated to sudden tranquillity and a feeling of complete isolation. There is a great stopping place and potential campsite on the north side immediately after the entrance.

The next section of coastline leads you to the entrance to Loch Laxford. Colourful cliff scenery along with numerous skerries and islands provide plenty of interest. To the south the impressive cliffs of Handa Island are clearly visible.

After paddling around Ardmore Point you enter Loch Laxford; this impressive loch with its abundance of islands cuts deep into the wilderness that is the far North West. The impressive conical-shaped mountain called Ben Stack dominates the distant view. It rises tall out the low-lying peat lands and is a stunning backdrop to the final stage of this paddle. Laxford derives from the Norse for 'salmon fjord' and the entire sea loch is designated a Special Area of Conservation, fitting for such a unique place.

The calmer waters of the sheltered loch now replace the rougher seas of the outer coastline. There is a splendid hidden landing place in the first bay you come across on the north side of the loch. This provides a welcome resting spot as well as offering great views of Ben Stack. Do not be tempted to head straight down the loch to the finish, but make the time to paddle across to the south side of the loch and explore the many islands and narrow passages. These are really interesting and provide a home to plenty of the fantastic wildlife that makes this loch its home.

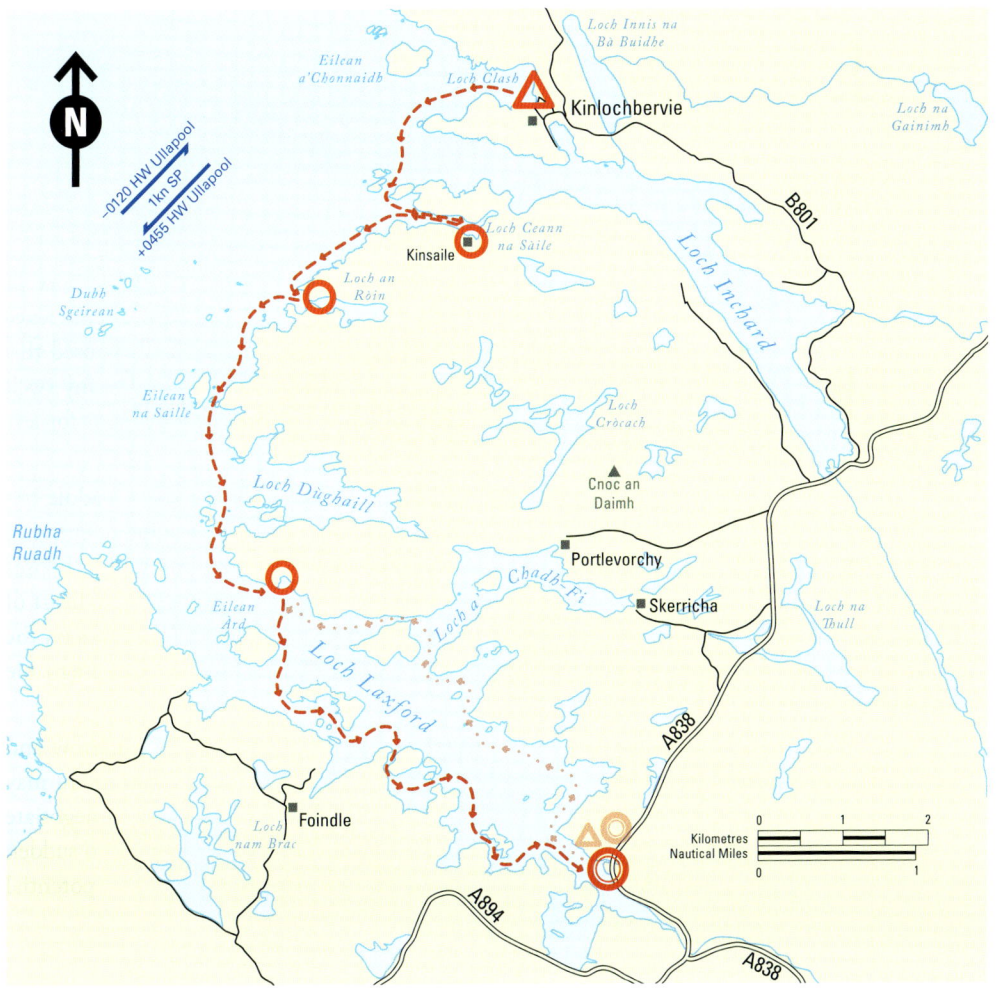

Eilean na Saille and the remote outer coast

Having fully explored the loch and hopefully been welcomed by much of its wildlife, the jetty towards the head of the loch comes into view. It provides the perfect finishing spot, with plenty of space to land and then spend some time savouring this very special and rarely visited corner of the far North West.

Tides and weather

There is little tidal movement along this section of coastline, so when planning the trip the main factors to take into account are the wind and swell. The outer coast section of this coastline is both remote and committing, so only consider this on days with light winds and small swell. Loch Laxford offers a lot of shelter and can be paddled in most conditions.

Additional information

At Kinlochbervie there is a shop and public conveniences, as well as hotels that offer food. The finish at Loch Laxford is very much 'in the middle of nowhere'!

Variations

If unsure about the conditions on the outer coastline, or if you prefer not to do the shuttle that is required, then a great day's paddling, or more, can be had within Loch Laxford itself. You can head out into the loch as far (or into as rough conditions) as is suitable, with the option of returning always available.

The impressive north coast of Handa

Handa Island

No. 3 | Grade B | 17km | OS Sheet 9

Tidal Port	Ullapool
Start	△ Scourie (NC 151 446)
Finish	○ Scourie (NC 151 446)
HW/LW	HW/LW at Scourie is around 10 minutes after Ullapool.
Tidal Times	On the west coast of Handa: The SW going stream starts at about 4 hours and 30 minutes after HW Ullapool. The NE going stream starts at about 1 hour and 45 minutes before HW Ullapool.
	In the Sound of Handa: The SW going stream starts at about 2 hours and 10 minutes after HW Ullapool. The NE going stream starts at about 4 hours and 15 minutes before HW Ullapool.
Max Rate Sp	Off the west side of Handa and in the Sound of Handa 2–3 knots.
Coastguard	Stornoway, tel. 01851 702013, VHF weather every 3 hours from 0710.

Introduction

Handa is a nature reserve as well as a Site of Special Scientific Interest (SSSI). Both of these designations are deserved, and there is no better way to experience this remarkable island than by sea

Handa Sound and a perfect beach to land on

kayak. On a calm day the cliff architecture and cave exploration is second to none. This, blended with the incredible amount of bird and marine wildlife along with stunning views toward the Point of Stoer and Cape Wrath, makes this a journey not to be missed.

Description

The sheltered golden sands of Scourie give a perfect launching spot. It also provides an ideal place to explore the mainland Lewisian Gneiss rock cliffs, as well as circumnavigating the sandstone rock cliffs of Handa.

Paddle along the southern coast for a short while until Handa Island comes fully into view. At this point head across the open water aiming for the beach on the south-eastern point of the island. Keep an eye out for seals, porpoises, dolphins and whales, as they can all be seen in this area. Soon you will arrive at the picture-postcard beach at Port an Eilein on Handa. It is well worth stopping here, as there is nowhere else to stop on the journey around Handa. It also gives an opportunity to take a walk on the island if time allows.

Handa was used as a burial ground by the mainland settlements in early times. In those days it was quite common to bury the dead on islands as it protected the bodies from scavenging wolves and, it was believed, from evil spirits that were unable to cross open water. These days, if you visit in the summer months, you may meet some of the five thousand visitors the island has a year, or one of the Scottish Wildlife Trust wardens who look after the island.

Leaving the beach, head along the south coast of the island to Bogha Mòr where the journey will change in character quite dramatically. The coastline ahead rears up to 100m sheer sandstone cliffs and if there is any swell it is here that it will be experienced. If the swell allows, keeping in close to the cliffs will reveal numerous caves and arches, all guarded by the thousands of seabirds that nest on the island. Guillemots make up many of these birds, as Handa is the largest breeding colony of these in Britain with about 100,000 birds. In addition to this you will see razorbills, puffins, shags, skuas and kittiwakes to name a few. May to July is the breeding season, so it is worth timing your paddle around Handa to be in these months to see the island at its best.

When you reach the dramatic vertical-walled bay that makes up the north-western corner of the island, you may also be able to explore the sea arch that forms its northern end. Just beyond this on the north coast is the immense 'Great Stack of Handa', which stands 115m high balanced on three giant legs of rock. If conditions allow, this is an incredible place to explore by kayak. This stack has been climbed by its north face and was first ascended in 1876 when Donald MacDonald went hand over hand across a rope attached to the mainland cliff, a brave stunt. Crossing the bay there is one more stack to explore before the cliffs slowly start to subside as the Sound of Handa is reached.

The Queen of Handa

At its busiest in the 1840s, 65 people lived on Handa surviving off the land and sea. They organised themselves in a similar fashion to the people of St Kilda. The oldest widow on the island was considered their 'queen', and the men of the island once held a daily parliament to decide the jobs to be done and who was to do them.

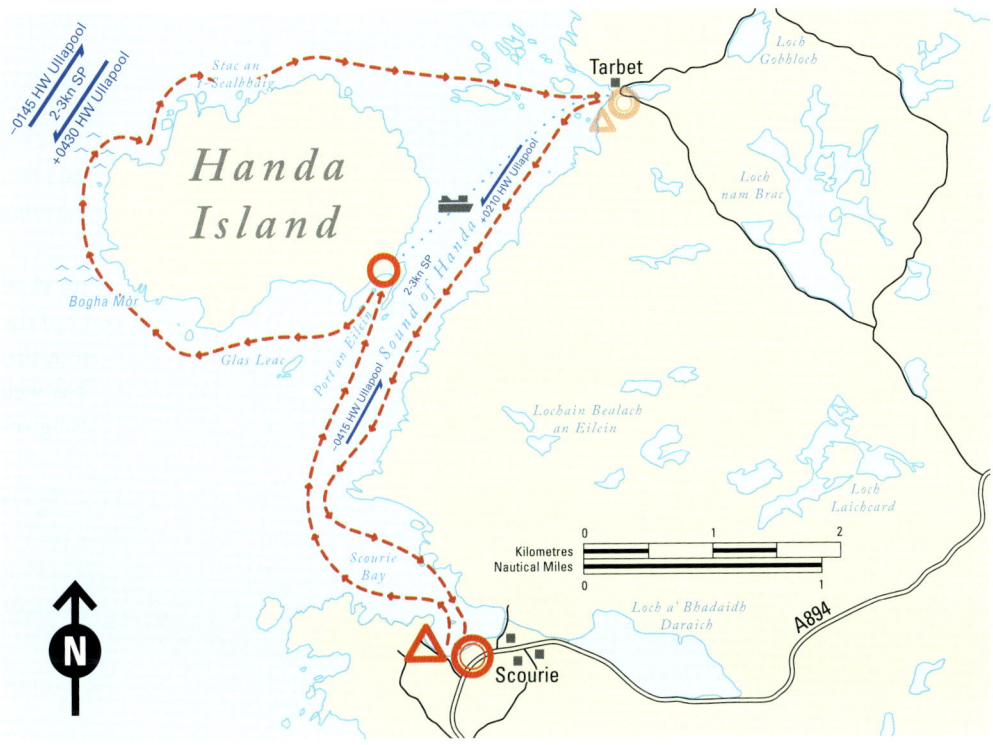

From here it is worth paddling across the northern entrance to the Sound and through the archipelago of skerries that guard the tiny village of Tarbet. A rest can be taken here and the café may be open for an ice cream. Refuelled and rested, heading down through the Sound of Handa is a great way to finish the journey. The sea stack the 'Old Man of Stoer' will be visible in the distance. On one side is another fantastic sandy beach and the sandstone of Handa, while on the other are the shaped Lewisian Gneiss rock cliffs of the North West Highlands. These cliffs provide further interest all the way back to the beach at Scourie.

Tides and weather

The west and north coasts of Handa are exposed to the full force of any Atlantic swell and this should never be underestimated. Add to this the numerous reefs, particularly at Bogha Mòr, and this can prove to be a very serious paddle in anything other than ideal weather conditions.

To make best use of the tide on this trip, time it so that the north coast is reached as the tide starts flowing in a south-westerly direction, about 4 hours and 30 minutes after HW Ullapool. This ensures tidal assistance up to this point, but also slacker water at the tidal races which form off the north and west coasts. The south-westerly flow will provide tidal assistance when returning through the Sound of Handa. Rough water can sometimes be experienced in the centre of the sound, particularly if there is a south-westerly wind against the tide.

If unable to make best use of the tide, it is possible to paddle around Handa at any state of tidal stream making use of the eddies that form, although this may be hard work on a spring tide.

Additional information

There is a shop, campsite and local amenities at Scourie. As well as the café at Tarbet there are also public toilets and the passenger ferry service to Handa. For non-paddling friends a trip to Handa using the ferry is a great day out, with a well-made path circumnavigating the island providing views of the cliffs, birds and maybe paddlers below! If you wish to camp on Handa permission is needed from the Scottish Wildlife Trust, 0131 312 7765. For more information about the trust and their work go to www.scottishwildlifetrust.org.uk

Variations

For a slightly shorter day, circumnavigating Handa starting and finishing at Tarbet works well; however it can be busy there in the summer for parking due to the ferry.

Badcall Bay with the Assynt mountains in the distance

Scourie to Kylesku

No. 4	**Grade B**	**20km**	**OS Sheet 15**
Tidal Port	Ullapool
Start	△ Scourie (NC 150 446)
Finish	○ Kylesku (NC 229 334)
HW/LW	HW/LW at Kylesku is around 5 minutes after Ullapool.
Tidal Times	Along this section of coastline: The SSW going stream starts at about 4 hours and 30 minutes after HW Ullapool. The NNE going stream starts at about 1 hour and 45 minutes before HW Ullapool.
	At the Kylesku Bridge narrows: The ingoing stream starts at about 5 hours and 55 minutes before HW Ullapool. The outgoing stream starts at about 30 minutes after HW Ullapool.
Max Rate Sp	Under the bridge 3 knots. Along the rest of the coast 0.5 knots.
Coastguard	Stornoway, tel. 01851 702013, VHF weather every 3 hours from 0710.

Introduction

This trip has a feeling of remoteness and isolation, spiced with plenty of variety. Cliffs and caves exposed to the full force of the Atlantic to start, a mass of sheltered and isolated islands follow, with a narrow fjord-like loch leading into the mountains to finish.

Kylesku road bridge overlooked by the impressive Quinaig

Scourie to Kylesku

Description

The beach in Scourie Bay provides the perfect launch spot, on a calm sunny day the water will be turquoise and the golden sands will be shimmering below as you paddle out of the bay. Leaving the bay you get a great view of the village behind, with the pointed peak of Ben Stack in the background. The sheltered, sandy bay soon gives way to the exposed rocky coastline that faces the Atlantic Ocean. Handa Island is obvious to the north, with the beautiful beaches of its southern shore. Lewisian Gneiss is the rock that makes up this exposed and intricate coastline providing fantastic shapes and colours to admire as you paddle past. Looking out to sea the Point of Stoer is obvious with the sea stack called the Old Man of Stoer standing tall and proud. The southern shore of Eddrachillis Bay adds to the scenery with Oldany Island visible. Don't expect to be able to land along this section of coastline; the cliffs drop vertically into the sea and the occasional bay is rocky and exposed. Passing Rubh' Àird an t-Sionnaich look out for the caves that are worth exploring before heading across the bay to the tallest cliffs of the day.

Beyond this section of exposed and dramatic cliffs the trip changes in character as you reach the mass of islands that mark the entrance to Badcall Bay. It is easy to lose yourself for many an hour in the tranquillity and remoteness of these islands. There are surprisingly few landing places on the islands, so it is worth considering heading into Badcall Bay where, on the north side, there are easy landings for a rest if required. The bay is used quite extensively for fish farming, a key industry for this area, but out amongst the islands there is only the wildlife. Leaving Badcall Bay another landing option is at Bàgh Leathann, where there are the remains of a remote croft. As beautiful a setting as it is, it is difficult to imagine how hard it must have been to survive in such

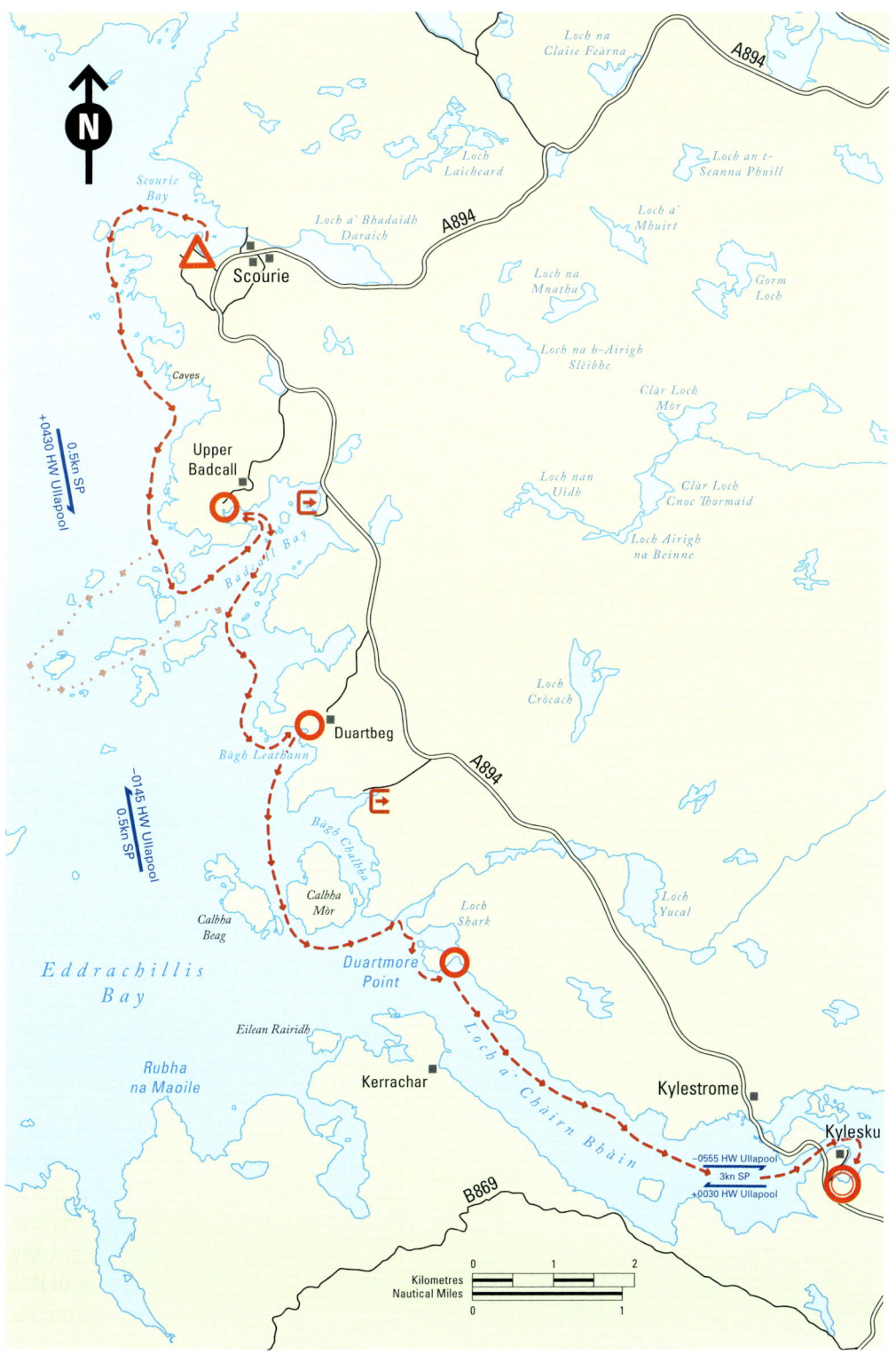

an unforgiving environment. Two final islands hide the entrance to Loch a' Chàirn Bhàin, but don't be tempted to take the short cut on the inside of these unless it is high tide.

The entrance to Loch a' Chàirn Bhàin is surprisingly narrow, given that it feeds such an extensive inland sea loch system. Duartmore Point marks its start, however do explore the beautiful rocky bay that forms at the river mouth just before this and the intriguingly named Shark Bay that follows. Neither of these provide great landing places, however once past the point there is a bay that provides a good place to stop. Throughout the second part of the trip the mountain that now towers over the loch has dominated the view. Quinag is arguably one of the more impressive mountains of the North West Highlands, and the kayakers' viewpoint while paddling up the loch is about the best.

On the final part of this trip up the loch to the finish at Kylesku, you would be forgiven for thinking you were in a Norwegian fjord. The views into the remote North West Highland mountains are expansive, and the mass of Quinag ever present. As the loch appears to come to a finish, the narrow channel that is crossed by the impressive Kylesku road bridge is revealed. Some tidal movement will be noticeable here, this narrow channel marks the gateway into the inner loch system of Loch Glendhu and Glencoul.

Having enjoyed paddling under the impressive bridge, Kylesku Hotel is passed with the slipway that was previously used by the car ferry. It is possible to land here, but it is often busy and at low water is not easy. There is a quieter spot with more parking just around the corner in the harbour, a small rocky beach in the back corner of the harbour bay that is the finish of the trip. A short carry leads to the harbour parking area.

Tides and weather

It is best to plan this trip to make use of the in-going tidal stream in Loch a' Chàirn Bhàin and under Kylesku Bridge. Under the bridge the faster flowing water is short-lived, and there is a large eddy on the north bank making it possible to paddle against the tide if required.

The start of this trip is very exposed to any Atlantic swell or westerly winds. This should be considered when planning as there are few escape opportunities along this remote coastline.

Additional information

There are plenty of amenities in Scourie along with a fantastic campsite overlooking the bay. In Kylesku there are no shops, however there are public conveniences and a hotel. Kylesku Hotel is extremely welcoming and offers a perfect place to enjoy a drink at the end of the trip; they also serve up some of the best local seafood in the area!

Glendhu

Loch Glendhu & Loch Glencoul

No. 5	**Grade A**	**20km**	**OS Sheet 15**
Tidal Port	Ullapool
Start	△ Kylesku (NC 229 334)
Finish	○ Kylesku (NC 229 334)
HW/LW	HW/LW at Kylesku is around 5 minutes after Ullapool.
Tidal Times	Under the bridge and within the lochs: The ingoing stream starts at about 5 hours and 55 minutes before HW Ullapool. The outgoing stream starts at about 30 minutes after HW Ullapool.
Max Rate Sp	Under the bridge 3 knots. Within the lochs 0.5 knots.
Coastguard	Stornoway, tel. 01851 702013, VHF weather every 3 hours from 0710.

Introduction

Lochs Glendhu and Glencoul provide one of the most impressive fjord-like locations in Scotland; it is easy to think you are in Norway when exploring these remote and beautiful lochs.

The old car ferry, Maid of Kylesku

Surrounded by wildlife and unique geology, along with historic tales of submarines and two bothies to explore, this is a trip that can be enjoyed over a few hours or a few days.

Description

The small, stony beach next to the harbour provides a quiet spot to launch, accessed by a short walk down the track from the harbour parking area. You will no doubt have already had some spectacular views of the lochs to be explored while driving to the put-in; so leaving the sheltered bay that forms the harbour there will be a sense of anticipation of what lies ahead. The old car ferry, the *Maid of Kylesku*, can be seen rotting away on the shore as you leave, abandoned here in 1967 when a newer ferry replaced it; the spectacular bridge seen today saw an end to the ferries in 1984.

Leaving the bay there will be tantalising views down into Loch Glencoul, but start by heading across into Loch Glendhu. Entering the loch there is a waterfall cascading down the hillside where there is a hydroelectric station. To the south Quinag towers over the lochs, like a protective sentinel. Looking down to the head of the loch the estate buildings and open bothy will be clear to see, along with the spectacular geology. These lochs sit in the heart of a 2,000 square kilometre area that has become Scotland's first Global Geopark. The view into the lochs is one of the most photographed in the world of geology due to the very visible Glencoul Thrust, one of the first thrusts in the world to be recognised as such. The band of Cambrian strata is easy to see as it gently dips beneath the Lewisian basement.

Kylesku Bridge

This bridge is unique in its appearance and provides an access lifeline to the remote far North West. It was opened on 8th August 1984 by the Queen and has received awards for its design. The bridge itself is concrete in structure with distinctive V-shaped legs supporting the curved road above. It sits 24 metres above the sea and has a 79-metre span, taking three years to build at a cost of four million pounds. Prior to the bridge a ferry was in place, the slipways being seen at Kylesku on the south side and Kylestrome on the north. The ferry can now be seen abandoned on the shore as the harbour is entered at Kylesku.

At the head of Loch Glendhu, take the time to enjoy the spectacular location. There is also the handy bothy alongside the locked estate hunting houses to provide some shelter if required.

On leaving Glendhu we move on to explore the second loch of the day, Glencoul. Look out for the seals that are often found on the south side of Loch Glendhu just before you turn the corner into Loch Glencoul. The scenery in the second loch of the day is no less dramatic then the first, there will no doubt be plenty of wildlife for company as you head towards the loch's inner

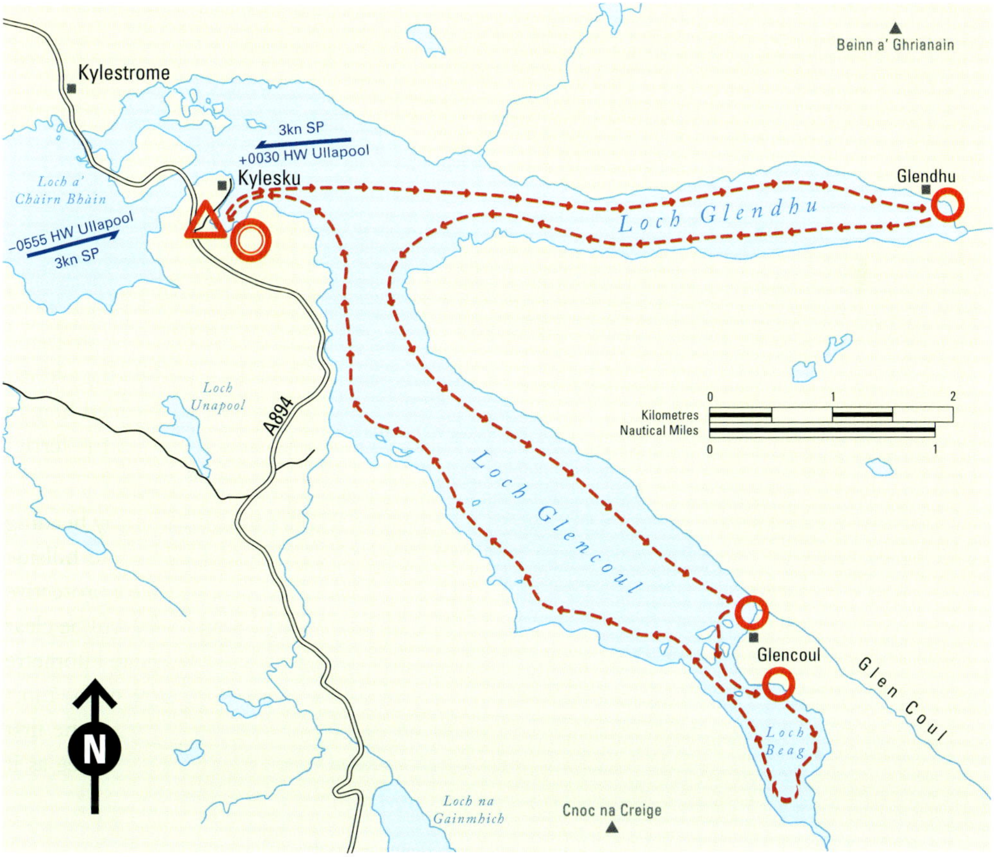

© Glendhu Bothy

sanctum, Loch Beag. This loch is guarded by some islands and a narrow entrance at the head of Loch Glencoul, overlooked by the grand bothy of Glencoul. Once in Loch Beag the peace and tranquillity is stunning. It is surrounded by steep mountainsides and the only sounds are made by the resident seals or the waterfalls cascading all around. Eas a' Chual Aluinn can be seen from the loch and is Britain's highest waterfall with a sheer drop of 200m. When in full flow it is over three times higher than Niagara Falls. It is well worth stretching the legs here, there is a reasonable landing with a path leading to the bothy on the north side of Loch Beag near the entrance. Alternatively there are landing opportunities beneath the bothy at the head of Loch Glencoul.

Paddling back along the southern shore of Loch Glencoul to Kylesku there are numerous small islands to provide interest. These islands are the home to numerous common seals. Look out for the plentiful birdlife and if you are lucky maybe even an otter or two. All too soon the end will be reached and the day's paddling will be over. All that will be left to do is enjoy some well-earned refreshments at the Kylesku Hotel, which has outdoor seating to take in the view of where you have just paddled.

Tides and weather

There is no tidal movement of note within the lochs, other than towards the narrows under the bridge where there are strong tidal streams to consider. The lochs offer good protection from the wind and it is usually possible to find a sheltered coastline to paddle along, although be watchful of downdrafts and the wind funnelling in very windy conditions. Despite the potential shelter offered within the lochs, they are still remote destinations with no easy escape, so consider this in the planning.

Loch Glencoul

X-Craft submarine training

The X-class was a World War II midget submarine class built for the Royal Navy during 1943–44. Known individually as X-Craft, the vessels were designed to be towed to where they would operate by a full size 'mother' submarine. When in location its small size would allow them to attack undetected, then return to the 'mother' submarine. Range was limited by the endurance and determination of their crews, but some crews were thought to have lasted 14 days on an attack mission. The XIIth Submarine Flotilla used the lochs to train in from 1943; a cairn on the north side of Kylesku Bridge was erected in 1993 to commemorate the 50th anniversary.

Additional information

Kylesku Hotel provides refreshments which includes some stunning seafood, much of which is harvested from the lochs just paddled. There are also public toilets. The nearest shops are at Scourie or Lochinver.

The bothies at the head of each loch provide shelter and the potential to stay overnight if desired. There is a good path to walk/bike into Glendhu if non-paddling friends want to meet up at the bothy. Alternatively there are boat trips from Kylesku in the summer months for non-paddling friends to enjoy the loch scenery and wildlife.

Looking into Loch Glendhu

Variations

If time is tight, or weather conditions dictate, then it is still well worth the paddle into just one of the lochs; Glencoul often offers a little more shelter. Alternatively, making a weekend of it and staying in one of the bothies is highly recommended, allowing some time for walking and further exploration.

Mountain bothies

Mountain bothies are unlocked shelters found all over Scotland that are maintained as places for people to stay in order to enjoy remote locations more easily. Some will be little more than a concrete floor with a watertight roof overhead; others will have separate rooms with wooden sleeping platforms, open fires, seats and tables. All however will be in a remote and spectacular location. These shelters often provide an ideal stopping place for sea kayakers and are well worth looking out for. The Mountain Bothies Association (MBA) is a charity that looks after the bothies; the work and maintenance associated with this is all done by a host of volunteers. The ethos of the MBA is "to maintain simple shelters in remote country for the use and benefit of all who love wild and lonely places". To find out more go to their website: www.mountainbothies.org.uk

Leaving Clashnessie towards Oldany Island, Handa Island in the far distance

Eddrachillis Bay & Oldany Island

No. 6 | Grade B | 24km | OS Sheet 15

Tidal Port	Ullapool
Start	△ Clashnessie (NC 057 309)
Finish	◯ Kylesku (NC 229 334)
HW/LW	HW/LW at Kylesku is around 5 minutes after Ullapool.
Tidal Times	At the Kylesku Bridge narrows: The ingoing stream starts at about 5 hours and 55 minutes before HW Ullapool. The outgoing stream starts at about 30 minutes after HW Ullapool.
Max Rate Sp	Under the bridge 3 knots, along the rest of the coast 0.5 knots.
Coastguard	Stornoway, tel. 01851 702013, VHF weather every 3 hours from 0710.

Introduction

This is a remote section of coastline that starts with an expansive sandy beach and finishes paddling under the dramatic Kylesku Bridge. Along the way there is a plethora of small islands and

One of the many common seals on Oldany Island

the beautiful Oldany Island to enjoy, with its resident seals and immaculate sandy beach, set in an idyllic bay looking across to the imposing mountain of Quinag.

Description

The expanse of Clashnessie's sandy beach with its views out to Oldany Island and the far North West beyond provides the starting place for this trip. Sheltered from the westerly swells this beach is generally surf free.

On leaving here you follow the coast towards Oldany Island. The rock is the ancient Lewisian Gneiss and provides plenty of interest along the route. Keep in close and look out for the arch along the way. If the conditions are good you may choose to head out and paddle around the outside of Oldany Island. This is a great experience and provides dramatic views across to the Point of Stoer and the north side of Eddrachillis Bay with Handa Island in the distance. The coastline is rugged with no landings, and off the tip of the island you will start to catch any swell coming in from the Atlantic. Head for the beautiful and somewhat hidden landing on the south-facing sandy bay set in amongst numerous small islands on the east coast, just past the tiny headland called Cnoc a' Mhoil Bhàin. If paddling around the outside of Oldany Island does not suit, the route on the inside of the island is equally spectacular. This follows a tiny channel that separates the island from the mainland; it provides wildlife in abundance, sheltered peace and solitude. The channel leads into a mass of tiny islands; weave your way through these, surrounded by many seals, to find the sandy beach landing already described. With its perfect beach, fairy tale-like little house and stunning views out to the imposing mountain of Quinag, you would be forgiven for not moving on from this place!

After the beach you paddle past many more islands along to the entrance to Loch Nedd. This narrow 'fjord-like' loch provides shelter for the small fishing community of Nedd; it also offers an alternative start/finish point. Continuing on, Eddrachillis Bay starts to narrow and the entrance channel to Loch a' Chàirn Bhàin is hiding around the corner. The coastline remains remote and rugged, with views across the bay to the islands off Badcall and beyond. As the end of Eddrachillis Bay is reached, the corner is turned and the view down Loch a' Chàirn Bhàin opens up, a relatively narrow loch leading into the heart of dramatic mountain scenery. Another beautiful stopping place to enjoy this view is at Kerrachar Bay.

Wedding on the beach

One June day a gathering of people was enjoying the beautiful sands at Clashnessie. Not that rare for this magnificent beach. However this time there were few buckets and spades, shorts or swimsuits; instead there were kilts aplenty along with fine dresses and hats to match. Landing on the beach this same day was a group of four sea kayakers, again not a rare sight for the beach. This time however one of the kayakers was wearing a tartan-effect paddle top and buoyancy aid, then stepping out of the kayaks all were kilted, with fine shoes being worn, and dress jackets at the ready to replace the paddle tops and buoyancy aids. It was the groom and his best men arriving for the special day on this special beach. Not long after this, the bride in her magnificent dress arrived walking bare foot in the sand; it was a day for all to remember in a location that can never be forgotten. The wedding was Doug and Lara's!

Clashnessie's magnificent beach

Kerrachar Man

In 1976 Eric MacLeod told his boss he was going to give up his successful career as an accountant and move to the middle of nowhere in the North West Highlands of Scotland to become a crofter. Needless to say most thought him mad! He had inherited a ruined croft at Kerrachar that was only accessible by boat or a trek across inhospitable moorland of over a mile. He boldly moved up with wife and two children to start a new life. It started by making a floating platform that could be towed behind a boat to transport a caravan to Kerrachar. This would give them somewhere to live while they built their house and slowly become crofters. Eric MacLeod and his family built the Kerrachar that can be seen today and lived for 16 years there before sadly leaving. His story is a good one and can be read in his book *Kerrachar Man*. For many years after Eric left Kerrachar, people came to see the beautifully ornate gardens that were grown by the new occupants. These gardens are now run down and overgrown; however the croft has new owners and the essence of Kerrachar lives on.

From Kerrachar the mountain scenery further along the loch draws you on, and you soon reach Eilean a' Ghamhna with its surrounding sheltered waters and fish/mussel farms. This form of farming provides a living for many in this area and is evident throughout the sea lochs. Just on from here the dramatic Kylesku Bridge comes into view, spanning the narrow channel and providing a road lifeline to the far north. If you have planned well there should be some tidal flow

The landing at Kerrachar

to help you on your way through the narrows and under the bridge. Just beyond the bridge are the Kylesku Hotel and the slipway that was used by the car ferry before the bridge was built. It is possible to land here, and it will be very tempting with only a few paces required for a well-earned pint in the pub. However there is a quieter spot with more parking just around the corner in the harbour. Entering the harbour you will see the old car ferry abandoned on the shoreline and just beyond this is a small rocky beach in the back corner of the bay which is the finish of the trip. A short carry leads to the harbour parking area.

Tides and weather

It is best to plan this trip to make use of the ingoing tidal stream in Loch a' Chàirn Bhàin and under Kylesku Bridge. Under the bridge the faster flowing water is only for a short distance and there is a large eddy on the north bank making it possible to paddle against the tide if required.

A large part of this trip offers good shelter from the wind and swell; however some sections are exposed to wind and swell from the north and north-west. This should be considered when planning, as there are few escape opportunities along this remote coastline. If conditions are not ideal for the entire trip consider the variations below that offer more shelter.

Additional information

There are no amenities at Clashnessie, however there is a small village shop at Drumbeg. The carry at Clashnessie beach is a long one at low water; consider using a trolley to make it easier. In

Kylesku Hotel, a welcome sight to finish the day!

Kylesku there are no shops, however there are public conveniences and a hotel. Kylesku Hotel is extremely welcoming and offers a perfect place to enjoy a drink at the end of the trip; they also serve up some of the best local seafood in the area!

Variations

Oldany Island makes for a great trip in its own right and can be done without the need for a shuttle. Starting and finishing at Clashnessie works well for this, with a circumnavigation of the island. Alternatively it is possible to start and finish at the small jetty opposite the island (NC 109 338); this provides an extremely sheltered option if conditions dictate. Please park considerately if starting here. If you wish to make the coastal journey shorter, then the head of Loch Nedd provides an alternative start or finish (NC 143 318). There is next to no parking at the small slipway, however a short way east of this there is a parking area down a short track on the grass overlooking the head of the loch.

The Old Man of Stoer | Giles Trussell

Point of Stoer

No. 7 | **Grade B** | **18km** | **OS Sheet 15**	
Tidal Port	Ullapool
Start	△ Clashnessie (NC 058 309)
Finish	○ Clachtoll (NC 039 272)
HW/LW	HW/LW at Clashnessie is around 5 minutes before Ullapool.
Tidal Times	Off Cluas Deas and the Point of Stoer: The SW going stream starts at about 5 hours and 10 minutes after HW Ullapool. The NE going stream starts at about 2 hours and 15 minutes before HW Ullapool.
Max Rate Sp	Off Cluas Deas and the Point of Stoer 2.5 knots.
Coastguard	Stornoway, tel. 01851 702013, VHF weather every 3 hours from 0710.

Introduction

This is without doubt one of the classic headlands of the North West Highlands, and a must for any paddler in the area. It provides the usual abundance of wildlife, spectacular cliffs and caves, limited landing spots, view to the Outer Hebrides, Stoer lighthouse and, of course, the 60m high Old Man of Stoer sea stack. In good conditions it is a comfortable day's paddle, allowing time for coastal exploring and making the most of this stunning headland.

Leaving Clashnessie

Description

Setting out from the golden sands of Clashnessie allows easy parking and access, along with the best views of the caves and 'Old Man' while paddling around the point. The first 4km gives a gentle introduction for what is to come, with small indented cliffs and the sandy bay of Culkein (an alternative start) en route. Keep your eyes and ears alert however as there is often an otter playing in the kelp or a peregrine screeching in the cliffs along this section. As you pass Rubh'an Dùnain you'll see a small natural arch up on the headland and the cliffs will start rearing up as they lead towards the point. Underneath these cliffs you'll soon come to Geodha an Leth-roinn, with some narrow caves on its southern side. This offers the last possible stopping point until 6km around the point, so it may be worth the boulder landing to rest and fuel up.

The next corner to turn is the point itself, and you are instantly rewarded with the expanse of the Inner Minch leading towards the Outer Hebrides, along with the Island of Handa to the north. The water will start to become livelier now with the swell and tide moving around the point. This will soon push you on a little further to get the first fantastic view of the Old Man of Stoer. As you paddle closer the grandeur of this stack becomes apparent, and in the right sea conditions, you'll be able to paddle easily between it and the mainland cliffs. While doing so you might well be able to say hello to climbers scaling the stack, which was first climbed in 1966. Moving on from here, the spectacular rock scenery continues for the next 4km, perhaps offering the most impressive cliffs of the journey, leading to the impressive Point of Stoer lighthouse.

Beyond the lighthouse the cliffs finish and the coastline changes to shingle and sand beaches. These offer a welcome landing spot for refreshment, prior to the final 6km of the journey. This

Point of Stoer lighthouse

takes us along a rocky coastline with some small caves at the entrance to the Bay of Stoer, another sandy beach and opportunity to stop. The trip finishes a short stretch further down the coast at the stunning beach of Clachtoll. Approaching the beach the impressive rock feature 'Split Rock' is easily seen lying beyond the bay. Landing at Clachtoll there will likely be others enjoying this gem of a beach. Behind you though will still be the views of the Outer Hebrides and of course those memories of the fantastic trip just completed.

Tides and weather

This is a major headland and as such is exposed to the wind, swell and tidal streams. Good planning is essential for this trip and a day with good weather and small swell is optimum. Arriving at the Point of Stoer and making use of the south-west tidal stream is recommended. There are eddies either side of the point, but these do not run too strongly.

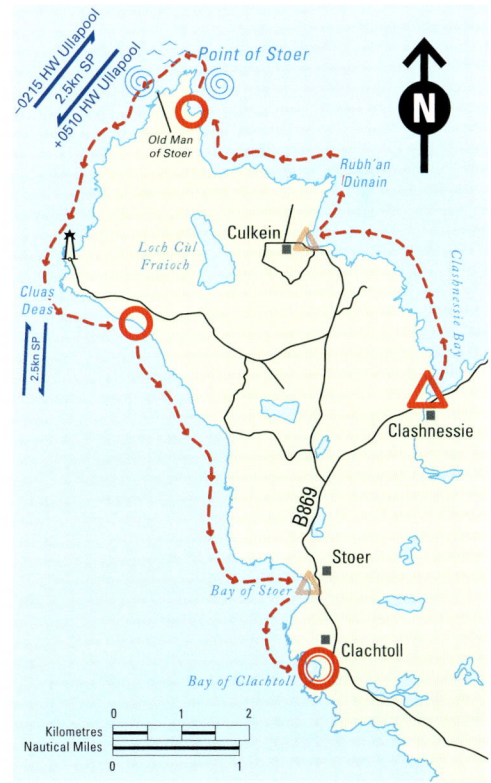

⊙ Heading out to the Point of Stoer

Additional information

There are no facilities at Clashnessie, however at Clachtoll there are public toilets and a campsite. When landing at Clachtoll it is sometimes easier to use the more northerly smaller beach, as vehicles can be driven down the track to collect the kayaks, making the carry shorter.

Variations

It is possible to start/finish at the Bay of Culkein (NC 038 332) or the Bay of Stoer (NC 038 283) if preferred. If doing so, please do not drive over the grass areas but carry the kayaks from the road. The trip can be paddled in either direction if tide or wind makes the recommended route less favourable. If it is a south-westerly wind then paddling out and back to the Old Man of Stoer from Clashnessie works well, perhaps cutting across and circumnavigating Oldany Island as well.

Achmelvich Bay

Loch Inver & Achmelvich

No. 8	**Grade B**	**17km**	**OS Sheet 15**	
Tidal Port	Ullapool
Start	△ Lochinver (NC 087 223)
Finish	◯ Lochinver (NC 087 223)
HW/LW	HW/LW at Lochinver is around 5 minutes before Ullapool.
Tidal Times	Tidal streams are insignificant in this area.
Max Rate Sp	Tidal streams are insignificant in this area.
Coastguard	Stornoway, tel. 01851 702013, VHF weather every 3 hours from 0710.

Introduction

A picturesque village with incredible mountain scenery as its backdrop leads to a wild island with great views and seals for company. Add to this a section of exposed Atlantic coastline, and then one of the most stunning beaches of the North West Highlands, and you have your trip.

Loch Inver and Suilven

Description

The slipway by the marina at the end of the road past the main harbour provides a perfect launch site to start the trip. Here you get great views looking across the water to the picturesque village of Lochinver; behind it the imposing mountain of Quinag dominates the landscape. Lochinver is one of the larger active fishing ports in Scotland, and you may well see Spanish and French trawlers coming and going as you leave the sheltered waters that make up the large natural inlet of Loch Inver. Heading out of the loch follow the southern shore, passing the odd small island. As you get out towards Kirkaig Point the views will really start to unfold; to the west is Rubha Coigeach and beyond this in the far distance are the Outer Hebrides. To the north you may get a glimpse of the lighthouse at the Point of Stoer, and behind you the towering mountain of Suilven. This mountain is one of the most distinctive in Scotland, and perhaps the most photographed. It is made of Torridonian Sandstone, sitting on the landscape of Lewisian Gneiss. The surrounding rocks were eroded during glaciation and what is left is the towering pillar-shaped mountain we see today.

Soyea Island is a wild place, with no easy landing. It acts as a natural barrier to the ocean swells and protects Loch Inver from them. On the route out to the island the old pyramid shaped metal beacon is seen to the east of the island, however don't be tempted to explore it and then miss out circumnavigating Soyea. Porpoises and seals will undoubtedly be the only company while paddling around the island. Off the western tip the ocean swell may well make its presence felt.

Returning to the mainland involves a short crossing, aiming towards the houses of Achmelvich that can be seen on the mainland shore. The views of Suilven are perhaps at their best from here.

It can be a bit difficult to make out Achmelvich Bay while paddling across to it, but once you arrive it is unmistakeable. The white sandy beaches that are found at the back of the bay are just stunning; the hardest choice of the day is which one to land on, or whether to land on them both. There is a campsite here so there will often be people sharing the beach with you, so look out for swimmers in the water as you land, or search out a bit of beach to enjoy for yourself. The crystal clear turquoise waters and pristine white sands will certainly have you feeling you have landed in paradise, the challenge is going to be leaving!

Heading back to Lochinver you can fully enjoy the expanse of mountains found in this corner of the North West Highlands. The shapes seen in the Lewisian Gneiss cliffs that create the rocky coastline also provide constant interest as they rise up out of the ocean. If time allows you may consider heading into the hidden inlet of Loch Roe, a tranquil escape from the more exposed outer coast. The village of Lochinver nestles in its dramatic setting and all too soon the trip will come to an end back at the slipway. All that is left now is to go into the village and enjoy some of the local refreshments that will be on offer; a visit to the 'pie shop' comes highly recommended.

Scotland's smallest castle

As you head around the first little headland and start going south when leaving Achmelvich, keep a sharp lookout for what has been described as Scotland's smallest castle. It is known as Hermit's Castle and the tiny structure can be seen perched on a rock overlooking a small inlet. Constructed in concrete, the castle was reportedly built in the 1950s by an English architect, David Scott, who spent only one night in it before leaving the area for good. The windows and doors have long gone so it does not look an appealing place to stay nowadays, despite its incredible views.

Tides and weather

There are no tidal streams of note in this area, so for this trip you need only consider the swell and the wind. Within Loch Inver there is reasonable protection from both, however Soyea Island and the section of coastline up to Achmelvich are very exposed to both wind and swell. Only choose to paddle this section of the trip in appropriate conditions.

Additional information

Lochinver offers a range of amenities including public toilets, shops, petrol station, pubs and cafés. It also has a good tourist information centre that can provide plenty of advice on the local area. Lochinver Larder is perhaps the best known of the cafés, its award winning pies have to be tasted to be believed. At Achmelvich there is a campsite and a youth hostel, both offering a great location to stay if visiting the area. There are public toilets available and it may be possible to get some refreshments at the campsite shop.

Variations

If conditions are not suitable to head to Soyea Island and Achmelvich, a trip around Loch Inver is still well worth considering. If you wish to extend the trip, heading on up to Clachtoll provides dramatic cliff scenery as well as some more spectacular beaches.

The impressive Assynt mountains from Rubha Coigeach

Rubha Coigeach

No. 9	**Grade B**	**17km**	**OS Sheet 15**
Tidal Port	Ullapool
Start	△ Achnahaird (NC 016 141)
Finish	⭕ Old Dornie (NB 983 112)
HW/LW	HW/LW at Old Dornie is around 5 minutes before Ullapool.
Tidal Times	Off Rubha Coigeach: The NE going stream starts at about 2 hours and 15 minutes before HW Ullapool. The SW going stream starts at about 5 hours and 10 minutes after HW Ullapool.
Max Rate Sp	Off Rubha Coigeach 2.5 knots.
Coastguard	Stornoway, tel. 01851 702013, VHF weather every 3 hours from 0710.

Introduction

Compared to some of the other headlands on the west coast, Rubha Coigeach is relatively small. Some say that "All the best things come in small packages", and this is certainly true of this journey. It has intricate sandstone cliffs, stunning views to the Hebrides and the unique Assynt mountains, plenty of wildlife and a real sense of remoteness. Add to this some tidal movement and exposure to any swell or weather, and it provides the perfect balance of challenge and beauty.

Cave just east of Rubha Coigeach

Description

From the road head that provides beach access and a great view of Achnahaird Bay, there is a short, steep track that leads down to a rocky inlet; this is the starting point for the trip. This was once an old slipway and remnants of it can still be seen, although it would not have been the easiest of places to launch and land each day. The spectacular views are immediately apparent as you head along the first section of low-lying cliffs. To the north the Point of Stoer is visible, and to the east the unique Assynt mountain formations, including the most dramatic of them all, Suilven. The cliffs start getting bigger at Rubha Duilich; look and listen for peregrine falcons here as they often nest in this area.

Camas Coille provides a landing opportunity, the only one until after the headland; so if a stop is required take the opportunity. All along this section there is a maze of low lying rocks and a small but prominent sea stack. Weaving in and out of them provides great sport. Keep an eye out for the 'eye of the needle' rocky headland as you start to approach the final bay before Rubha Coigeach. This small natural hole in the rock marks the approach to some of the best caves on this trip. Take the time to enjoy them; they both have hidden surprises! The natural bay just before the headland does not provide an easy landing, but it does offer some sheltered water to take in the surroundings before carrying on around the headland. The sea will be a bit more lively as the headland is rounded, the swell and tide may well be apparent. The views will open up in dramatic fashion as the expanse of the Minch, and beyond this the Outer Hebrides, come into view.

Soon you will reach Faochag Bay that has a beautifully sheltered stony beach as a landing place on its north side. With great views and short-cropped grass to lie out on, it may be difficult to rouse yourself to leave when the time comes. The intricate sandstone cliffs continue as the trip heads south. This is a popular venue for rock climbers so be sure to say hello as you pass beneath them. There is plenty of interest in Camas Eilean Ghlais; if you are lucky there may even be an otter along with the seals that make this their home. There is a sandy beach to land here if another stop is required, if not continue on around the final little headland to Reiff Bay. It will come as no surprise that reefs guard the bay, so if any swell is around be mindful of this as you approach. This bay has a beautiful sandy beach with idyllic houses overlooking it, the majority of them being holiday homes. It is possible to finish here but the parking is limited, so it is best to continue the journey on to the jetties at Old Dornie. This is no hardship as the cliffs and spectacular scenery continues, now with great views down though the magical Summer Isles. One of the bigger cliffs paddled beneath is 'Pig Cliff'. See if you can spot the stone pig on the hillside above. It may well be tempting to head on and explore the stunning beach on Isle Ristol, and perhaps even some more of the island. If time allows this is recommended, if not the sheltered natural harbour and jetties at Old Dornie are a perfect finishing spot.

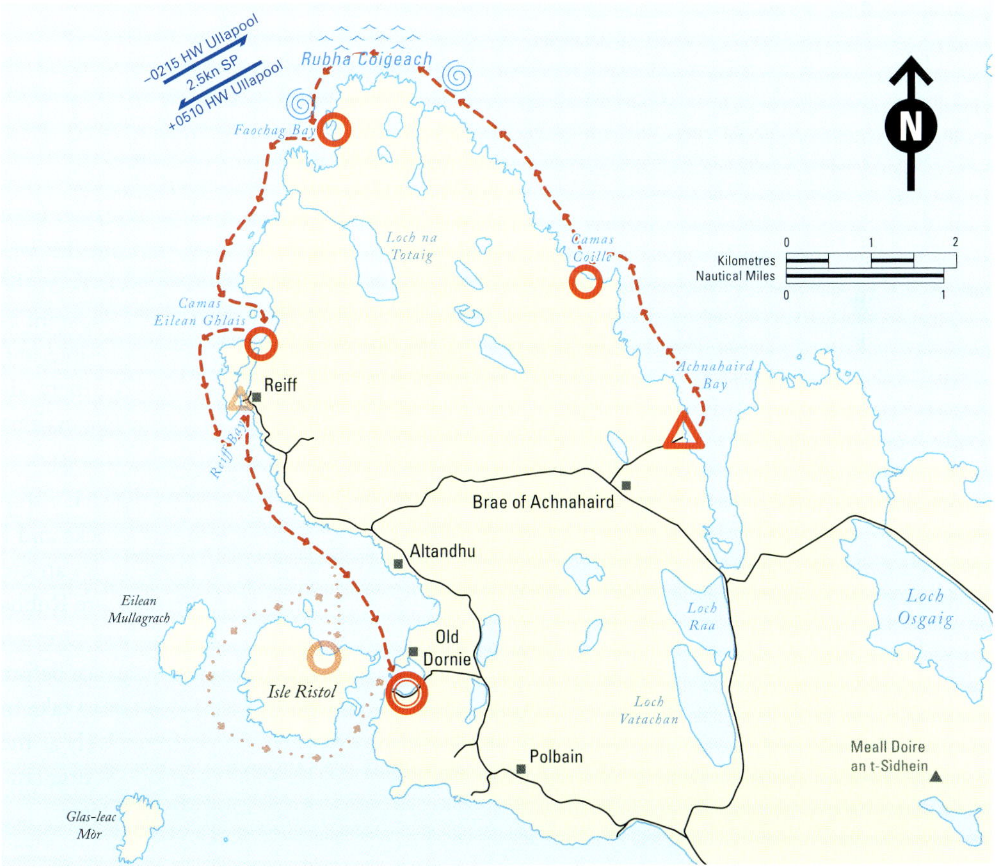

Sea stack near Camas Coille

Tides and weather

Rubha Coigeach does not offer many landing places and is exposed to weather and swell. Add to this the tidal movement, and it is clear that a good weather forecast is necessary for this trip. On the eastern coast of the headland the tides are not noticeable. Off the headland there is tidal movement and associated eddies, with the western side experiencing slight tidal movement. It is best to time this trip to make the most of the tidal movement off the headland and down the west coast.

Additional information

There are no amenities at either the start or finish. There is a well-serviced campsite at Altandhu, which is handily adjacent to the pub which serves great food. The nearest shops and fuel station are in Achiltibuie.

Variations

If a westerly wind puts the west coast out of your comfort zone, it is well worth paddling out to the headland and back on the eastern side. This can provide excellent shelter as well as stunning scenery and rock architecture.

The trip can be extended by exploring some of the northern Summer Isles (see following chapter).

Tanera Beg's sandstone arch

Summer Isles – North

No. 10 | **Grade A** | **24km** | **OS Sheet 15**

Tidal Port	Ullapool
Start	△ Achiltibuie (NC 013 096)
Finish	○ Achiltibuie (NC 013 096)
HW/LW	HW/LW at Achiltibuie is around 5 minutes before Ullapool.
Tidal Times	In the vicinity of the Summer Isles: The direction and the times of the small amount of tidal flow is variable.
Max Rate Sp	0.5 knots.
Coastguard	Stornoway, tel. 01851 702013, VHF weather every 3 hours from 0710.

Introduction

The Summer Isles are a sea kayaker's paradise. There is a wealth of islands, coastlines and wildlife to enjoy. With no real tidal concerns and relatively sheltered waters, it is a perfect place to spend some time. This trip takes in the main islands on the Summer Isles which offer some amazing arches, caves and beaches. A week could easily be spent exploring this area, let alone the islands further south.

Crossing to Eilean Mullagrach

Description

At the put-in at the beach to the east of Achiltibuie pier there is ample parking on the grass, looking out to Tanera Mòr. A 3km crossing takes you across Badentarbat Bay to the Summer Isles, so called because they were used for summer grazing by the crofters. Tanera Mòr is the largest and only inhabited island of the Summer Isles and its perfect large natural harbour, the Anchorage, is where you will first arrive. The Anchorage is a very different place today from what it would have been in the late 1700s. At this time up to 200 fishing vessels would be found in the bay, bringing the herring into the fishing station at Tigh an Quay where the old pier is. Nowadays the only boats found here are usually leisure boats, and the only inhabitants on the island are there for the tourist trade. It is worth landing to stretch the legs and explore the old schoolhouse and post office if time allows. From the Anchorage head around the south of the island to Mol Mòr, where you will get a taste of the fantastic colours and shapes of the sandstone cliffs of these islands. The views from here extend across the southern Summer Isles and beyond, a trip for another day perhaps.

Heading across to Tanera Beg aim for the south-eastern extremity where you will find a beautiful sandstone arch. This stands delicately over the sea and can be paddled through at high water. From here there is a choice, paddling into the tranquil sheltered lagoon found between Eilean Fada Mòr and Tanera Beg, or paddling up the western coastline of Tanera Beg. The lagoon offers small bays, coral sands and seals lazing on seaweed-covered rocks; the western coast offers a huge cave at its south-western corner and then rugged cliffs exposed to the elements. It's a difficult choice as both are great options. If time and fitness allow, do both! There is no landing on the western coast, so ensure a rest is taken on one of the landing places found at the southern end of the lagoon if deciding to head this way. On either route keep an eye out for sea eagles that can be seen in this area.

Leaving Tanera Beg the trip continues across to Glas-leac Mòr; look out for the seals hauled out on the rocky skerry just south-east of the island. There is a storm beach with potential landing on the east side of this island, but it is usually easier to continue on to Isle Ristol for an easy landing. From Glas-leac Mòr be sure to head across to Eilean Mullagrach and paddle up its east coast, as here you will find the biggest sea arch on the Summer Isles. Having found the giant arch head across to the north coast of Isle Ristol and take the time to explore the caves found here before heading to the stunning beach on its northern coast. Here you will find a well-earned resting spot. With its azure blue waters and peaceful setting it is one to savour. When you eventually manage to leave the beach the last bit of the journey takes you through the narrow gap formed between Isle Ristol and the mainland. On a spring tide at low water this may be a short portage, but other than this it is paddleable. The cliffs and interest continue back to the finish at Achiltibuie. The fantastic views down through the Summer Isles and inland towards the grandiose backdrop of the Assynt mountains will no doubt keep any weary arms going for the last few kilometres.

Tides and weather

With no real tidal streams in and around the Summer Isles, weather is the only consideration when planning your trip. Once amongst the islands they offer a lot of shelter from any wind or swell. Getting across to each island and around the more exposed parts of the islands will require planning, with attention being paid to the prevailing wind and swell.

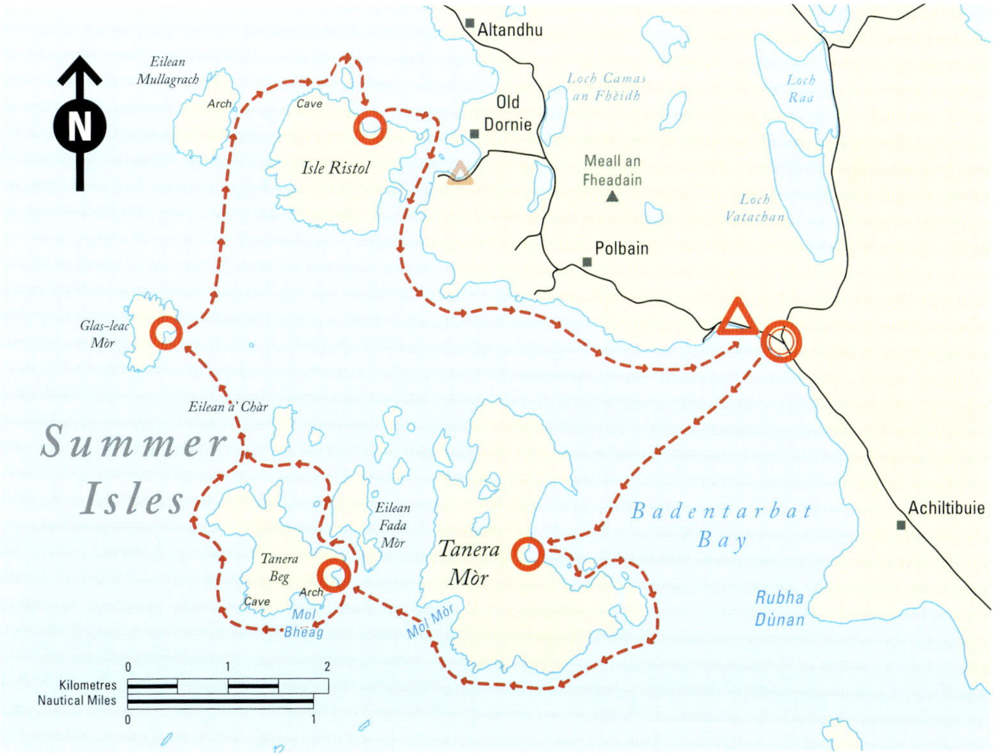

Isle Ristol's 'other' beach

Additional information

There are some public toilets at the road junction just south from the put-in. Achiltibuie has good amenities including a shop, petrol station and hotel with a public bar. If there are non-paddlers in the group there are regular boat trips to the Summer Isles in the summer season from Achiltibuie pier.

Variations

If wanting a shorter day, then just paddling around Tanera Mòr and Beg is recommended. If then wanting to explore Isle Ristol, Eilean Mullagrach and Glas-leac Mòr, then doing this as a separate day trip from the jetties at Old Dornie (NB 983 112) works well. It is also possible to make the trip a multi-day journey and take in rest of the Summer Isles to the south or Rubha Coigeach to the north. See the previous and following chapters for more information.

Priest Island

Summer Isles – South

No. 11	**Grade B**	**31km**	**OS Sheet 15**
Tidal Port	Ullapool
Start	△ Badenscallie (NC 036 062)
Finish	◯ Badenscallie (NC 036 062)
HW/LW	HW/LW at Badenscallie is around 5 minutes before Ullapool.
Tidal Times	In the vicinity of the Summer Isles: The direction and the times of the small amount of tidal flow is variable.
Max Rate Sp	0.5 knots.
Coastguard	Stornoway, tel. 01851 702013, VHF weather every 3 hours from 0710.

Introduction

These southern islands of the beautiful archipelago of the Summer Isles have a remote and 'out there' feel about them. They include perhaps the jewel in the crown of the Summer Isles, Priest Island; an RSPB nature reserve and home to a wealth of wildlife as well as spectacular cliffs, caves and sea arches. With small crossings, stunning scenery and islands in abundance this is a trip to be savoured on a good weather day.

© Eilean Dubh's 'palm tree retreat'

Summer Isles – South

Description

Looking out across to the first island of the day, Horse Island, the beach at Badenscaille burial ground provides the perfect location to start. At low water it can be quite a carry, so perhaps consider this in the day's timings. The narrow gap that dries between Horse Island and Meall nan Gabhar offers the only real landing spot on the island and is worth heading to first. From here, head down the east coast where the most dramatic cliffs on the island can be enjoyed. In the distance the mountain of An Teallach is clearly seen, standing proud of all that surrounds. From the southern tip of Horse Island it is well worth the slight detour to take in the small islands of Càrn nan Sgeir and Meall nan Caorach. These are home to a host of wildlife including seals and otters, have stunning views across all of the Summer Isles, and offer a perfect landing spot to take in the vista.

From this small cluster of islands, the first of the slightly longer crossings of the day leads to the group of islands south of Eilean Dubh, which includes the intriguingly named Bottle Island. Like Priest Island these islands are also managed by the RSPB as a nature reserve, so you will no doubt be greeted by plenty of the nesting residents. As with all of these magical islands, the sandstone cliffs provide constant interest as you explore and weave in and out this cluster of skerries and islets. From here there is the final short crossing to reach Priest Island, the remotest of the Summer Isles and some would say the most special. Head to the sheltered landing spot at Acairseid Eilean a' Chlèirich. Once landed it is worth taking some time to explore the island, however take care in this as there are numerous ground nesting birds on this RSPB-managed haven for wildlife.

Continue the island exploration by paddling around the southern and western coastlines. The fantastically deep red colours and ornate shapes of the Torridonian Sandstone will be clear to see, along with the geos and caves that make up the western coastline. Being exposed to everything, there may be a lively sea to contend with as you make your way to the northern point. Here you will find the dramatic cave and arch that make up the tip of the island, and this is followed by Toll Eilean a' Chlèrich (Priest Hole).

This marks the point to leave this magical island and start heading back, taking in another island along the way, Eilean Dubh. Although relatively small, the island is one of the highest of the Summer Isles, so what it lacks in size it makes up for in stature. There are more cliffs and geos to explore, along with an idyllic sheltered bay which makes for a perfect landing spot on the north-eastern corner of the island. The surprise here is a jetty and well-maintained chalet, with its own palm tree in amongst pines and lush vegetation. This was built by the island's owner Dr Van Arman and clearly provides an amazing place to get away from it all, as well as a perfect place for weary paddlers to stop and stretch their legs.

From Eilean Dubh the final crossing of the day takes you back to the west coast of Horse Island. Paddling up this and then around Meall nan Gabhar provides some final sandstone cliffs and geos, along with seals and birdlife to enjoy before finishing the trip at the beach at Badenscallie.

Tides and weather

There are no tidal considerations for this trip, so the weather is the main concern. All the islands have limited landing places, involve open crossings, and are exposed to potential winds and rough seas from all sides. Therefore good weather conditions are recommended.

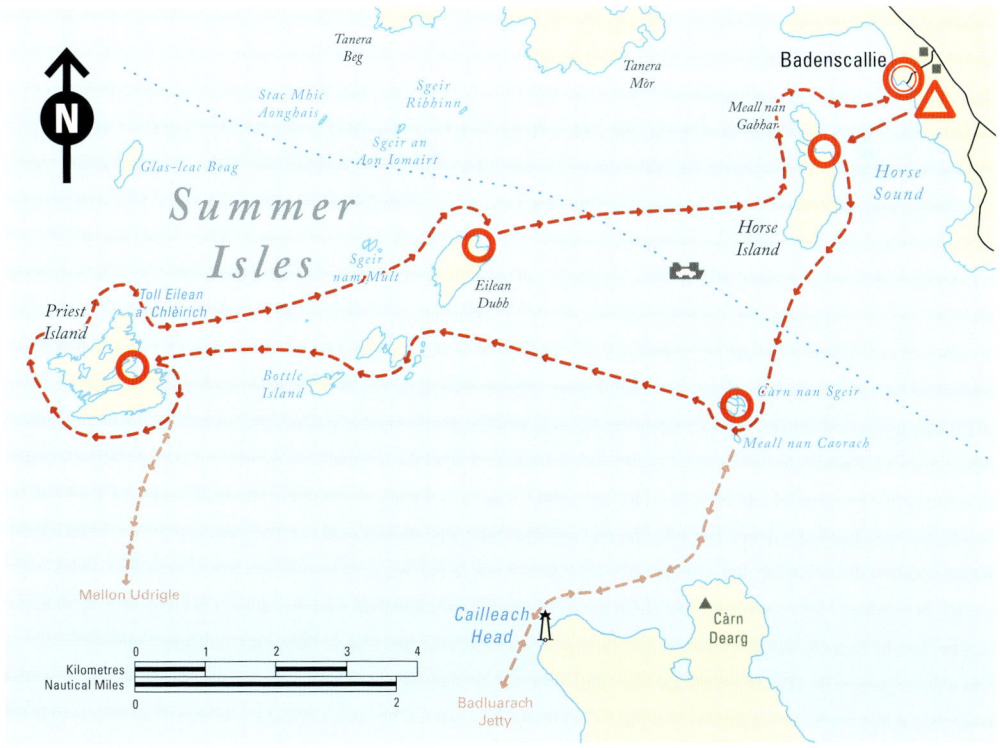

Eilean Dubh's cliffs with Tanera Mòr beyond

Additional information

There are no amenities at Badenscallie. The nearest are at Achiltibuie, including a good shop, petrol station and hotel with a public bar.

Variations

There are two alternative places to start this trip from on the mainland to the south, one at Mellon Udrigle (NB 892 958) and the other Badluarach jetty (NB 996 947). Both will involve a longer crossing to get out and back to the islands; Mellon Udrigle has a stunning beach to start and finish the trip from. It is also possible to make the trip a multi-day journey and take in the rest of the Summer Isles to the north, see the previous chapter for more information.

Island Years

It was the naturalist Dr Fraser Darling who gave Priest Island its fame when he lived on the island in the 1930s and wrote his book, *Island Years*. The island was inhabited long before he stayed there though, with the remains of prehistoric stone circles built by settlers of an even more distant past still evident today. There are also the remains of a ruined bothy that is the site of an ancient chapel. This was used as a Christian retreat and is how the island acquired its name. Today the only real evidence of habitation is the shelter that the RSPB wardens use on their visits to the island.

Loch Broom and Ullapool

Isle Martin & Loch Broom

No. 12 | Grade A | 14km | OS Sheet 19

Tidal Port	Ullapool
Start	△ Ardmair (NH 107 983)
Finish	○ Ullapool (NH 126 938)
HW/LW	As at Ullapool.
Tidal Times	In Loch Broom: The ingoing stream starts at about 6 hours and 5 minutes before HW Ullapool. The outgoing stream starts at about 5 minutes before HW Ullapool.
Max Rate Sp	In Loch Broom 0.5 knots.
Coastguard	Stornoway, tel. 01851 702013, VHF weather every 3 hours from 0710.

Introduction

Isle Martin has towering cliffs on the north coast, sheltered bays which otters and seals make their homes, and an interesting history. Add to this the small lighthouse at Rubha Cadail and finishing in the North West Highland's main town of Ullapool, a bustling centre of boats, tourists, cafés and ferries, and you have a fine day out.

© Rubha Cadail

Isle Martin & Loch Broom

Description

There is usually plenty of roadside parking at Ardmair, which provides easy access to the beach. While launching it will be hard not to notice the fact that the beach is made of perfectly round and flat small stones; when it comes to stone 'skimming' this place is as good as it gets!

The trip starts by circumnavigating Isle Martin, so head across to the southern coast to do this in an anticlockwise direction, this ensures there are some good landing places when you need them, later in the day. The island is named after St Martin who is reputed to have established a monastery on the island around 300–400 AD. There is an impressive stone cross on the island that is worth looking out for. Heading up the west coast the cliffs will start rearing up out of the sea as you reach the north-western tip. This sets the scene for the impressive cliffs that are just around the corner.

As you explore the northern coastline not only will the cliffs impress; the view will as well. The Summer Isles are visible to the north-west and if lucky you will have the Outer Hebrides in the far distance beyond. To the north the towering mountain of Ben Mor Coigach rises straight up from the seashore. With its majestic cliffs and resident birdlife, the northern coastline of the island is stunning, and as it is not visible from the main road at the start, it is a real hidden gem. There is a tranquil landing spot at the north-eastern corner, somewhere to have a bite to eat while watching the seals, and if lucky otters, playing in the small sheltered bay it overlooks. From here the cliffs finish and a pleasant low-lying coastline leads to the sheltered bay that forms the natural harbour for the island.

Having explored ashore, head back across to the mainland and Rubha Cadail. The small white lighthouse is clear to see as the low-lying headland is reached. This light was built in 1952 and marks the entrance route to the port of Ullapool. Loch Broom now leads down to this busy yet picturesque town. The distant views of the Hebrides will be replaced with the inland view of Ullapool as it protrudes out into the loch, with the mountains of An Teallach, Beinn Dearg and Sgùrr Mòr forming a huge natural amphitheatre at the head of Loch Broom. There are plenty of places to stop if required while paddling down the loch, and it is also worth keeping in close to the shore as large ships and ferries come and go from Ullapool.

The finish in Ullapool will be a contrast to the rest of the trip; landing on the stony beach somewhere along Shore Street is one of the few landing options here. Stepping out of your kayak you will no doubt have plenty of spectators, however you will also have next to no distance to go to find one of the many cafés or pubs for some well earned refreshments.

Tides and weather

There is no tidal movement around Isle Martin worthy of consideration and only a small amount in Loch Broom. This area is relatively sheltered from any swell so it will just be the wind to consider in the trip planning. If it is possible to plan the trip to have the wind in your favour and the small amount of tide going into Loch Broom to assist then this is ideal. It is however no problem to plan this trip based on the wind direction alone.

Fishing and flour

In the 18th century the island was a busy place, and at its peak there were around 100 people living on the island, mostly working in its own herring station and customs house. As with so many places however this all ceased by 1813 when the fish stocks had irreversibly dwindled.

In the late 1930s the herring station was converted into a flourmill. Wheat was brought to the island by sailing ship and then flour was transported to Ullapool. This flour was then distributed to bakeries across the north of Scotland in flour sacks that were labelled 'Isle Martin Flour Mills'. The workers were ferried to the island daily until the mill eventually closed in 1948.

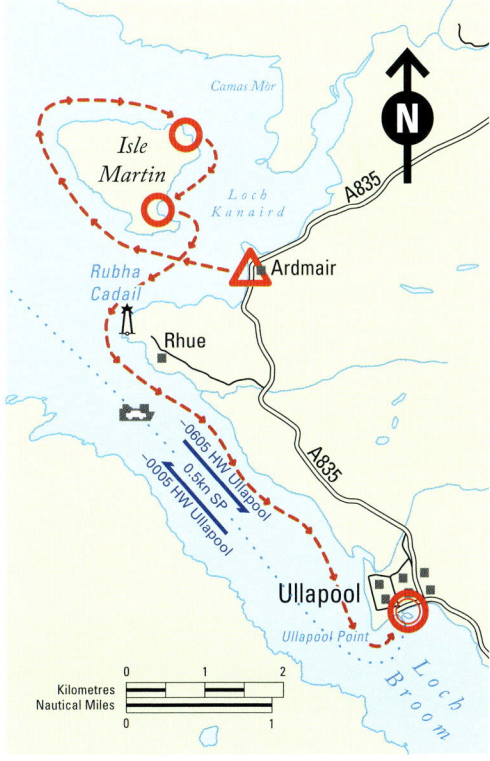

The ornate sandstone of Isle Martin

Additional information

Shore Street, where the trip finishes, runs from Ullapool Point past the ferry terminal to the sailing club, and it is often difficult to find parking on it, particularly in the summer. If this is the case consider parking in the main signposted car park and then just picking the kayaks up at the end of the trip. There is a turning circle at the end of Shore Street, or limited off the road stopping by the sailing club to do this. Alternatively, consider staying in the campsite; this is perfectly located to enjoy the town, and with its own beach surrounding it provides a perfect launching or landing spot. Ullapool has a full range of amenities including toilets with public showers.

Variations

To avoid the need for a shuttle, start and finish at Ardmair, circumnavigate Isle Martin, and take in the lighthouse at Rubha Cadail. This makes for a great half-day out.

Wester Ross

Introduction

Wester Ross takes in the coast from Ullapool down to Kyle of Lochalsh and is an area well known for its spectacular mountain scenery, along with remote coastlines, accessible bays and sea lochs cutting deep into the landscape. Rubha Rèidh is the standout headland of this area, with a stunning beach nestled into its northern coastline. Either side of this can be found the more sheltered open bays of Gruinard and Gairloch, both with a wealth of beaches and wildlife.

The whole area is overlooked by towering mountains. The Torridon mountains are arguably the most spectacular of the area, and a trip out of Shieldaig into the relatively sheltered waters of Loch Torridon allows you to paddle right beneath these mighty giants.

The isolated and beautiful Applecross peninsula, south from here, has its own unique charm. If you are looking for sheltered islands, sandy beaches and otters aplenty, then Plockton and the Black Isles is a must.

The area is full of human history as well, much of it, particularly around Loch Ewe, linked to wartime days. Gruinard Island also harbours a dark secret linked to the Cold War era (see Trip 14).

Having moved on from its past, the area thrives on tourism and ensures it welcomes all who visit. Around every corner there are cafés, pubs and restaurants to be enjoyed, with the villages of Gairloch, Shieldaig, Applecross and Plockton at the heart of this.

Tides and weather

This area receives a reasonable amount of shelter from Skye and the Outer Hebrides, so unless the swell is running from the north, the coastline is not too badly affected. In windy conditions it is obvious where will be exposed, however the area offers a lot of options for more sheltered trips when conditions are unfavourable.

In general there is very little tidal movement in this area. Ruabh Rèidh would be the only notable exception, but on the whole the wind will usually be the dominant factor when planning trips in this area.

Shieldaig Island

Cailleach Head and the southern Summer Isles

Cailleach Head

No. 13	**Grade B**	**20km**	**OS Sheet 19**

Tidal Port	Ullapool
Start	△ Badluarach (NG 996 947)
Finish	◯ Badluarach (NG 996 947)
HW/LW	HW/LW at Badluarach is around the same as Ullapool.
Tidal Times	In the entrance to Little Loch Broom: The ingoing stream starts at about 6 hours and 5 minutes before HW Ullapool. The outgoing stream starts at about 5 minutes before HW Ullapool.
Max Rate Sp	At the entrance to the loch 1 knot.
Coastguard	Stornoway, tel. 01851 702013, VHF weather every 3 hours from 0710.

Introduction

Cailleach Head translates as 'headland of the old woman'. Who the lady was or when she lived is a mystery. The headland lies at the tip of a long finger of land that separates Loch Broom from Little Loch Broom known as the Annat peninsula. It is a remote and infrequently visited section of coastline with wonderful views and abundant wildlife.

© Cailleach Head

Description

The journey begins at Badluarach jetty, which is where the passenger ferry goes over to Scoraig, a village you can't drive to. Start by paddling across Little Loch Broom to Scoraig. It was re-populated in the 1960s and now has an almost self-sufficient community, with a primary school and a population of about 100. The village is not supplied by mains electricity from the national grid so they produce their own by harnessing energy from wind, water, and solar power. The community depends upon the sea and coast around the Annat peninsula for food, as the land is not the most fertile. Fish farms are a source of income for some in this area, and source of concern for others who see the fish farms doing more harm to the environment than good. If choosing to land at Scoraig and have a look around, be sure to look out for the old lighthouse that used to be at Cailleach Head. It was moved from the headland when replaced by the current light, and then rebuilt in the village where it has now been converted into a museum for the village and surrounding area.

Leaving the village, the shoreline steepens into cliffs and the lighthouse is soon reached. It is a small and slightly disappointing affair, the hill it stands on providing the height as opposed to the structure of the light itself. The views will more than make up for the lighthouse though, as the expanse of the Summer Isles will now be coming into view, as well as hopefully the Outer Hebrides beyond. The landing jetty that used to supply the lighthouse is not marked on the map, but look carefully and you will discover it about a kilometre beyond the light. The bay of Camus na Ruthaig is an out-of-the-way place and the chances of seeing an otter or divers are high; it offers a stopping opportunity if required. For the birdwatcher this headland is an important site as it's one of the few places where all the 'divers' have been seen: great northern, red-throated, black-throated and white billed. The next headland of Càrn Dearg is grander in stature than Cailleach Head itself and has some sizable cliffs halfway up.

Around the headland Fèith an Fheòir is reached; this is an easy place to land and a convenient turning point for the trip. If wishing to continue a little further, the remote tiny settlement of Achmore is worth a look. A couple of families make this their isolated home. Heading back from here the views across Loch Broom will be dominated by the impressive mountain of Ben Mor Coigach, rising steeply up from the loch's shores. Keep an eye out for wild goats, red deer and free-ranging horses while returning along the Annat peninsula,;these can often be seen quite close to the shore.

Reaching Cailleach Head, cross over the mouth of Little Loch Broom to Stattic Point. Here you will have views of Gruinard Island and Greenstone Point, and perhaps be able to make out some of the fantastic beaches that are found in the Gruinard Bay area. The cliff scenery from Stattic Point back to the jetty is dominated by a very richly-coloured conglomerate rock that is made up of huge stones. The rock has eroded to form a few caves that will provide continued interest until you reach the finish back at Badluarach jetty.

Tides and weather

There are no tidal streams of consequence on this trip, despite the fact it goes around reasonable-sized headlands. The wind and any swell from the west or north are the main considerations when planning. If there is an easterly wind this can be funnelled up Little Loch Broom and may prove stronger than forecast.

Additional information

There are no amenities at Badluarach, the nearest being in Dundonnell or Laide. There is a reasonable amount of parking at the jetty, but please be careful and try to leave plenty of room close to the jetty for those going about their normal way of life.

Variations

It is possible to extend this trip into a long day or multi-day trip by crossing to the southern Summer Isles and exploring Càrn nan Sgeir, Eilean Dubh and Bottle Island. See Trip 11 for more information.

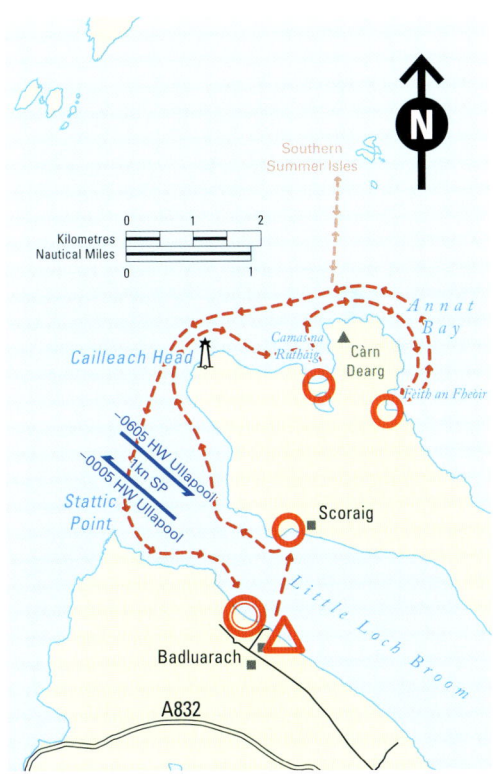

Camas na Ruthaig and Coigeach

Laide jetty and Gruinard Island

Gruinard Island

No. 14	**Grade A**	**18km**	**OS Sheet 19**
Tidal Port	Ullapool
Start	▲ Laide (NG 902 925)
Finish	◯ Laide (NG 902 925)
HW/LW	HW/LW at Laide is around 5 minutes before Ullapool.
Tidal Times	Gruinard Bay: the tides are weak and variable within the bay.
Max Rate Sp	0.5 knots.
Coastguard	Stornoway, tel. 01851 702013, VHF weather every 3 hours from 0710.

Introduction

Gruinard Island's dark history is hard to believe when the bay in which it sits provides such wonderful surroundings. Gruinard Bay has stunning beaches and coastlines, along with a wealth of wildlife including some resident sea eagles. The island itself offers interesting cliffs and great views, helping the terrible fate it suffered fade into a distant memory.

Camas a' Chruthaich and Gruinard Island

Description

The tiny jetty at Laide, made of the colourful red rock that makes up this section of coastline, is an idyllic starting point for the trip. There is next to no parking here, so please drop off the kayaks and find suitable parking further along the road. Once afloat follow the coastline towards the spectacular beaches at the head of Gruinard Bay. While doing so you will get a flavour of the area, with views across to Gruinard Island and Cailleach Head beyond. There will no doubt be some of the numerous beaches visible and in the distance, and looking out of the bay the Summer Isles come into view. The coastline has a rocky foreshore with steep hillside above; at its foot there will often be seals hauled out on any exposed rocks. The occasional small, secluded sandy beach gives a taste of what's to come. As you paddle past the small headland of Leac Innis nan Gobhar, the golden beach at the head of the bay is revealed. The mountain of An Teallach in the distance forms an impressive backdrop for what can only be described as 'breath-taking' scenery.

If you choose to land on the beach you will likely be sharing it, as there is easy access from the road. Perhaps it is best to enjoy it from the sea and head across to Camas a' Chruthaich. This is hidden behind a few small islands and a headland, however it is, in my view, the 'beach of the bay'. Hopefully you will have this one to yourself to sit and spend some time taking in the surroundings. Once you have had your fill, it is time to head across to Gruinard Island.

Head up the east coast of the island first. This low-lying coastline is often very sheltered, giving a chance to paddle in close and enjoy seeing the life below the crystal clear waters. The northern point of the island will no doubt have livelier sea conditions, as well as extensive views. Keep an eye out here for the bay's resident sea eagles; I once saw three sat on the rocks on the north-western corner of the island.

The west coast offers some great rock hopping as well as beautifully-shaped red cliffs, which continue until the coastline takes a more south-easterly direction. At this point, if a landing place is needed, a stony beach can be found at the southern tip of the island, however this is also the obvious point to head back across to the jetty at Laide. This 4km crossing will give you time to reflect on the beauty of the island just explored and its dreadful history.

The poisoned island

Gruinard Island was the site of a military operation that can only be described as 'unbelievable'. Due to fears of chemical weapons being used in the Second World War, the British carried out some research and trials. These were conducted on Gruinard Island where, in 1941, a canister of Anthrax spores was exploded near a group of secured sheep. In a few days the sheep all died and their bodies were dumped over the cliff and covered in rocks; one drifted away and infected other sheep nearby. Over the following years the military realised the extent to which Anthrax had poisoned the island; to deal with it they simply put up a sign saying, 'Landing is prohibited'! Finally, in 1987 the MOD were shamed into action, and £500,000 was paid to decontaminate the ground with 280 tonnes of formaldehyde and removal of topsoil. Anthrax spores are extremely hardy and can survive many years, however sheep and wildlife seem to be able to live happily on the island again, though you may want to think twice before camping there!

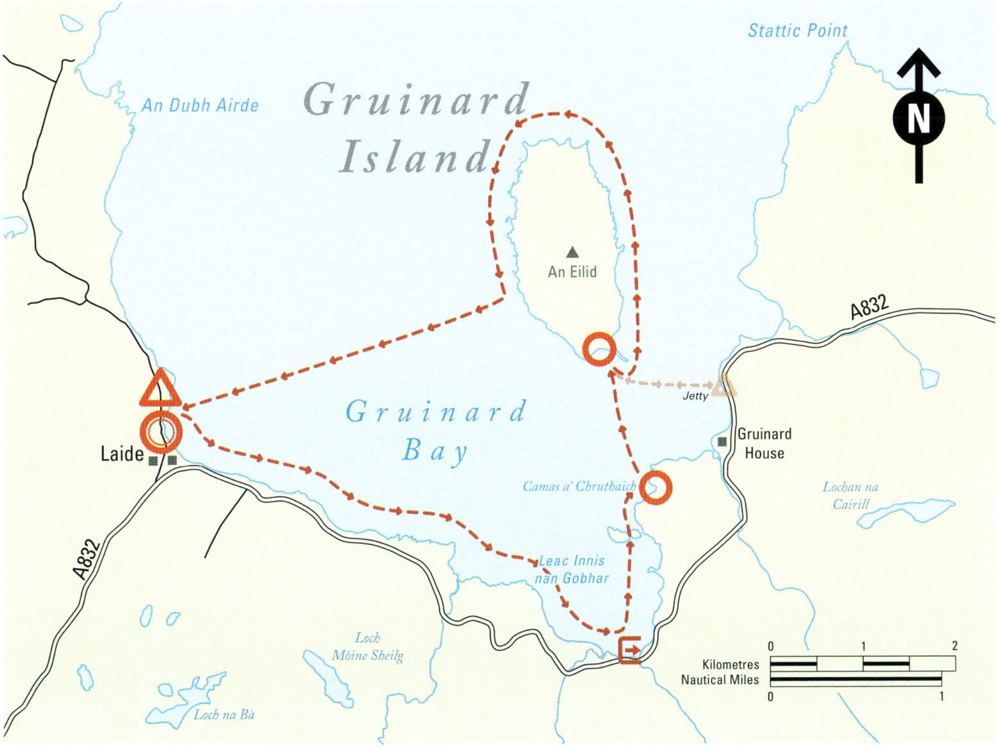

Colourful cliffs on Gruinard Island

14 Gruinard Island

Tides and weather

There are no tidal streams in Gruinard Bay, so the wind and swell are the only considerations. The bay is relatively sheltered and has numerous landing opportunities. So as long as the wind is not offshore from the south or excessively strong, some form of trip is usually possible. Any swell from the north or north-west can make some of the beach landings awkward.

Additional information

Laide has a campsite, a small shop from which provisions and ice creams can be bought, and one of the few petrol stations in the area. Please be considerate when using the jetty, especially when parking.

Variations

For a shorter day out, an alternative jetty to launch from can be found at NG 961 926. This is an ideal spot if you just wish to paddle around Gruinard Island. Parking is on the edge of the main road and it is a bit of a walk down to the jetty, so it is not as easy as starting from Laide, but it is quite feasible.

Mellon Udrigle

Greenstone Point & Loch Ewe

No. 15 | Grade B | 20km | OS Sheet 19

Tidal Port	Ullapool
Start	△ Mellon Udrigle (NG 893 958)
Finish	○ Aultbea (NG 867 888)
HW/LW	HW/LW at Aultbea is around 10 minutes before Ullapool.
Tidal Times	Between Greenstone Point and the entrance to Loch Ewe: The SSW going stream starts at about 5 hours after HW Ullapool. The NNE going stream starts at about 2 hours and 30 minutes before HW Ullapool.
	Within Loch Ewe: The ingoing stream starts at about 6 hours and 5 minutes before HW Ullapool. The outgoing stream starts at about 5 minutes before HW Ullapool.
Max Rate Sp	Between Greenstone Point and the entrance to Loch Ewe 1–2 knots. In the narrows within Loch Ewe 0.5 knots.
Coastguard	Stornoway, tel. 01851 702013, VHF weather every 3 hours from 0710.

Loch Ewe and Aultbea

Introduction

A stunning, sandy beach at the start as well as a few more on the route, added to a remote headland with dramatic views of the surrounding North West Highlands and across to the Hebrides, makes this a fine day out. Finishing in Loch Ewe with its wealth of wartime history adds a unique historic perspective.

Description

The beach at Mellon Udrigle is truly sensational, with Caribbean-like sands and sea and the North West Highlands mountain landscape as backdrop. This is a launch site that will not be forgotten, and as you head off on the trip it will seem a shame to leave it behind.

The first small headland on the route to Greenstone Point is Rubha Beag and this boasts some of the taller cliffs of the trip, with some geos and skerries to explore along the way. Beyond this, the sheltered bay of Leac Mhòr with its few remote houses is the last possible stopping place until Slaggan Bay at the entrance to Loch Ewe. Heading on to Greenstone Point itself the cliffs are surprisingly low-lying for such a major headland, however they do provide opportunities for some exploration. The grandeur of the surrounding views more than makes up for the lack of grandeur in the cliffs. Inland there is a mountain landscape, while out to sea there are the Summer Isles, the Point of Stoer in the distance, and the Outer Hebrides out to the west. A square high point of rock with a small cairn on its top marks Greenstone Point.

Wartime lookout station with Loch Ewe behind

Greenstone Point & Loch Ewe

On passing Greenstone Point the next headland of Rubha Rèidh and its lighthouse comes into view, with low-lying cliffs and barren moorland continuing until Gob a' Gheodha is reached. Here the cliffs rise a bit in stature and this marks the entrance to Slaggan Bay, where there is a welcome stopping place on another beautiful beach. Facing west this beach may well provide a bit of surf to negotiate in order to land. Slaggan was once a crofting settlement that supported a school and teacher. The ruined house seen today was where the last family lived, but when it burnt down in the early 1940s the family left and Slaggan became deserted.

The tallest cliffs of the day are encountered on leaving Slaggan Bay, with some caves to explore as the entrance to Loch Ewe is reached. On either shore of the entrance you will see the remains of numerous wartime lookout stations and gun emplacements that act as a reminder to the loch's historic past.

Soon after entering the loch you reach the small headland of Rubh' a' Choin. Look out for the ornate little bridge and a military lookout converted into a small house on the rocky island that makes up this headland. The beach at Mellon Charles offers another stopping opportunity, this proving a strange contrast of military remains alongside a beautiful beach. From here you can finish the trip by either paddling the short distance to Aultbea, or heading across to the cliffs at the northern end of the Isle of Ewe and circumnavigating the island. Whichever route you choose, the stunning mountain scenery of An Teallach, Slioch and the Torridon mountains provides an amazing view while paddling the last few kilometres into Loch Ewe. At the finish at Aultbea there is plenty of parking and a choice of landing spots, along with a handy ice cream shop.

Greenstone Point

Loch Ewe – base of the Arctic convoys

From 1939 until 1945, during World War II, Loch Ewe was a safe haven for naval vessels and merchant ships. Its depth, size and seclusion with convenient access to the Atlantic made it a perfect location. Merchant ships laden with supplies sailed from Loch Ewe under naval protection on the renowned Arctic convoys to Murmansk and Archangel in Russia. In the 1940s the loch was described as being a 'sea black with ships', there being so many you could walk from one side of the loch to the other without getting your feet wet. A total of 481 merchant ships and over 100 naval escort vessels left Loch Ewe for Russia as part of 19 Arctic convoys. Many of the men leaving in these convoys never returned, the German U-boats and bombers or the inhospitable weather and dangerous seas claiming many lives. A memorial stone commemorating those who lost their lives can be seen at Rubha nan Sasan (NG 815 923), unveiled by the Russian Convoy Club in 1999.

With the constant threat of espionage and undercover German operations, everyone in the area had to carry passes in and around Loch Ewe. Those travelling into the area had their passes checked at Inverness and again at Achnasheen, where the red hut used can still be seen.

Slaggan with the Outer Hebrides

Tides and weather

A small amount of tide runs down the west side of Greenstone Point and into Loch Ewe; ideally the trip should be planned to take advantage of this. The headland is very exposed to the wind and swell and this should be the priority when planning the trip, as it will have a greater effect than the tide. A north or north-westerly swell provides the biggest challenge, and may make landing at Slaggan Bay very difficult.

Additional information

At Mellon Udrigle there are no amenities, however there is a basic campsite, an amazing location to use as a base for a few days. Aultbea offers a range of amenities including a shop, pub and public toilets. When landing at Aultbea there is the harbour, but there is also a slipway with large parking area at the signposted picnic spot a few hundred metres to the west of the harbour. If interested in the wartime history of the loch, it is well worth driving the road around the loch to Rubha nan Sasan (NG 815 923) where a memorial stone can be found. Along the road you will find numerous information boards as well as have opportunities to see the old lookouts and gun emplacements.

Variations

The trip can be made longer or shorter by including the circumnavigation of the Isle of Ewe at the end. Starting and finishing at Aultbea and paddling around the Isle of Ewe make for a pleasant short trip if conditions are too windy for the headland. Mellon Udrigle also provides a great starting point to paddle out to Priest Island and the southern Summer Isles, see Trip 11 for further information.

Rubha Rèidh's cliffs and sea stacks

Rubha Rèidh

No. 16	**Grade B**	**32km**	**OS Sheet 19**

Tidal Port	Ullapool
Start	△ Big Sand (NG 759 777)
Finish	◯ Midtown (NG 823 847)
HW/LW	HW/LW at Midtown is around 10 minutes before Ullapool.
Tidal Times	Off Rubha Rèidh: The NE going stream starts at about 3 hours and 50 minutes before HW Ullapool. The SW going stream starts at about 2 hours and 50 minutes after HW Ullapool.
	In the entrance to Loch Ewe: The ingoing stream starts at about 6 hours and 5 minutes before HW Ullapool. The outgoing stream starts at about 5 minutes before HW Ullapool.
Max Rate Sp	Off Rubha Rèidh 3 knots. In the entrance to Loch Ewe 0.5 knots.
Coastguard	Stornoway, tel. 01851 702013, VHF weather every 3 hours from 0710.

Introduction

Rubha Rèidh is the most dramatic and challenging of the Wester Ross headlands and features a committing coastline with tidal streams as well as cliffs, arches and sea stacks. It also hides a fantastic sandy beach, with views across to the Outer Hebrides as well as the surrounding cliff architecture. On a fine day this trip is a classic.

© Rubha Rèidh lighthouse

Rubha Rèidh

Description

If time and fitness allow it is well worth paddling the entire headland of Rubha Rèidh as described. This provides a fantastic journey that takes in the exposure of the west and north coastlines as well as the calmer waters of Loch Ewe. To do this, start the trip at the jetty by the large sandy beach and camp/caravan ground at Big Sand. This is accessed through the camping site where you will need to stop at reception to obtain permission and pay a small fee.

From the jetty, head up the coastline between Longa Island and the beach to reach the cliffs that start to rear up out of the sea at Rubha Bàn. Keep an eye out overhead as sea eagles have been seen in this area. Port Erradale with its raised beaches provides a break in the cliffs and a chance to stop if required, however heading onto the small jetty at Melvaig may be preferable. The jetty at Melvaig provides an alternative start and is situated on the only section of lower-lying coastline this headland offers until Loch Ewe.

Shortly after Melvaig the boulder shore changes into cliffs that gradually gain in height the further north you go. There are some caves to explore on the way up to the lighthouse. The lighthouse was built by David Stevenson of the famous lighthouse building family in 1910. It is now fully automated and the lighthouse buildings house an outdoor centre, hostel and small visitor centre. There is a small jetty just to the north that used to provide sole access to the light before the road was built in 1962, but to land here you need relatively calm seas. The cliffs and sea stacks just beyond the jetty are some of the most spectacular of the trip, and they come to an end at the stunning beach of Camas Mòr. Stopping here is a must; the location, surrounding scenery, perfect sands and emerald green waters make this perhaps the best of all Wester Ross's many beautiful beaches.

The northern coastline of Rubha Rèidh is a wild and remote place. The west coast stretches as far as the eye can see, with the headlands of Greenstone Point, Rubha Coigeach and the Point of Stoer prominent, and to the west the Outer Hebrides with the Shiant Islands are clearly visible. This coastline leads to the entrance to Loch Ewe, and although the cliffs are not as grand as already paddled, there are some small islands that provide shelter for seals and wildlife. Rubha nan Sasan marks the entrance to Loch Ewe and it is easily identified with its numerous World War II lookout buildings and gun emplacements. This is a clear reminder of the role this loch played in the Arctic convoys. Not far beyond this lies Cove, with its small and well-hidden natural harbour and a natural arch. This provides a place to stop if necessary, but you may prefer to continue on to one of the sandy beaches at either Camas Allt Eoin Thòmais or Gaineamh Smo.

The final part of the journey leads into the heart of Loch Ewe, with its sheltered waters and low-lying coastlines. The backdrop of An Teallach, Slioch and the Torridon mountains, some of the most dramatic mountains in Scotland, will make the last few kilometres pass easily. The jetty at Midtown provides an easy place to land, and Poolewe with its café and pub is only a short drive away.

Tides and weather

Rubha Rèidh has fairly strong tidal streams that can form particularly rough seas if the wind is blowing against them. This trip is best planned to make use of the main tidal stream around the headland. Ideally you would have tidal assistance in Loch Ewe as well, but this is not essential as the streams here are weak. Weak eddies form either side of the headland. The headland is also very exposed to wind and swell from most directions, so a good weather day is recommended for this trip.

Additional information

There are no amenities at the start or finish of the trip, however both Poolewe and Gairloch possess a wide range of cafés, pubs, shops and public toilets. The Bridge Cottage café in Poolewe and the Mountain Coffee Company café in Gairloch come well recommended. As well as the campsite at Big Sand there is also a very basic camp field behind the beach at Gaineamh Smo, both offering a great place to make a base for a weekend. Please be sure to stop at the reception and pay the small amount asked to use the jetty at Big Sand.

Variations

This trip can be made as long or short as is preferred with a variety of options to start or finish. In addition to those described, alternative start/finish places can be found at: Melvaig (NG 739 863), Cove (NG 810 905) and Firemore (NG 817 883).

Gairloch

Loch Gairloch & Longa Island

No. 17	Grade A | 23km | OS Sheet 19
Tidal Port	Ullapool
Start	△ Charlestown (NG 808 751)
Finish	◯ Charlestown (NG 808 751)
HW/LW	HW/LW at Charlestown is around 10 minutes before Ullapool.
Tidal Times	Loch Gairloch: The ingoing stream starts at about 6 hours and 20 minutes before HW Ullapool. The outgoing stream starts at about 20 minutes before HW Ullapool.
Max Rate Sp	In Caolas Beag 0.5 knots.
Coastguard	Stornoway, tel. 01851 702013, VHF weather every 3 hours from 0710.

Introduction

Sandy beaches, quiet coastlines, sheltered waters, waterside pubs and wildlife aplenty, all set in the unique North West Highlands mountain scenery, makes for an idyllic day out.

© Loch Gairloch and the Torridon mountains

Description

There are plenty of places to start this trip from, depending on how far or where you want to go, however the slipway at Charlestown is almost ideal. At low water it can dry out, so try and avoid launching or landing at this time if possible. The main pier is still used by fishing, leisure and tourist boats alike. Before the road was built this was the only access to this area.

On leaving Charlestown, head across the loch to the narrow inlet that separates Eilean Horrisdale from the mainland. The views into the Torridon mountains to the south-east will gradually unfold, and these mountains provide the spectacular backdrop for the rest of the day. The narrow inlet remains hidden until the last minute and then gives access to the sheltered tranquillity of Badachro Bay. This was once a busy fishing village with much of the cod that was caught being cured in a station on Eilean Horrisdale. Nowadays it is justifiably popular with leisure craft and visitors, not least because of the waterside Badachro Inn, which serves great food and of course liquid refreshments. Spend some time exploring the picturesque houses that surround this natural harbour before heading back out into the main loch and along its southern coast. There is abundant wildlife, hopefully seals or otters, to be seen on this uninhabited section of coastline. As the coastline starts to head south, cut across the entrance of Loch Gairloch to Longa Island. On this 3km crossing you get some of the best views looking back towards the village and its sandy beaches.

Longa Island was named in the times when Vikings ruled this area (up until 1264), its name translates into 'boat island'. Despite its close proximity to habitation it has a remote and wild feel about it, with plenty of cliffs and small bays to explore, all home to birds, seals and otters. The outer coast is the most exposed part of the trip and the water could well be a bit rougher here.

Clan Mackenzie

On the hillside overlooking Charlestown is the grand Flowerdale House, the home of the Mackenzie clan who have owned the land since 1494 when King James IV granted it to them. During the 19th century and the infamous Clearances the Mackenzies of the day refused to evict a single tenant, despite the estate running at a loss. As a result, other evicted tenants from the Highlands came to settle in Gairloch and a thriving community has been maintained ever since.

It is said that in the 1500s, when a ship was seen from their rival clan, the MacLeods, a Mackenzie archer shot an arrow from Flowerdale and at 800 metres managed to kill the lookout on the ship's mast!

On leaving Longa head across to the sandy beach at Big Sand; this is an ideal place to stop if a rest hasn't been taken on the island. From here a low-lying rocky coastline leads towards Gairloch. There is a small slipway as the main village is reached, with a pretty row of old cottages overlooking it. This gives easy access some of the numerous cafés that Gairloch has to offer, just turn left and head up the hill a short distance.

The route back to Charlestown follows the coastline, past the beaches that Gairloch is renowned for. The finest of the beaches is found next to a small promontory called An Dùn, once

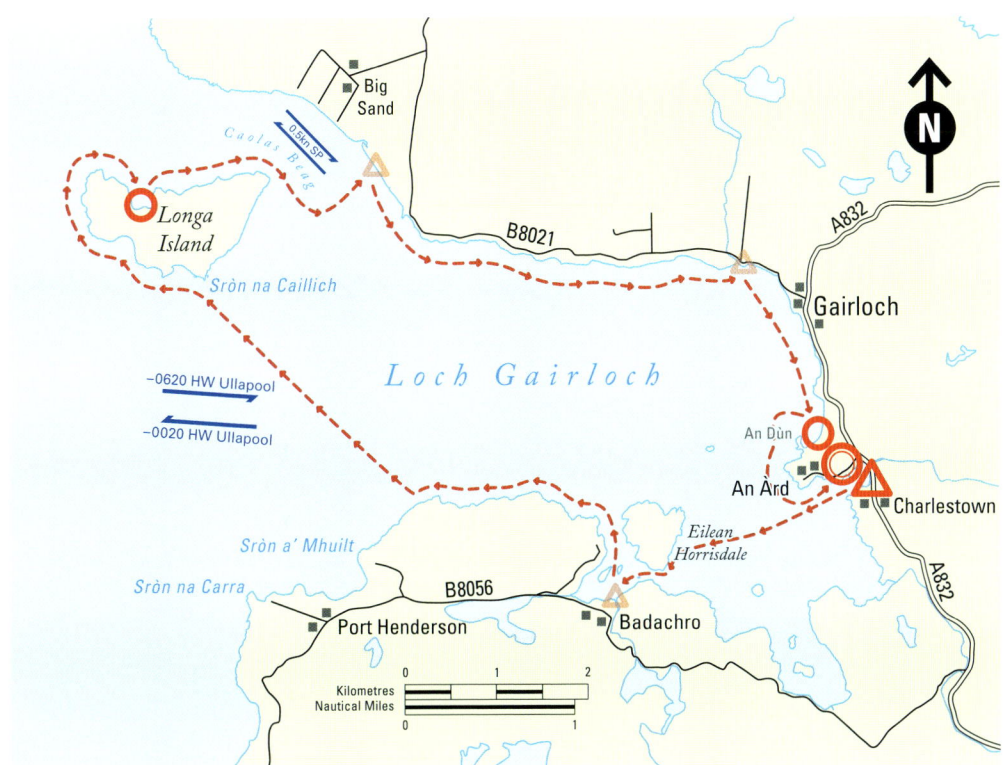

a fort where the MacLeods managed to hold out during one of their numerous battles with the Mackenzies. From here a short paddle leads back to the start, with the views of the Torridon mountains providing a fitting finale. At Charlestown, look out for the quaint old bridge that is seen up the river beyond its modern replacement. This leads to the Old Inn which is an ideal place to head for some well-earned refreshments.

Tides and weather

There are no tidal streams of note in the loch so the trip should be planned taking into consideration the wind. Care should be taken when crossing the loch or heading around Longa Island if the wind is strong, particularly if offshore. Within the loch, shelter can usually be found in most conditions, particularly in the Badachro area.

Additional information

Gairloch and Charlestown have ample amenities, including public toilets at the pier in Charlestown. There are numerous cafés and pubs to choose from, however the Old Inn at Charlestown and the Badachro Inn are of particular note, along with the Mountain Coffee Company café in Gairloch (just up the hill from the small slipway). In Gairloch there is a heritage museum and information centre.

Variations

Within the loch there are three alternative launch/landing sites giving options to modify the trip to suit the weather: Badachro (NG 783 737), Gairloch slipway (NG 796 773) – this has limited parking, and Big Sand (NG 759 777) – accessed through the camp/caravan site (please stop at reception to ask permission and pay a small fee).

Charlestown or Badachro also provide the starting point if wishing to paddle to Red Point and back. This low-lying headland has some fine beaches on its north and south sides. This variation can be extended by heading to Craig (NG 774 638) which was once the UK's most remote youth hostel and is now a mountain bothy.

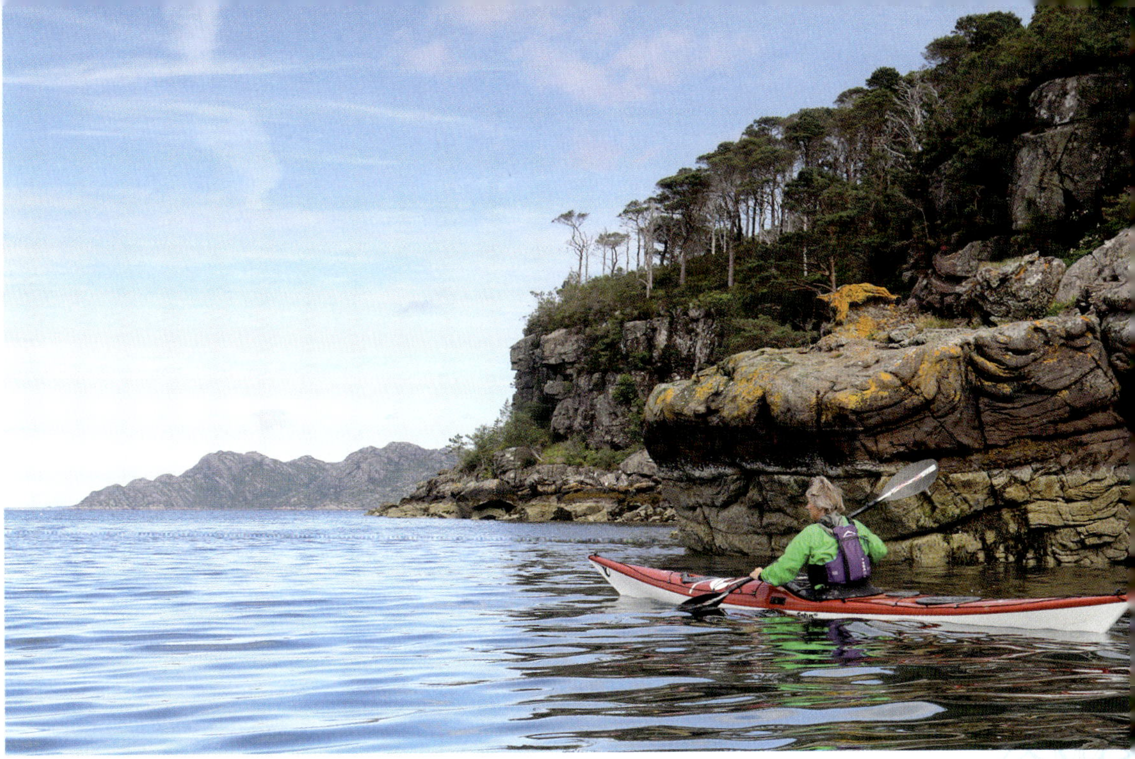

Shieldaig Island

Shieldaig & Torridon

No. 18	**Grade A**	**20km**	**OS Sheet 24**
Tidal Port	Ullapool
Start	△ Shieldaig (NG 815 536)
Finish	○ Shieldaig (NG 815 536)
HW/LW	HW/LW at Shieldaig is around 15 minutes before Ullapool.
Tidal Times	In the narrows of Loch Shieldaig: The W going stream starts at about 20 minutes before HW Ullapool. The E going stream starts at about 6 hours and 20 minutes before HW Ullapool.
Max Rate Sp	In the narrows of Loch Shieldaig 2 knots.
Coastguard	Stornoway, tel. 01851 702013, VHF weather every 3 hours from 0710.

Introduction

The combination of the picturesque village of Shieldaig set on the shores of the sheltered loch with its own pine-covered island, alongside the towering Torridon mountains, makes for a stunning sea kayaking destination.

© Loch Shieldaig, Upper Loch Torridon and Liathach

Description

The village of Shieldaig is often cited as being one of the most picturesque in Scotland. The jetty on the south side of the village provides a perfect launch site and from the sea you will get the best views of this fantastic place. The white houses align the shore in perfect symmetry looking out onto the wooded island that takes the village's name. To start the trip, head across to Shieldaig Island before heading north to the narrow channel that separates Loch Shieldaig from Upper Loch Torridon.

Men for war, wood for ships

The village itself was founded in the 1800s with a view to training up seamen for the Royal Navy in the war against Napoleon. Grants were provided by the Admiralty to support housing and boat building, and Shieldaig flourished. The village never really provided seamen for the navy due to Napoleon's demise in 1815. The village did prosper from its fishing fleet and the abundance of herring (from which the loch and the village's Viking name derives).

Shieldaig Island is covered with mature Scots pine, planted in the 19th century with seeds taken from Speyside. The trees were grown to provide timber and spars for boats and fishing.

Shieldaig Island provides a home for much wildlife, including herons that provide the symbol for the village. Most noticeable are the resident sea eagles that are found on the west side of the islands, occupying a former herons' nest. These huge birds with their wingspan of up to 2.5 metres are an incredible sight.

At high water it is possible to paddle through the narrow gap that separates Eilean a' Chaoil and the mainland in the channel that links Loch Shieldaig and Upper Loch Torridon. Here you will find a small boat shed and house above, only accessible by foot or from the sea.

Entering Upper Loch Torridon you may experience a small amount of tidal flow. The views into the loch and the mountains that surround it are stunning; Beinn Alligin, Liathach and Beinn Eighe are the three tallest and most dramatic mountains rising out of the north side of the loch. The pretty shore-side hamlet of Inveralligin provides a good place to head to, the quaint houses all nestled into the hillside at the foot of the towering Beinn Alligin. There is a jetty here with easy landing.

From here, head back to Loch Shieldaig following the remote and rugged northern coastline. Just past the narrows there is a landing spot at the small promontory called Rubha na h-Àirde Glaise. Ruins of an old settlement can be found here. Follow the coastline on towards Loch Diabaig; along the route you will pass a few remote houses that are well maintained and clearly used as holiday getaways, not a bad place to escape to for a while.

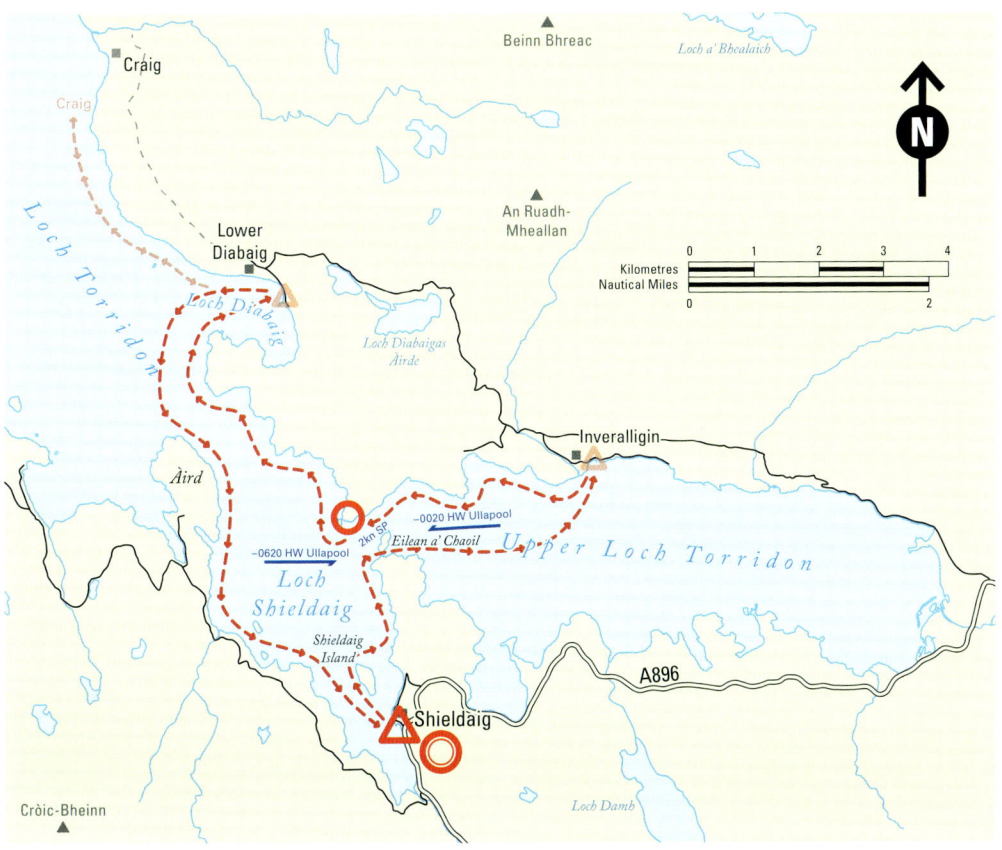

The headland that forms Loch Diabaig rises nearly 150 metres out of the loch; although a steep hillside as opposed to cliffs, it still makes for a dramatic gateway into the loch. The hamlet of Diabaig really is at 'the end of the road', clinging to the shores of this steep-sided fjord-like loch. The hillsides are steep and craggy, with very good rock climbing on the crags. If you land at the jetty it is well worth considering visiting the perfectly situated Gille Brighde Café and Restaurant which offers fantastic locally-sourced food and drink.

Leaving Diabaig it is time to head back to Shieldaig. Paddling across to Àird and along the south side of Loch Shieldaig, with its sheltered pine-clad coastline and islands to weave in and out of, is recommended. Keep an eye out for the resident sea eagles, particularly as you paddle down the west side of Shieldaig Island to finish the trip. On landing in Shieldaig the only thing left to do is to spend some time enjoying this wonderful village and a visit to the great little café called Nanny's is the best place to start.

Tides and weather

There is some tidal movement in the narrow channel that separates Loch Shieldaig from upper Loch Torridon. This can be easily paddled against if necessary by using the eddies that form along both of the shores. The majority of this trip is sheltered from the worst of the winds and any swell, however if heading out as far as Diabaig it becomes exposed to any winds and swell from the west.

Additional information

Shieldaig has public toilets at its northern end as well as a pub, café and basic campsite. When parking at the jetty please be mindful of other users. Inveralligin has no amenities, but Diabaig has a fantastic café/restaurant that is worth making the time to enjoy. In nearby Torridon village there is a selection of pubs and cafés as well as a visitor centre and public toilets with showers.

Variations

This trip can be made as long or as short as required, whether it is just an hour around Shieldaig Island or a weekend exploring the lochs more thoroughly. To extend the trip further, then heading to Craig (NG 774 638), which was once the UK's most remote youth hostel and is now a mountain bothy, makes for a good overnight trip.

Cliffs on the peninsula's south coast

Applecross Peninsula

No. 19	**Grade B**	**61km**	**OS Sheet 24**
Tidal Port	Ullapool
Start	△ Shieldaig (NG 815 536)
Finish	○ Ardarroch (NG 837 396)
HW/LW	HW/LW at Applecross is around 10 minutes before Ullapool.
Tidal Times	In the narrows of Loch Shieldaig: The W going stream starts at about 20 minutes before HW Ullapool. The E going stream starts at about 6 hours and 20 minutes before HW Ullapool.
	In the Inner Sound: The S going stream starts at about 5 hours and 5 minutes after HW Ullapool. The N going stream starts at about 55 minutes before HW Ullapool.
	In Caolas Mòr: The SE going stream starts at about 5 hours and 50 minutes after HW Ullapool. The NW going stream starts at about 10 minutes before HW Ullapool.
Max Rate Sp	In the narrows of Loch Shieldaig 2 knots. In the Inner Sound and Caolas Mòr 1 knot.
Coastguard	Stornoway, tel. 01851 702013, VHF weather every 3 hours from 0710.

Introduction

The isolated Applecross peninsula has all the ingredients for a fantastic journey, which should be savoured over a few days. It has stunning mountain scenery and views across the Inner Sound

The coral beaches at Coillegillie

Applecross Peninsula

to the Isle of Skye and beyond. Add a remote coastline with cliffs and beaches, wildlife, a picturesque village with waterside pub halfway around, and it all adds up to make for a perfect trip.

Description

The Gaelic name for the Applecross peninsula is a' Chomraich, which means 'the sanctuary'; an apt name for this very special place. The journey starts at the jetty on the south side of the attractive village of Shieldaig and sheltered paddling leads you away from the village past Shieldaig Island. Look out for the resident sea eagles as you pass the island, they occupy a former heron's nest on the west side of the island. Loch Shieldaig is a beautiful place and as you paddle across it the dramatic Torridon mountains that overlook it will become ever more visible.

After passing Àird you enter the more open Loch Torridon; on a clear day the distant Outer Hebrides can be seen on the horizon. The small island of Eilean Mòr is home to numerous sea birds, which will be making themselves heard as you pass. If you need a rest there are plenty of places to stop as you explore this coastline, as is the case for the whole of this trip.

Rubha na Mòine is the next obvious feature, this has some of the best cliffs of the trip so far. When you reach the northern tip of the Applecross peninsula the views across the Inner Sound unfold. The Island of Rona with its distinctive lighthouse stands out, with Skye forming the backdrop. The bay called Ob na h-Uamha (bay of the cave) is well worth exploring. The cave from which the bay gets its name is up above the shore and clearly has been used as a shelter for many years. At the back of the bay a stream cascades off a rocky ledge, and there are usually plenty of common seals for company. The beach marked on the maps at Ob Chuaig is a bit of an

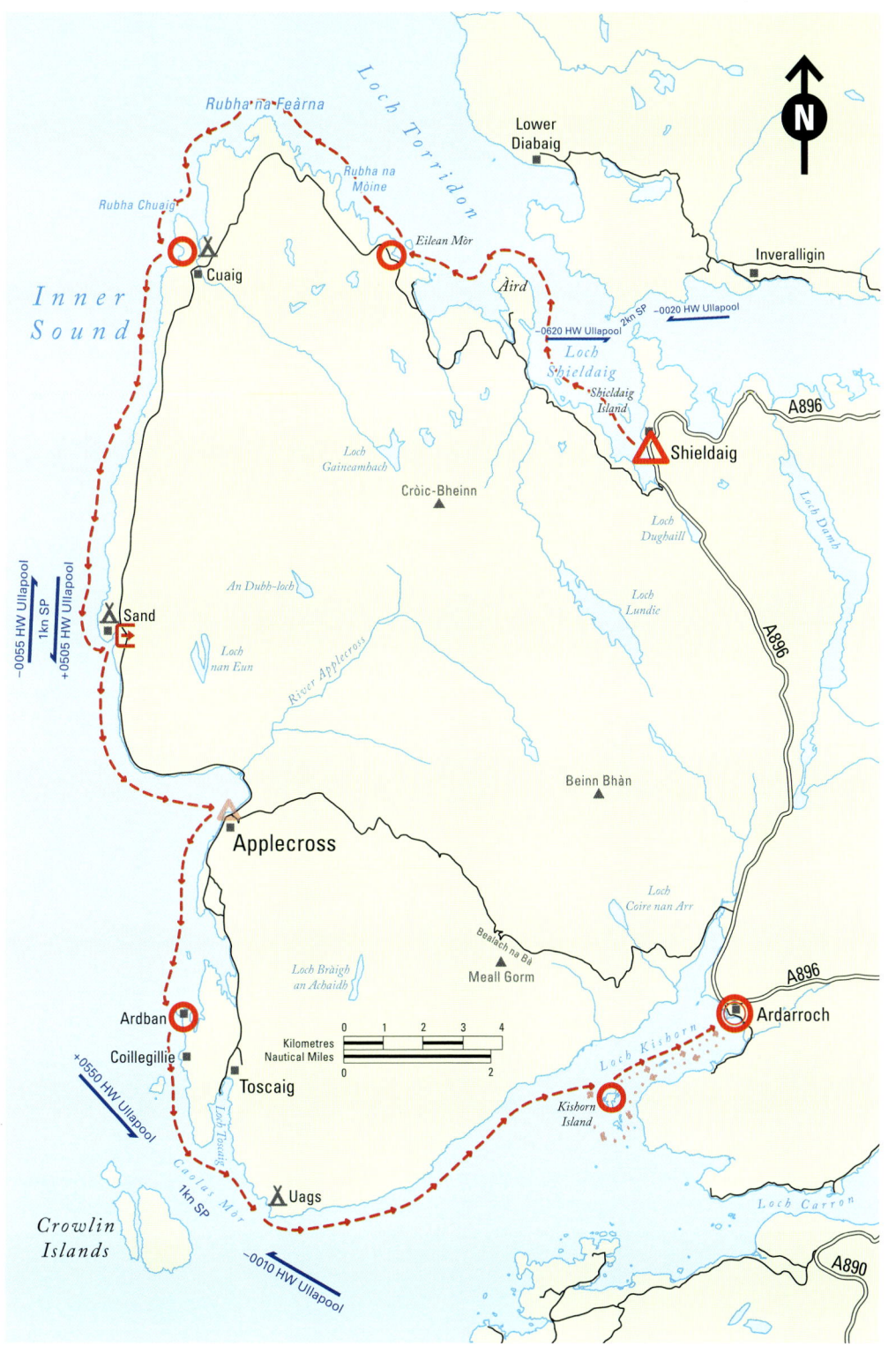

Applecross village

Applecross Peninsula

anti-climax, so continue on just past Rubha Chuaig to a much better sandy beach. This provides a perfect resting place or a campsite.

The coastline continues with low-lying cliffs and views of the Cuillin mountains of Skye.

Just before you reach the spectacular beach at Sand you pass the naval base that monitors underwater activity in the Inner Sound, a strange sight on such a remote coastline. It is well worth spending some time at the spectacular beach at Sand; at its northern end there is some great camping as well as an unlocked shelter. This was home for the TV presenter Monty Halls during his popular TV series 'Great Escape' in 2009. As it is the halfway point of the trip it makes a logical place to spend the night.

Not far beyond Sand is the picturesque village of Applecross. The village sits along the shore of the bay with steep hillsides rising up behind it to the infamous mountain pass called the Bealach na Bà. If time allows it is well worth having a look around. With a pub offering great food and refreshments it might just be too good to miss!

South from Applecross the coastline has numerous islands and inlets to explore. The unique coral beaches found at Ardban and Coillegillie should not be missed; they are a stunning place to land and enjoy for a while. As you paddle between the Crowlin Islands and the peninsula look out for Uags bothy, which is another great place to take a rest or spend a night if required.

The final part of the journey leads into Loch Kishorn. The spectacular Cuillin mountains will now be behind and the view will be replaced with the many mainland mountains. It is well worth the effort of exploring the Kishorn Islands on the way to the finish at Ardarroch, as these are

The shelter at Sand

home to plenty more wildlife in a beautiful setting. Approaching the finish, the Bealach na Bà will be seen taking its improbable route over the mountains; to the north of this is Beinn Bhàn with its impressive high mountain corries. The landing at Ardarroch is at the north-eastern corner of the beach where the road is very close – at low water it may be quite a walk so plan for this.

A cave for a home

One of the caves north of Sand was once home to a lady who came from the Isle of Barra many years ago. She could only exit the cave at low water and she made her living by gathering shellfish and then carrying them into Applecross to sell. She was later given land in the bay in order to build a place to live in; the place is named Re-Aulay and can still be seen today.

Tides and weather

There is very little tidal movement on any of this trip, so the main consideration is the wind and the swell. Although the road is never too far away and there are plenty of landing places, it would be awkward to escape from many parts of this trip; so look for lighter winds to enjoy the trip. If a northerly swell is forecast this can funnel down the Inner Sound.

Sand and the Isle of Raasay

Additional information

Shieldaig has public toilets at its northern end as well as a pub, café and basic campsite. When parking at the jetty please be mindful of other users. Applecross has public toilets as well as a campsite. The Applecross Inn is well renowned for its food, and if time allows the Potting Shed café in the walled garden of Applecross House is also well worth a visit. At Ardarroch there are no amenities, however be sure not to miss the Kishorn Seafood Bar just up the road which has an amazing selection of local seafood.

Variations

From Ardarroch a short day out to explore the relatively sheltered Kishorn Islands is well worth considering. The trip can be extended by exploring the Crowlin Islands as well, see Trip 20 for more information.

The Red Cuillins of Skye from the Crowlin Islands

Crowlin Islands

No. 20	**Grade B**	**16km**	**OS Sheet 24**

Tidal Port	Ullapool
Start	△ Toscaig (NG 710 378)
Finish	○ Toscaig (NG 710 378)
HW/LW	HW/LW at Toscaig is around 10 minutes before Ullapool.
Tidal Times	In Caolas Mòr and around the Crowlin Islands: The SE going stream starts at about 5 hours and 50 minutes after HW Ullapool. The NW going stream starts at about 10 minutes before HW Ullapool.
Max Rate Sp	In Caolas Mòr 1 knot.
Coastguard	Stornoway, tel. 01851 702013, VHF weather every 3 hours from 0710.

Introduction

The tightly clustered Crowlin Islands, situated off the remote Applecross peninsula, possess a unique natural harbour and fine views across to Raasay, Rona and the Cuillins of Skye. With a short crossing to the island and plenty of wildlife for company, a visit to these relatively sheltered islands makes for a fine day out.

The natural harbour of the Crowlin Islands

Description

The old pier at Toscaig is a sheltered launch spot and provides the shortest crossing to paddle out to the Crowlin Islands. For many years the pier was used for the ferry service that provided a lifeline for the Applecross peninsula, bringing in mail and supplies as well as passengers to and from Kyle of Lochalsh. With the only other access the notorious Bealach na Bà, this ferry was an essential link to the outside world for the Applecross communities at the time. After paddling out of the shelter of Loch Toscaig it is worth exploring the coastline south for a while. There is plenty of interest, wildlife, and the magical Uags bothy. Overlooking a small sheltered bay this beautifully located bothy is an ideal place to stop, stretch your legs and take in the great views of the Crowlin Islands, with the Cuillins of Skye beyond.

From Uags a two-kilometre crossing will take you to Eilean Mòr (big island), which as the Gaelic names states is the largest of the three islands that make up the Crowlin Islands. Head west along the south coast of Eilean Mòr to the narrow gap that separates it from Eilean Meadhanach (middle island) and forms the natural harbour. Time your arrival here to avoid low water, as at this stage of the tide the entrance dries and it is not possible to kayak between the two main islands. At this southern entrance to the natural harbour there is an ideal place to stop and take a rest if needed; it also provides the best camping spot on the islands.

Head on through this beautiful natural harbour between the islands, which possibly gives them their name. In Gaelic 'Crowlin' translates into 'eye of the needle channel' which as you will see is very apt. While threading the needle, enjoy the peace, shelter and hopefully the wildlife that this unique channel offers. After exiting the harbour on the northern side, head on around Eilean

Beag (little island). Paddling around this island you will be rewarded with the trip's best views up the Inner Sound to Raasay, Rona and the Applecross peninsula, along with ornate sandstone cliffs. On the western side look out for the old cable handrail, which used to help men access the light positioned higher up the steep shoreline. You paddle under the light as you travel around the exposed northern tip of this island. There is a beach made up of perfectly smooth and rounded stones on this coastline which is a good place to stop and enjoy the surroundings.

Having explored Eilean Beag, paddle down through Caolas Mòr on the east side of the islands. As you paddle down the coastline of Eilean Mòr, look out for the numerous sea urchins, especially at low spring tides. Soon you will arrive at the last landing site on the Crowlins at Camas na h-Annait. This bay gets its name from the small church that was once situated next to it, along with the cottages of the 40 islanders who once lived here in the 1840s. Having landed and had a rest, the short crossing back to Toscaig awaits; a fine finish to a day exploring this unique little cluster of islands.

Tides and weather

The tidal streams in this area are negligible, so timing the trip to ensure that the natural harbour can be paddled through is of more importance. The islands provide reasonable shelter from the wind and swell, however considering the small crossing to get to them and the more exposed west and north coastlines, it is best to plan for lighter winds with minimal swell from the north.

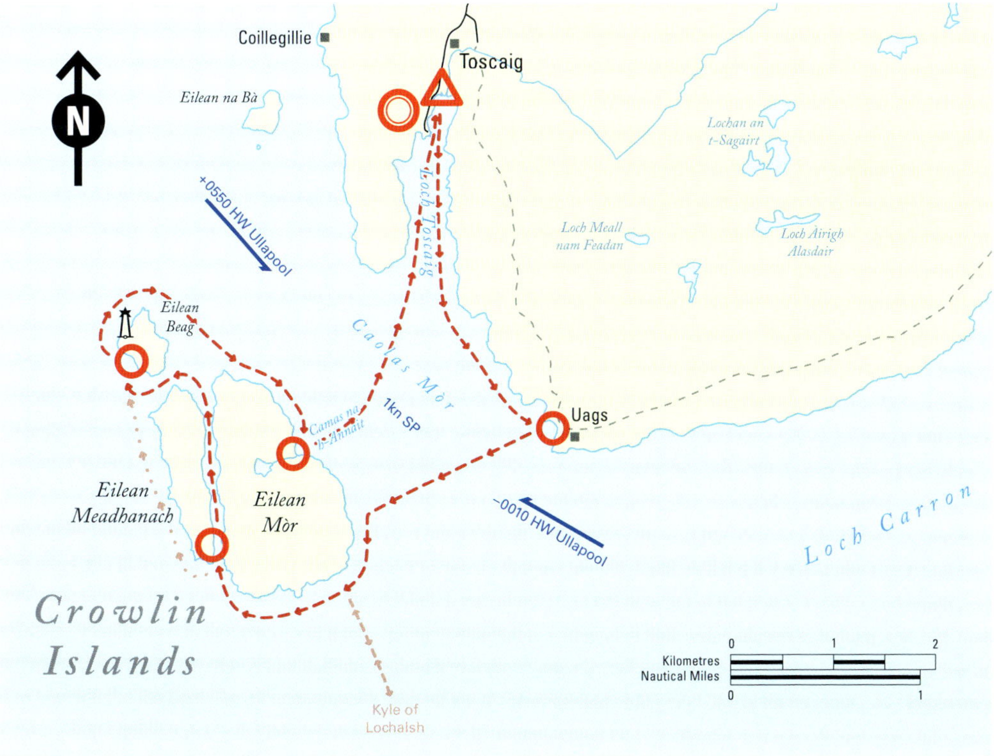

The Crowlin's colourful cliffs with Raasay behind

Additional information

There are no amenities at Toscaig and at low water the put-in is a little bit awkward. The nearest amenities are a shop at Camusteel along with a campsite, public toilets, cafés and a fine pub in Applecross.

Variations

To avoid the long drive over the Bealach na Bà to Toscaig, an alternative place to start the trip is from Kyle of Lochalsh (NG 761 271). This requires a longer crossing and negotiating some tidal water in Kyle Akin under the Skye Bridge, information can be found about the tidal streams in Trip 21.

Leaving Plockton

Plockton & The Black Islands

No. 21 | Grade A | 15km | OS Sheets 24 and 33

Tidal Port	Ullapool
Start	△ Plockton (NG 804 334)
Finish	○ Kyle of Lochalsh (NG 761 271)
HW/LW	HW/LW at Plockton is around 15 minutes before Ullapool.
Tidal Times	In Kyle Akin: the W going stream starts at about 3 hours and 30 minutes after HW Ullapool. The E going stream starts at about 3 hours before HW Ullapool. (These times are based on spring tides; they can vary from this on neaps as well as wind, barometric pressure, rain and snowmelt having an effect.)
Max Rate Sp	In Kyle Akin 3 knots.
Coastguard	Stornoway, tel. 01851 702013, VHF weather every 3 hours from 0710.

Introduction

Starting in the picturesque village of Plockton, this trip goes on to explore a mass of islands, idyllic beaches and sheltered bays. With wildlife never too far away, and the Cuillin mountains of Skye providing an impressive backdrop, this is a trip worth taking some time over.

📷 The islands of Loch Carron

Description

Plockton is without doubt a contender for Britain's prettiest village, with its sheltered waters and seafront palm trees you would be easily mislead into thinking you were somewhere other than the North West Highlands. Unsurprisingly it has been used in various television series and films, with the TV series *Hamish Macbeth* perhaps being the best known. The village dates mostly from the 19th century, when it was established as a planned fishing community in an attempt to stem the tide of emigration from the Highlands. Seeing what a busy tourism-based community it is now, the village has certainly prospered since its initial conception.

As you set off from its sheltered waters, take the time to explore the wooded bay in which the village is situated; look for the tiny, hidden sea loch under the railway line. Leaving the bay, the impressive Duncraig Castle stands out; built in 1866 by Sir Alexander Matheson, who acquired a vast fortune trading in the Far East. To the west of the bay there is the small lighthouse on Eilean a' Chait with its tiny lean-to cottage where the lighthouse keeper lived. Due to the small size and basic nature of the keeper's accommodation, a separate cottage was built for his wife and family; this can be seen on the adjacent island as you paddle by. From here the coastline provides a wealth of small islands separated by crystal-clear sheltered turquoise waters. It is the kind of place you could spend many hours exploring and taking in the surroundings. There is wildlife all around, and if lucky you will see some otters as they are frequently seen in this area. On the route be sure to look out for the 'secret beach', an idyllic white sandy gem found on a small island, and a perfect place for a first stop of the day.

The islands continue all the way down the coastline, as do the sheltered bays and wildlife. The views across to the island of Skye are dominated by the mighty Cuillin mountains, towering above all that surrounds. To the north, the Crowlin Islands which sit off the Applecross peninsula are visible, and beyond this and up the Inner Sound are the islands of Raasay and Rona. The view is breath-taking. As you arrive at the slightly larger Black Islands that sit in Erbusaig Bay, the Skye Bridge will come into view. Although a man-made structure in surroundings of natural beauty, it is still an impressive sight to behold. These islands, or the bay in which they sit, provide another fine place to take a rest with a choice of landing places and views that require time to absorb.

The trip finishes with further islands all the way to the Skye Bridge that links the mainland to Eilean Bàn. Passing under the bridge some tidal movement will be noticeable, however close to the mainland shore this should not be too strong and does not produce any rough water to speak of. While passing under the bridge, look out for the 'otter tunnels' that have been built that allow the otters to pass under the road safely. Hopefully you will have seen one or two on the journey down to the bridge. The finish point is at the large slipway in Kyle of Lochalsh, where the car ferries departed from prior to the bridge being built in 1995. Kyle of Lochalsh still sees a lot of boat traffic with tourist boats as well as workboats, so be mindful of this while coming in to land.

Tides and weather

The numerous islands on this trip provide plenty of shelter from wind and swell, enabling this trip to be considered in many conditions. That said, to see the islands and crystal clear waters at their best, calm conditions are recommended. Tidal streams will be encountered under the Skye Bridge when entering Kyle Akin and should be considered in the planning. These tidal streams

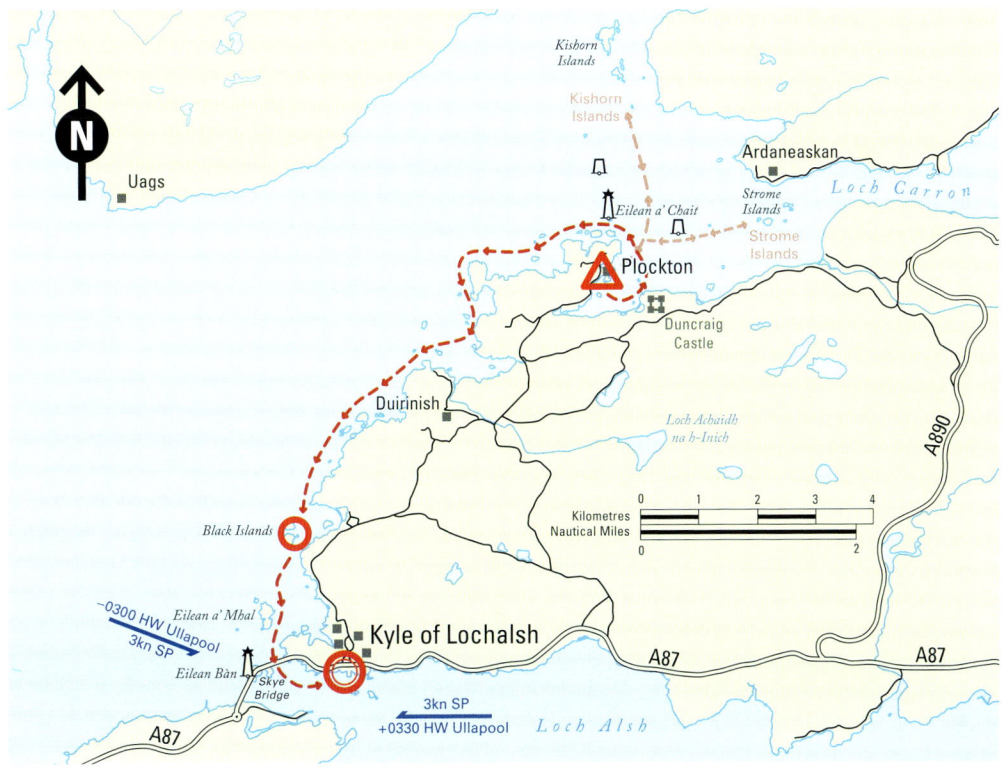

Heading to the Black Islands with the Cuillins of Skye beyond

are weaker and less rough on the mainland side where the trip goes, and there are plenty of eddies to make use of if necessary. Plan to pass under the bridge with an east going tide, however be aware that the tidal stream times in this area will often vary due to local anomalies.

Additional information

Plockton has cafés, craft shops, public toilets and the pub is well renowned for its seafood. Kyle of Lochalsh has a large supermarket as well as a full range of amenities and public toilets at the get-out.

Variations

To avoid the need for a shuttle, starting and finishing at Plockton or Kyle of Lochalsh makes for a great day out that can be made as long or short as desired. Plockton also provides a good starting point to explore the Kishorn Islands and Strome Islands.

Skye and Raasay

Introduction

When it comes to Scottish sea kayaking, the island of Skye is one of the most iconic destinations. This status is well deserved as it offers something for everyone. Whatever your paddling standard there will be a 'classic' sea kayak journey waiting for you on Skye. These could include the major headlands of Dunvegan, Rubha Hunish and Neist Point, or the remote and committing coastlines where the eagles soar high above and the whales swim deep below at Talisker and Kilt Rock. Alternatively it could be the sheltered waters and coral sands of Loch Dunvegan and Loch Eishort that appeal, or the tidal waters of Kyle Rhea. The islands of Raasay, Rona and Scalpay are easily reached from Skye and provide a great place to explore for a week or more. Whatever the interest, there is enough here to keep even the most active sea kayaker happy for many a year.

The inland mountains that Skye has to offer, along with the view of the Outer Hebrides, will always be a spectacular outlook to enjoy. In the north it is the Quiraing and Storr mountain range that dominate the inland landscape and in the south the mighty Black Cuillin of Skye. The latter has provided mountaineers with challenges for generations.

It is also an island rich in history, often based around clan rivalries and associated myths and legends. These can be seen and experienced along much of the coastline and add to the special 'Skye' experience.

Tides and weather

Being an island it will always offer a more sheltered coastline, so whatever the weather there should be somewhere to hide. Despite being in the comparative lee of the Outer Hebrides, do not underestimate the sea states that the Minch can throw at the unwary paddler. Northerly and south-westerly swells in particular can bypass the Outer Hebrides and land on Skye's coastlines with their full force.

The tidal streams flow up the west coast of Skye and across the southern and northern tips; around the headlands and in the narrows there are tidal races and eddies. In places these tidal streams can reach quite a speed and demand respect.

Kilt Rock waterfall | Giles Trussell

Portree

Inside Passage  22

No. 22 | Grade A | 45km | OS Sheets 23, 32 and 33

Tidal Port	Ullapool
Start	△ Kyleakin (NG 752 264)
Finish	ⵔ Portree (NG 486 438)
HW/LW	HW/LW at Kyleakin is around 40 minutes before Ullapool.
Tidal Times	In Kyle Akin: (Times are based on spring tides; they can vary from this on neaps, and wind, barometric pressure, rain and snowmelt may have an effect.) The W going stream starts at about 3 hours and 30 minutes after HW Ullapool. The E going stream starts at about 3 hours before HW Ullapool.
	In Caolas Scalpay: The NW going stream starts at about 1 hour and 10 minutes before HW Ullapool. The SE going stream starts at about 5 hours and 5 minutes after HW Ullapool.
	In the Narrows of Raasay: The N going stream starts at about 55 minutes before HW Ullapool. The S going stream starts at about 5 hours and 5 minutes after HW Ullapool.
Max Rate Sp	In Kyle Akin and the Narrows of Raasay 3 knots. In Caolas Scalpay 1 knot. Along the rest of this coastline 0.5 knots.
Coastguard	Stornoway, tel. 01851 702013, VHF weather every 3 hours from 0710.

© Skye Bridge and Eilean Bàn | Donald Macpherson

Inside Passage

Introduction

A journey called 'The Inside Passage' fires up the imagination. The name evokes images of a voyage that sneaks its way up a coastline, weaving between islands and spectacular scenery. A journey that takes a while, so that you can lose yourself in the environment and spend time admiring the wildlife. A journey that is relatively sheltered from the elements and accessible to many. This is that journey, enjoy.

The Skye Bridge

The bridge opened in 1995 as a toll bridge. With the ferries ceasing when the bridge was opened, controversy raged over the excessive tolls required for all those wishing to get to Skye. Eventually public opinion won the day and in December 2004 the tolls were abolished.

If time allows, consider stopping at the island nestled under the bridge called Eilean Bàn. This island was owned by the author Gavin Maxwell who is most famous for his book *Ring of Bright Water*, an autobiographical account of his time spent living on Skye and his interaction with the otters. The island is a wildlife haven which inspired Maxwell in many of his writings, and is now an otter sanctuary with a museum dedicated to him. Before Maxwell's time the island housed the lighthouse keepers, and although the light was decommissioned in 1993 with the building of the bridge, it is still a well-kept listed building.

Description

The trip starts at Kyleakin in the south and finishes at Portree in the north, making use of the more sheltered waters between Skye and the islands of Pabay, Scalpay and Raasay. It is possible to do it in a day, but ideally it should be done over at least two to be thoroughly enjoyed.

The stony beach next to the large car park is the launch site, and as you set off from Kyleakin the view is dominated by the Skye Bridge. Hopefully some tidal flow will whisk you along as you pass under the bridge, which despite its controversial past is a fantastic feet of engineering.

The journey follows the coast towards the small low-lying island of Pabay. This is a relatively exposed part of the trip, yet with the advantage of fantastic open views up the Inner Sound and many islands and mountains. Pabay translates into 'Priests Isle' with the remains of a 13th century chapel on the island, which at low tide nearly doubles in size! If a café stop is required there is also the village of Broadford just opposite.

The 'inside passage' continues up between the island of Scalpay and Skye, passing through the narrows of Caolas Scalpay. There is tidal movement here to hopefully help you on your

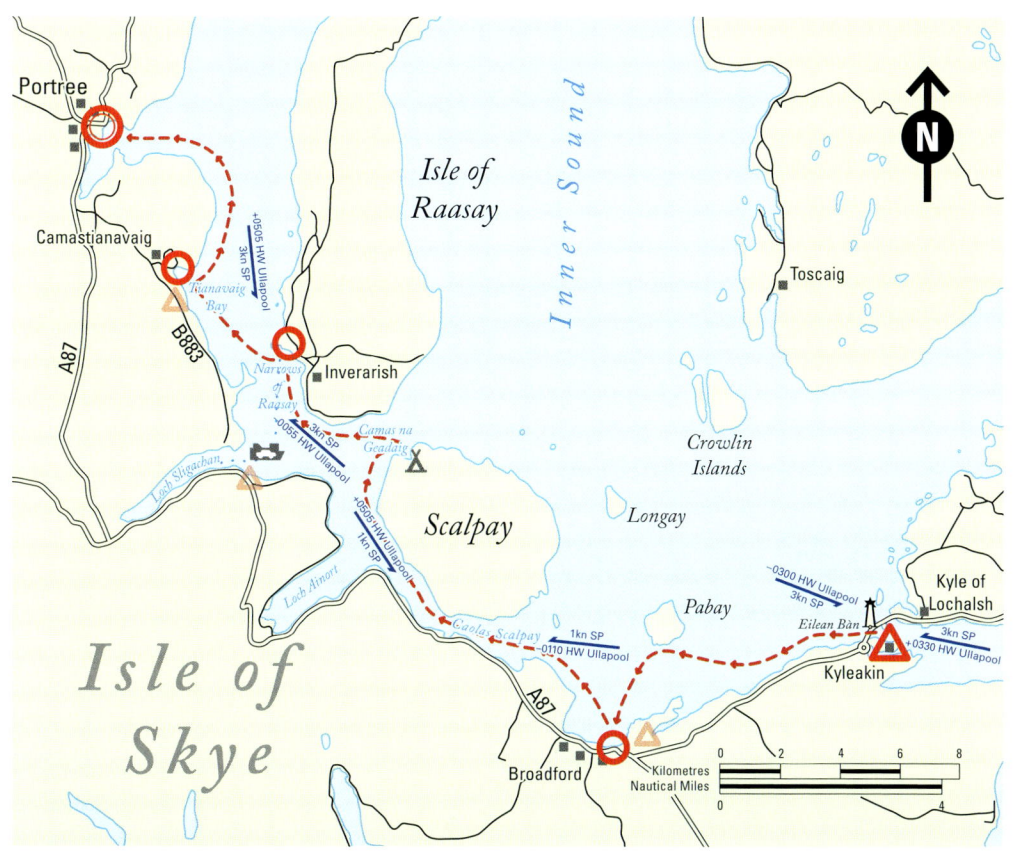

© Scalpay with Raasay behind from Caolas Scalpay

Inside Passage

way. Hugging the Scalpay shoreline gives a sense of isolation, with the Red Cuillin mountains looking down on you. There are plenty of stopping opportunities here, but the small thumb of land protruding into the loch at Corran a' Chinn Uachdaraich provides a great vantage point. Continuing onwards, Raasay and the steeper coastlines of northern Skye will start to dominate the view. On the north of Scalpay at Camas na Geadaig there is an idyllic stony beach landing, which is an ideal place to camp. Look out for the old raised 'lazybeds' from which the bay gets its Gaelic name. The crofters used to grow their crops in the poor ground by heaping up the small amount of soil and adding seaweed to make these raised beds for growing.

The Island of Raasay and its narrows is the journey's next destination, where again the tide will hopefully help you on your way. The unusual flat-topped peak of Dùn Caan, the island's highest point, will be clearly visible as you paddle into Churchton Bay. This is where the ferry lands (so keep an eye out for it) and is also the main hub of the island. There is an opportunity here for a leg stretch and explore, with a shop in Inverarish. Raasay House, an outdoor centre, is the obvious building seen as you leave the bay. From here it is time to head back to the main Skye coastline and the bay at Tianavaig is worth aiming for; a great place to land after the short crossing from Raasay.

Paddling around the dramatic headland north of Tianavaig provides a spectacular finish to the journey. Here steep slopes lead to crags and cliffs that are the home of the resident sea eagles. There are incredible views of the unique landscape of north Skye's Trotternish peninsula. Here the imposing mountain range is known as the Quiraing, and looking carefully you will be able

Skerries near Skye Bridge | Donald Macpherson

to make out the rock pinnacle high up on the scarp slopes known as the 'Old Man of Storr'. Entering the large natural bay that leads to Portree, it is clear how it got its Gaelic name of 'king's port'. Stay close to the coastline to discover Scarf Caves and perhaps consider a final stop at Camus Bàn, with its lovely beach, before the journey has to finish.

It is worth paddling into the colourful port of Portree itself for a look, but the best place to land is on the stony beach just north of the port, next to the River Chracaig.

Tides and weather

In all the narrow passages on this journey there is tidal flow. Although it is possible to paddle these at any state of flow it is best timed to have tidal assistance. Although there is good shelter for much of the trip, southerly and northerly winds can produce a reasonable sea state. It is worth noting that a northerly swell will have a significant effect on the final headland north of Tianavaig. Also in the area north of Caolas Scalpay there can be localised strong winds and downdraughts.

Additional information

There is a full range of amenities in Kyleakin, Broadford and Portree, a few amenities on Raasay and nothing of note elsewhere on the trip.

Cuillins of Skye from Scalpay

Variations

This journey can be broken down into many options, all worthwhile in their own right. Exploring Eilean Bàn and the Skye Bridge is a great short trip, Pabay or Scalpay are day trip possibilities from Broadford, visiting Raasay a day trip from Sconser, and the headland north of Tianavaig is an amazing trip on its own.

On the journey itself there are variations possible depending on time and weather. The outside coast of Scalpay is the obvious one, however consider taking in the Crowlin Islands as well. If an extra few days are available, then continuing on around Raasay and Rona make for a great week's paddling.

Eilean Fladday, Raasay with North Skye beyond

Raasay and Rona

No. 23 | Grade B | 78km | OS Sheet 24

Tidal Port	Ullapool
Start	△ Sconser (NG 525 323)
Finish	◯ Sconser (NG 525 323)
HW/LW	HW/LW on Raasay is around 25 minutes before Ullapool.
Tidal Times	In Caol Mòr: The E going stream starts at about 5 hours and 50 minutes after HW Ullapool. The W going stream starts at about 10 minutes before HW Ullapool.
	For the east coasts of Raasay and Rona: The N going stream starts at about 55 minutes before HW Ullapool. The S going stream starts at about 5 hours and 5 minutes after HW Ullapool.
	In Caol Rona: The NW going stream starts at about 1 hour and 10 minutes before HW Ullapool. The SE going stream starts at about 4 hours and 50 minutes after HW Ullapool.
	In the Narrows of Raasay: The S going stream starts at about 5 hours and 5 minutes after HW Ullapool. The N going stream starts at about 55 minutes before HW Ullapool.
Max Rate Sp	In Caol Mòr 1–2 knots. On the east coast of Raasay and Rona 1 knot. In Caol Rona 2 knots. In the narrows of Raasay 3 knots.
Coastguard	Stornoway, tel. 01851 702013, VHF weather every 3 hours from 0710.

© Raasay's east coast, looking to Dùn Caan | Giles Trussell

Introduction

The paddle around the islands of Raasay and Rona is a deservedly popular journey. It offers two contrasting islands with a common theme of unrivalled wildlife and views across to the Quiraing of Skye. Being sheltered from the westerly winds by Skye this area often has better weather and lighter winds in which to enjoy the journey. This trip can be done in three days, but considering what is has to offer many would choose to take longer.

Description

Setting off from the ferry terminal at Sconser provides the quickest access across to Raasay to start the journey. After the short crossing to the southern extremity of Raasay, head through Caol Mòr, passing the light at Eyre Point. This leads to the remote and inaccessible east coast of the island. This entire coastline has no road access and has steeply-wooded hillsides and cliffs throughout. The uniquely-shaped highest point of Raasay, Dùn Caan, is prominent and, with luck, one of the golden eagles often seen in this area may be soaring high above. Up to about Brochel Castle the cliffs and rocks are made of sandstone with a variety of shapes and reddish colours. Paddling around Rubha na' Leac a great view of these cliffs and Dùn Caan unfolds, with a nice landing spot in the bay below the deserted clearance village of Hallaig. Leaving here you pass a dramatic waterfall on the way to Brochel Castle. The road running 2km north of Brochel to Arnish is the famous 'Calum's Road'.

Leaving Brochel, the island turns more rugged, and the ancient Lewisian Gneiss rock type gives the island landscape a different, rougher feel. Just before the tiny passage between the northern tip of Raasay and Eilean Tigh there is a good sheltered stopping place with a small stony beach. From this beach there is a choice of excellent camping spots along with a bothy five minutes walk to the south.

Paddling across Caol Rona in the early morning sun is a magical experience, followed by continuing up the sunny east coast of Rona. With views across to the North West Highlands on one side, and the remoteness of Rona on the other, it is a special place. After about three kilometres look carefully on the hillside about thirty metres up for the ancient Church Cave. This is where the islanders once worshipped prior to the island church being built in 1912. Although not an easy landing place, it is worth the effort to explore this unique place of worship, with stone pews and a natural font which receives water in the form of drips from the roof above. Further up the coast, the imposing Rona lighthouse comes into sight as the northern tip is neared, as well as ever increasing evidence of the NATO station which is situated here. This northern area of Rona is perhaps the most special with a mass of skerries and inlets sheltering many common seals, and otters as well. At the backs of these inlets there are often places to stop to get out and explore the area further. About six kilometres down the west coast of Rona, hidden behind Eilean Garbh is Acairseid Mhòr, a sheltered loch that has an inlet tucked into the south-east corner. This is a fine place to camp for the second night. This big, natural harbour was once the base for smugglers many years ago.

The final part of the journey takes you back across Caol Rona and through the sheltered Caol Fladda between the west coast of Raasay and Eilean Fladday. If it is getting towards low tide it is better to go around Eilean Fladday. Beyond this is the small bay of Rubha Crion at the end of Calum's Road. This is a good stopping place, as well as an alternative starting point

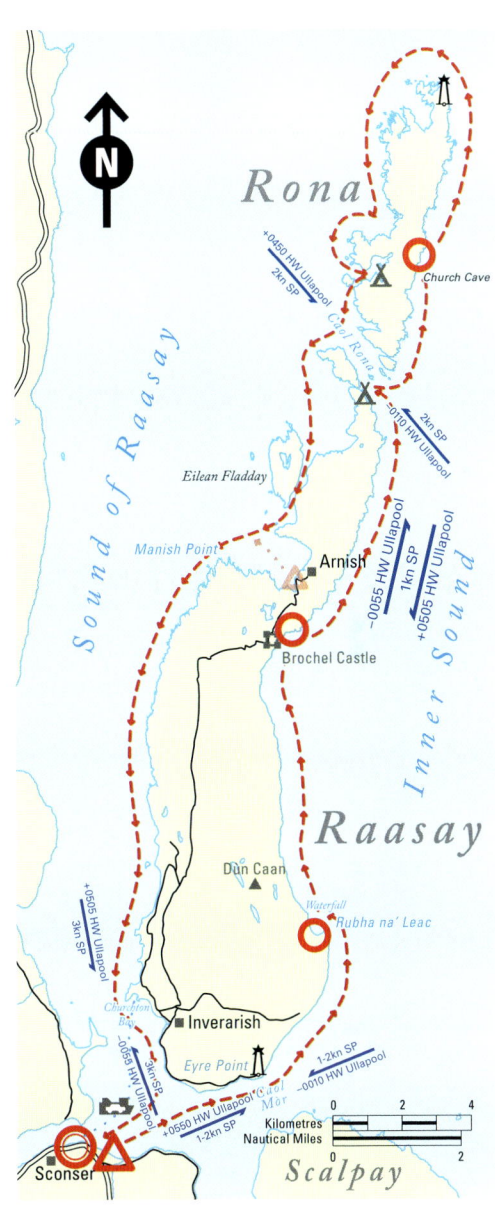

if you just wish to paddle around Rona for a day trip. Continuing down the coast the strangely-shaped Quiraing hills will be over your shoulder to the right. Look out for the sandstone through cave past Manish Point. With the occasional small rocky beach for a stop if required, the houses by the Narrows of Raasay will soon be reached. This will then just leave the short crossing back to Sconser to finish a fantastic journey.

Tides and weather

The tidal streams produce no rough water to talk of, and generally do not affect the trip unduly. Being aware of them will make life easier but it is always possible to make way with or without the tide.

The islands of Raasay and Rona generally offer relatively sheltered conditions in all but the worst of weather. Having said this, the area is still fairly committing. There are no easy escape routes and a crossing back to Skye would only lead to a coastline with no roads. A northerly wind with associated swell causes the biggest challenge in this area.

Additional information

There is a post office and shop in Inverarish, but other than this there are no amenities available on this trip.

Variations

There is an alternative launch site at Rubha Crion, Arnish (NG 592 480) at the north end of Raasay where there is a small slipway. From here it is possible to do a day trip circumnavigation of Rona if less time is available.

Calum's Road

Calum MacLeod was the Arnish postman, and in the 1960s the eight families making up the community were going to leave, as they had no road access to their village. The council had refused to help, so armed with a four-shilling book on road building, Calum built his own road by hand. When he finally finished he was awarded the British Empire Medal, but by then he and his wife were the only remaining inhabitants. He unfortunately died shortly after in 1988. If you ever drive along Calum's Road, now covered in tarmac by the council, be sure to have the tune *Calum's Road* by the band Capercaillie playing on your music system. This is a tune that can bring a tear to a glass eye, knowing the effort one man went to, with his bare hands, to try and save his community from disappearing.

Natural arches near Leac Tressirnish | Giles Trussell

Kilt Rock

No. 24 | **Grade C** | **30km** | **OS Sheet 23**

Tidal Port	Ullapool
Start	△ Portree (NG 486 438)
Finish	○ Staffin (NG 495 683)
HW/LW	HW/LW in Portree is around 25 minutes before Ullapool.
Tidal Times	Between Portree and Staffin: The N going stream starts at about 1 hour and 15 minutes before HW Ullapool. The S going stream starts at about 4 hours and 40 minutes after HW Ullapool.
Max Rate Sp	Along this section of coast 0.5 knots.
Coastguard	Stornoway, tel. 01851 702013, VHF weather every 3 hours from 0710.

Introduction

This is a section of remote Skye coastline that offers a big day out with no escape possible, dramatic scenery all around, and the impressive Kilt Rock with the cascading waterfall to finish. The only company you'll have here will be eagles above or whales below, all regularly seen in the area.

Kilt Rock

Description

Start at the stony beach at Portree that looks across to the brightly-coloured houses surrounding the busy harbour. This, along with the large natural sheltered inlet that forms Portree (king's harbour), is in stark contrast to the solitude, commitment and exposure to follow.

As the shelter of the bay is left so the view starts to open out, with the imposing headland of Tianavaig that is home to sea eagles to the south, and steep cliff-topped grassy slopes to the north. As you paddle north the Sound of Raasay will be on your right with great views across to Raasay and Rona, behind you the Cuillin mountains will be visible, and ahead the unrelenting steep, grassy cliff-topped slopes will stretch ahead as far as the eye can see. This steep coastline has an 'untouched by man' feel about it. An occasional stream tumbles into the sea with the odd small cave, and the rock architecture high above is varied and dramatic. Holm Island is soon visible in the distance. Although not overly spectacular, the island is one of the more obvious features along this coastline and a small beach on the western side provides a possible landing place.

Storr Lochs Power Station

This hydroelectric power station is clearly visible with the pipes descending 150m down the steep hillside from the lochs above. The station was opened in 1952 and is still producing electricity today. Alongside the pipes is the only working railway line on Skye; used to service the power station, it is not open to the public.

Just beyond Holm Island, Bearreraig Bay, a large bay nestled beneath the surrounding steep coastline, is another good place to stop. The bay is well known for the fossils that have been found here over the years.

Leaving Bearreraig the steep coastline continues and the first of the caves to explore appear. Beyond these caves at Rigg there is a great landing spot with a cascading waterfall alongside.

The old fishing station at Leac Tressirnish, which develops a natural harbour at low tide formed by a perfectly 'harbour-shaped' rock ledge, is another good place to land. It also marks the start of the best section of coastline for arches and caves to explore. Take your time not to miss any as quite a few are well hidden!

Inver Tote follows, with its waterfalls, stony beach landing and large ruined building showing evidence of an industrial past.

Digging for Dynamite

Large deposits of diatomite (locally known as cailo) were found in the nearby Loch Cuithir in 1886. Diatomite is a whitish, clay-like deposit made up of microscopic shells of diatoms. It has wide-ranging industrial uses including the production of paints, filtering beer and the manufacture of dynamite. In 1899 the Skye Diatomite Company was established to extract the diatomite from the loch and then transport it by railway to Inver Tote bay below. The wagons on the railway were pulled by hand all the way to the drying, heating and grinding shed that can be seen on the shore today. From here the diatomite was shipped as far away as South Africa.

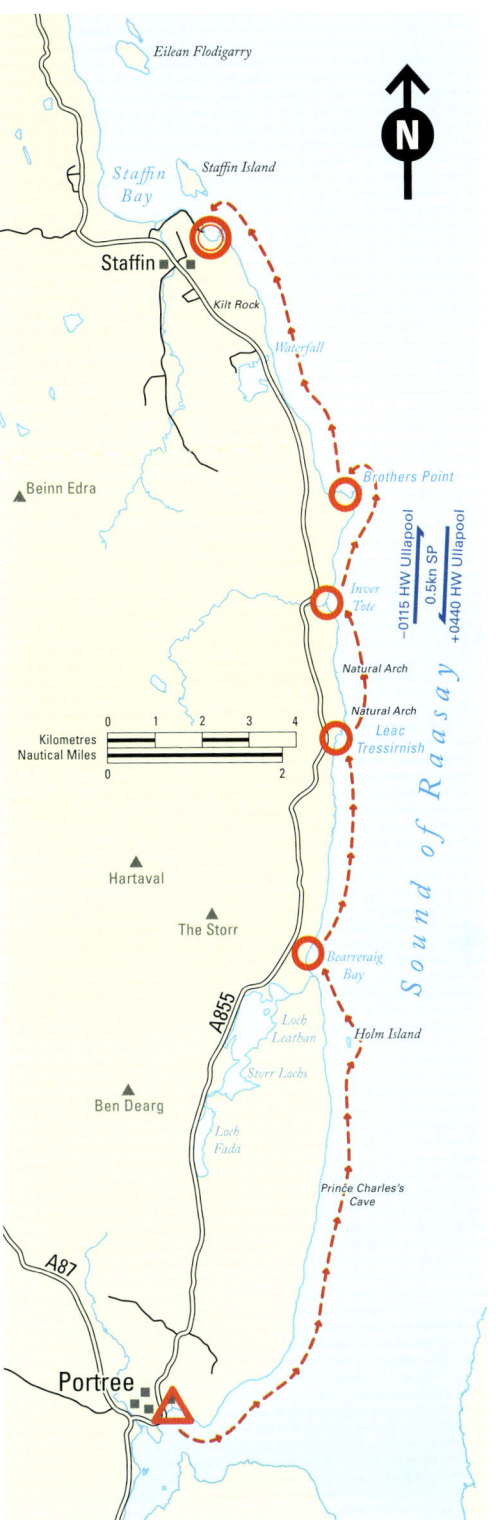

At the small low-lying peninsula of Brothers Point archaeologists have found evidence of hunter-gatherers, Iron Age warriors and medieval monks. Whether it gets its name from the 'brotherhood' of monks who once lived there, or two brothers who lost their lives when their boat was smashed on the rocks during a wild winter storm, nobody knows. It makes for another interesting spot to land with a rocky beach on the northern side being best. Whales are often seen off the point so keep a look out!

As with all great trips, the best is left to last ... Kilt Rock. The vertical basalt columns that form this impressive feature are said to resemble a kilt, hence its name. Just before arriving at the cliffs you pass Skye's most dramatic and well-known waterfall. Look out for the tourists in the viewing platform high above, the sea kayakers view is definitely the better one! While paddling beneath Kilt Rock look out for rock climbers, as these basalt columns give some of the finest rock climbs of their type in Britain. These final dramatic cliffs provide a fitting conclusion to a spectacular paddle, with the slipway at Staffin only a short distance beyond.

Tides and weather

There is minimal tidal movement to consider on this trip, so plan it around the prevailing winds. Being on the east coast this trip offers relative shelter, however with no easy escape look for a day with calm conditions. With strong westerly winds downdraughts and funnelling will be experienced. Any swell from the north will have a big effect on this coastline.

Additional information

There is a full range of amenities in Portree, and in Staffin there is a good shop as well as an excellent café at the Columba 1400 centre. There are some excellent walks to view this coastline from, including out to Brothers Point and Bearreraig Bay.

Variations

Starting at Staffin and paddling out to Brothers Point and back is a great day out if a shorter, less committing paddle is preferred.

Rubha Hunish with Fladda-chùain and the Outer Hebrides beyond

Rubha Hunish

No. 25 | Grade C | 26km | OS Sheet 23

Tidal Port	Ullapool
Start	△ Staffin (NG 495 683)
Finish	○ Duntulm (NG 408 736)
HW/LW	HW/LW in Duntulm is around 30 minutes before Ullapool.
Tidal Times	Off Staffin Island: The N going stream starts at about 1 hour and 15 minutes before HW Ullapool. The S going stream starts at about 4 hours and 40 minutes after HW Ullapool.
	Between Eilean Trodday and Rubha na h-Aiseig: The W going stream starts at about 2 hours and 25 minutes after HW Ullapool. The E going stream starts at about 4 hours before HW Ullapool.
	Off Rubha Hunish: The SW going stream starts at about 2 hours and 10 minutes after HW Ullapool. The NE going stream starts at about 4 hours and 30 minutes before HW Ullapool.
Max Rate Sp	Off Staffin Island 0.5 knots. Between Eilean Trodday and Rubha na h-Aiseig 2.5 knots. Off Rubha Hunish 3 knots.
Coastguard	Stornoway, tel. 01851 702013, VHF weather every 3 hours from 0710.

Approaching Rubha Hunish

Introduction

Rubha Hunish is one of the classic headlands of Scotland. The trip has everything you would expect including exposed coastlines, majestic cliffs, tidal races, caves and arches. While paddling around this northern tip of Skye you will see the Western Isles to one side and the mainland coastline stretching to Cape Wrath on the other. With Rubha Hunish also being a good place to see whales, it is a trip guaranteed to excite.

Description

Setting off from the pier at Staffin leads you to a small crossing to Staffin Island. This island is the home of many nesting gulls, oystercatchers and curlews, which will surround you as you paddle past.

From here, head to Eilean Flodigarry and the impressive basalt cliff that guards its southern end. Passing under the cliff, watch out for the reefs as you go between it and Sgeir na h-Èireann. This area of sheltered water is the home of many common seals that will come out to play as you paddle past. There is no simple landing here due to seaweed-covered rocks, however it is as easy a landing place as you are going to get for a while so a stop is recommended.

On leaving Sgeir na h-Èireann head across to the cliffs at Creag na h-Eiginn. For the next four kilometres the basalt rock architecture is quite stunning; there are caves and arches hidden around every corner and it is one of the best sections of cliffs to explore on Skye. Shortly after you start paddling along the cliffs, opposite Clach nan Ràmh you will pass under Flodigarry Cliffs, which is a popular climbing venue. Here there is a fantastic cave with many through routes and tunnels depending on the tide. There will be plenty more caves to explore as you continue, but ensure that you do not miss the dramatic arch and caves in the area by Stac Buidhe. As you cross Kilmaluag Bay you will see to your left Port Gobhlaig, which gives an alternative starting or finishing point. There is a rocky beach on the north side of this bay providing a convenient landing site; it also has the remains of an old fishing station.

Having rested and eaten it is now time to head on to the climax of our journey, paddling round the northern tip of Skye. You will soon pass Rubha na h-Aiseig where the first of the tidal streams squeeze between this headland and Eilean Trodday. At the same time the view will open out, from right to left you will see the mainland of Scotland with Cape Wrath in the far distance, the Shiant Islands to the north with Lewis to the right and Harris to the

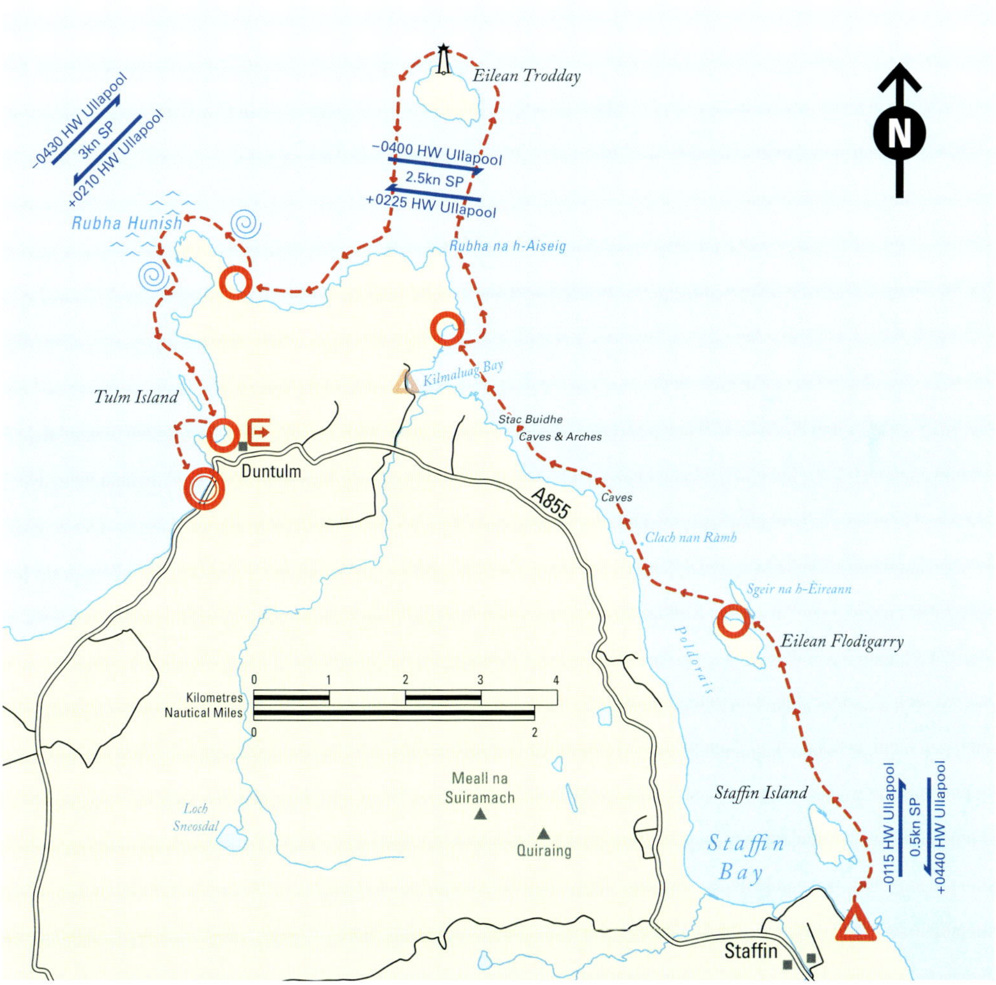

The old coastguard lookout

Rubha Hunish

left behind. The sea state will probably liven up, as this section of coastline is exposed to all weathers. Above there will be gannets circling and diving and below you may be lucky enough to see a minke whale. From Rubha na h-Aiseig it is well worth heading out across the tide to paddle around Eilean Trodday. The north-western coastline of this island is spectacular, with an impressive sea stack along with a huge cave you can paddle through. There are no easy landings on the island so once the cliffs have been explored it is on to Rubha Hunish. You can stay out from the cliffs and get the most assistance from the tidal stream, but I would recommend heading back to the north Skye coastline to explore it further, as there are still a few more hidden caves and stacks. Just before going around Rubha Hunish there is a possible rocky landing place at the western end of the bay if a rest is needed. This spot provides an amazing camping place, as well as a chance to stretch the legs and walk up to the old coastguard lookout high above, now converted into a bothy.

Following the basalt cliffs round to Rubha Hunish there are two final sea stacks to weave in and out of before the tide takes you round the headland. If there is any wind and swell from the west this will provide some rougher conditions, but the bays can usually offer some shelter. Continue down the coast past Tulm Island, choosing the dramatic west side or the sheltered east. The island is covered with bird life, and otters have been seen on the sheltered eastern side. The imposing ruin of 15th century Duntulm Castle guards the final small headland you will pass before reaching the finish. A rocky beach landing (though there is sometimes a small amount of sand to land on at the northern end) will be the final challenge. If this is looking too difficult in

Landing at Kilmaluag Bay

the conditions, an alternative is at Port Duntulm, but this is a long walk finishing in the hotel car park. If this option is chosen please be courteous to the hotel owners and guests.

Tides and weather

Reasonably strong tidal streams flow off the northern tip of Skye and planning is essential to ensure they assist. These are strongest off Eilean Trodday and Rubha Hunish. On the north-east going tide off Rhubha Hunish and on the east going tide off Trodday these will form a tidal race, at other times these will just produce eddies and confused water. If concerned about this, plan the trip on a neap tide and/or make use of slack water in this area. Eddies form in all the bays in this area, but all can be paddled against reasonably easily. To complete this trip you will paddle on all aspects of coast, each being very exposed to any wind or swell. Therefore settled weather is best for the trip.

Additional information

In Staffin there is a shop as well as an excellent café in the Columba 1400 centre. There is also a hotel in Duntulm that offers food and drink to non-residents. If you have the energy there is a good walk to the lookout overlooking Rubha Hunish, which is now a bothy managed by the Mountain Bothies Association. The walk starts at the telephone box and provides amazing views of the area.

Sea stacks south of Kilmaluag Bay | Giles Trussell

Variations

The four-kilometre section of coastline south of Port Gobhlaig is arguably one of the best on Skye, it makes an exceptional morning paddle with the sun on the cliffs. It can be done by paddling from Staffin and finishing at Port Gobhlaig (NG 436 751), or simply starting and finishing from Port Gobhlaig. It is often a very sheltered section of coast compared to going around Rubha Hunish and has no tidal movement of note. For a shorter paddle around Eilean Trodday and Rubha Hunish, starting at Port Gobhlaig instead of Staffin works well.

For a longer paddle, taking in the offshore islands of Fladda-chùain makes for an exceptional trip. Careful tidal planning will be required for this (see Trip 27) and camping out on the islands is worth considering.

Perfect conditions to cross the Sound of Shiant | Giles Trussell

Little Minch & the Shiant Islands

No. 26	**Grade C**	**70/60km**	**OS Sheets 23 and 14**
Tidal Port	Ullapool
Start	△ Camas Mòr (NG 370 706)
Finish	○ Camas Mòr (NG 370 706) or Tarbert (NG 157 998)
HW/LW	HW/LW the Shiants is around 20 minutes before Ullapool.
Tidal Times	Off Ru Bornesketaig: The NE going stream starts at about 4 hours and 15 minutes before HW Ullapool. The SW going stream starts at about 2 hours and 10 minutes after HW Ullapool.
	Off Fladda-chùain: The E going stream starts at about 4 hours before HW Ullapool. The W going stream starts at about 1 hour and 55 minutes after HW Ullapool.
	South end of Shiant Isles: The NE going stream starts at about 3 hours and 30 minutes before HW Ullapool. There is slack water at about 1 hour and 40 minutes after HW Ullapool. The SW going stream starts at about 2 hours and 55 minutes after HW Ullapool.
	Sound of Shiant: The NE going stream starts at about 3 hours and 15 minutes before HW Ullapool. The SW going stream starts at about 3 hours and 10 minutes after HW Ullapool.
	Sound of Scalpay: The E going stream starts at about 5 hours and 30 minutes before HW Ullapool. The W going stream starts at about 55 minutes after HW Ullapool.
Max Rate Sp	Off Ru Bornesketaig 2 knots. Off the N and S ends of Fladda-chùain 2.5 knots. Off the S end of the Shiants 3 knots. In the Sound of Shiant 2.5 knots. In the Sound of Scalpay 2 knots.
Coastguard	Stornoway, tel. 01851 702013, VHF weather every 3 hours from 0710.

© Evening on the Shiant Islands, Harris beyond | Giles Trussell

Little Minch & the Shiant Islands

Introduction

To set off from Skye and cross the Minch to the Outer Hebrides has got to be one of the classic crossings. Add to this the islands off the north of Skye and the unique Shiant Isles and this is a remarkable paddle. With the option of continuing on from the Shiants to Tarbert and getting the ferry back, you have your perfect journey. For this trip to be successful it will take careful weather watching for the right conditions and good tidal planning to make it as easy as possible.

Description

When setting off from the small pier at Camas Mòr there will always be a feeling of apprehension. "Will the weather hold and have the tides been worked out correctly?" will be part of it, but, "Will I need to go to the toilet on the three hour crossing to the Shiants?" will be the main part! Leaving Camas Mòr head for the rocky island of An t-Iasgair where there is no landing, but good rock architecture and plenty of nesting kittiwakes, puffins, guillemots and razorbills. From here you will have the tide at your back and get a gentle push for the 6km to Fladda-chùain; watch out for large boats and submarines in this channel. Before heading to the only easy landing spot half way up the west side of the islands where there is a small ruined building and stone-cleared landing inlet; consider exploring the other islands. Lord Macdonald's Table is a must, with a natural arch separating it from Gearran Island. Having rested and explored the wildlife of Fladda-chùain (look out for the big black rabbits), you'll be ready to head to the Shiant Isles that you can hopefully see in the distance.

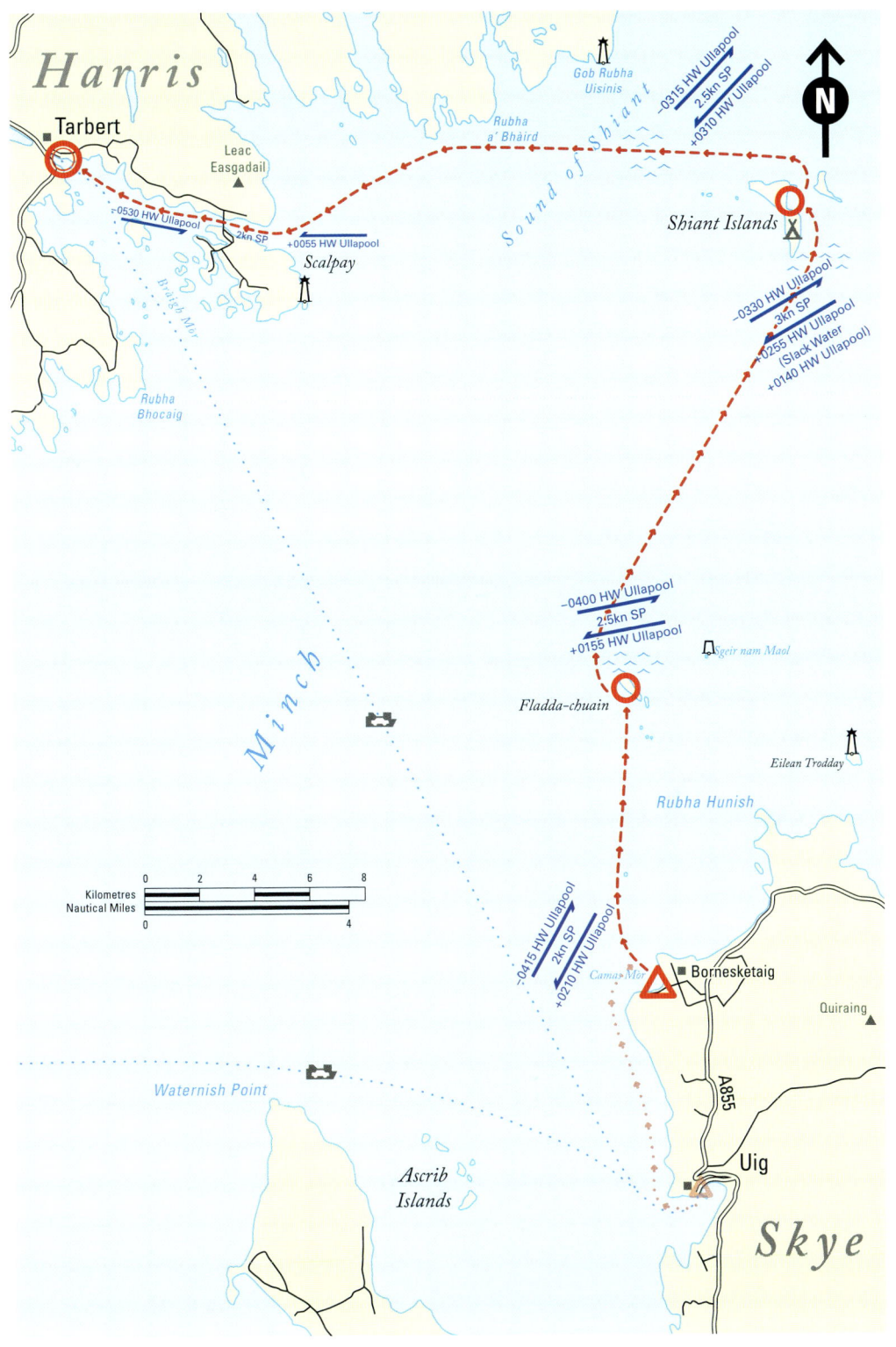

Cave exploring on the Shiant Islands | Giles Trussell

With some help from the tide and hopefully the weather, the crossing should take no more than three hours. With the expanse of the Western Isles arcing from back left to dead ahead and the disappearing Skye and mainland behind, the time will soon pass. As the Shiant Isles come into closer view, so will the number of puffins increase, and the calls of thousands of sea birds will soon be heard from the islands. On reaching the towering sides of the southern island of the Shiants, Eilean an Taighe, head up to the isthmus where it joins Garbh Eilean to land. The eastern side gives the most shelter and from here there is good camping on the northern tip of Eilean an Taighe. The locked hut used by the sheep farmer when visiting the island is also found here. It is well worth the effort spending some time exploring the island on foot. There are crofts scattering the hillside, which housed up to five families until 1901. Since then it has been uninhabited. Paddling around the other islands that make up the Shiants you will be rewarded with a wealth of birdlife, seals, impressive basalt cliffs and arches. In itself it is a memorable paddle and if you can manage the rocky landing required, then landing on Eilean Mhuire will offer more of the history of the Shiants. This is the most fertile of the islands and it also has plenty of signs of habitation, of particular interest is the ruined chapel dedicated to the Virgin Mary.

From the Shiants the trip described continues on to Tarbert, though you do have the option of heading back across the Minch to Skye. Our route takes you past Galta Mòr, the most westerly of the Shiants, and across the Sound of Shiant to Harris, which is the more mountainous southern half of the Isle of Lewis. Planning to make the best use of the tide helps, and the headland of Rubh a' Bhàird is a good place to aim for. This gives you options for landing in the inlets to the west of the headland. Paddling down the Harris coastline, with perhaps only a lone stag watching from the moors, will convey the sense of remoteness that the Western Isles have. Paddling past

The anchorage and landing on the Shiant Islands | Giles Trussell

Eilean Mòr a' Bhàigh and on underneath the bridge in the Sound of Scalpay takes you into East Loch Tarbert. You may wish to pull into the naturally sheltered North Harbour of Scalpay for a rest, or if a ferry is being caught then the final paddle into Tarbert beckons.

You will be able to carry your kayak aboard the ferry, usually paying the charge for a bike, and then it will be a relaxing journey back to Skye. On arriving in Uig there is the final bit of paddling to get back to Camas Mòr, thus completing an unusual paddling circuit.

Tides and weather

To carry out this trip some detailed tidal planning will be required. It is worth considering using tidal vectors for the crossings to get most effect from the tide, and paddle no further than required. There are useful tidal diamonds on the charts to help with this, however on neap tides the drift is not too great if vectors were not used. For the crossing to the Shiants it is best to time it so as to arrive at the Shiants at slack water; making use of the north-east going stream provides most tidal assistance. This will mean the sea state will be easy for a tired paddler at the end of a three-hour crossing. Timing it like this means that you will have to paddle through the tidal race which forms off the north end of Fladda-chùain, and it will push you in a NE direction if you are not careful. On neap tides however it is certainly not a violent race and is no more than a few hundred metres wide.

Crossing the Sound of Shiant will again take careful tidal planning but once across there is negligible tidal movement until the Sound of Scalpay is reached. This is only in the narrows however, and as it may be hard to plan the trip to get there before it starts running east, it is good to know that it is relatively easy to eddy hop up the narrows even on a spring tide.

Approaching the Shiant Islands | Giles Trussell

Due to the nature of the trip, and the crossings generally going slightly across the tidal streams, it is worth planning to do this trip on neap tides. It is also clear that this trip takes in some very exposed water, so a settled spell of weather with minimal winds is also required.

Additional information

To get information and timetables for the Tarbert to Uig ferry contact Caledonian MacBrayne Ferries on www.calmac.co.uk. There are no amenities at Camas Mòr, but at Tarbert and Uig there are plenty. To help with the ferry crossing it is worth using a kayak trolley.

The Shiant Islands are owned by the Nicolson family and there is a good book called *Sea Room: An Island Life* by Adam Nicolson, about their history. In planning this trip using the Admiralty Chart 1794, North Minch – Southern Part is worthwhile.

Variations

The Shiant Islands are an amazing place to explore, it is worth spending two nights camping on the islands to allow a full day to paddle around them. If you don't wish to continue to Tarbert and have to use the ferry, just paddling out and back to the Shiants from Camas Mòr is still a great trip. Alternatively you could paddle back from Tarbert to Camas Mòr, this involves a 30km crossing of the Minch.

The final ten kilometres from Uig back to Camas Mòr at the end of the trip can feel a long way – you may want to leave a car at Uig to avoid this!

Dawn start heading to Fladda-chùain

Fladda-chùain  27

No. 27 | Grade C | 28km | OS Sheet 23

Tidal Port	Ullapool
Start	△ Camas Mòr (NG 370 706)
Finish	O Camas Mòr (NG 370 706)
HW/LW	HW/LW at Camas Mòr is around 30 minutes before Ullapool.
Tidal Times	Off Ru Bornesketaig: The NE going stream starts at about 4 hours and 15 minutes before HW Ullapool. The SW going stream starts at about 2 hours and 10 minutes after HW Ullapool.
	Off Fladda-chùain: The E going stream starts at about 4 hours before HW Ullapool. The W going stream starts at about 1 hour and 55 minutes after HW Ullapool.
	Off Rubha Hunish: The SW going stream starts at about 2 hours and 10 minutes after HW Ullapool. The NE going stream starts at about 4 hours and 30 minutes before HW Ullapool.
Max Rate Sp	2 knots off Ru Bornesketaig. Off the N and S ends of Fladda-chùain 2.5 knots. Off Rubha Hunish 3 knots.
Coastguard	Stornoway, tel. 01851 702013, VHF weather every 3 hours from 0710.

Puffins that nest on Fladda-chùain

Introduction

With tidal waters, open crossings and offshore islands, this trip has all the ingredients for a great day out. Add to that the wildlife, an incredible through cave and spectacular scenery, and the trip becomes a classic. Careful planning and good conditions are required to enjoy this trip, but with all of this in place this is a paddle not to be missed.

Description

Starting from the slipway at Camas Mòr you will be looking straight out over the first ten kilometres of paddling to Fladda-chùain. To get there, head first to the small basalt cliffs of Ru Bornesketaig, before crossing to our first islands of the day. These are the rocky skerries around An t-Iasgair, which translates into 'fisherman's rock'. There is no landing place on these islands, so the basalt cliffs and grass summit remain the domain of the sea birds. In the spring there will be puffins, guillemots, razorbills and kittiwakes all nesting on this small cluster of rocks. The next five kilometres crosses the open sea to the islands around Fladda-chùain. As on all of the open crossings, you are paddling through one of the main shipping lanes of the Minch, so keep a watchful eye over your shoulder.

The first island of this group that you will come across is Lord Macdonald's Table, which has a fantastic cave that can be paddled through to the other side of the island. Having paddled through this you will pass the basalt columns of the Cleats, before heading around Gaeilavore Island and on to Fladda-chùain. By now it will be clear what an amazing breeding ground for sea birds the islands are, as you will have paddled past puffins, guillemots, Arctic terns and skuas to name a few. These stunning islands have some of the best birdlife that Skye has to offer.

At Fladda-chùain an easy landing place is found at a small natural inlet midway up the southwestern side of the island. The island has been inhabited in the past and the only evidence of this today is the ruin of a chapel. This is believed to have been founded in Columba's time, and built by a huge monk known as O'Gorgon. All you will find living on the island these days are the birds, as well as giant black rabbits! The views across to the Shiant Isles and Hebrides on one side, on to Cape Wrath in the other direction, and the north of Skye in front, are just stunning.

Leaving the sheltered little landing, head on around Fladda-chùain and it will then be time to make the crossing back to Skye, heading for Tulm Bay. Keep an eye out for whales and dolphins while paddling as this is a frequent feeding area for them. After the tidal crossing the shelter

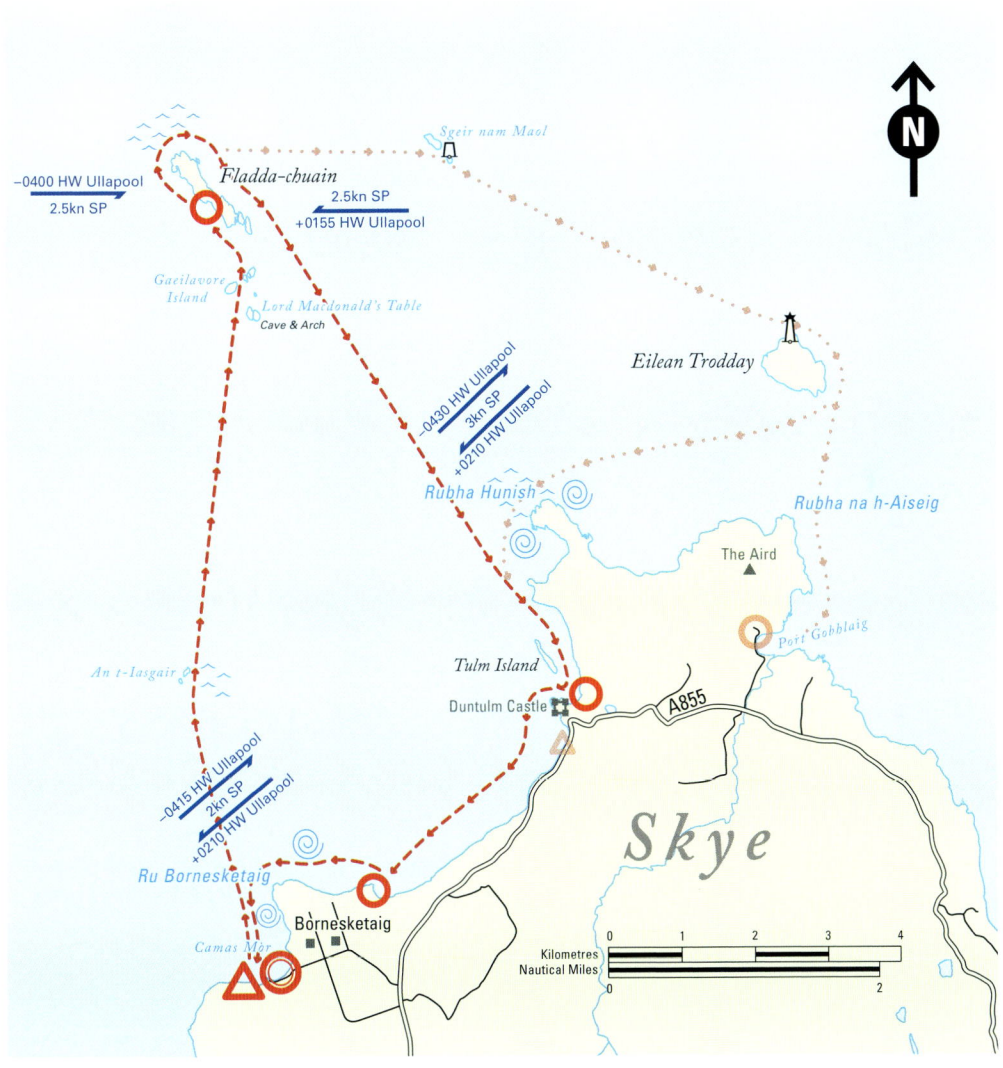

Group heading out to Fladda-chùain with the Outer Hebrides beyond

found in this bay will be a welcome relief; there will be plenty of birds on Tulm Island to welcome you and maybe even an otter if you are lucky. There is an easy place to land in the corner of the bay at Port Duntulm, overlooked by Duntulm Castle.

Legend has it that the castle was abandoned after the infant son of the chieftain fell from a window and was dashed on the rocks below. The nursemaid in charge was punished by being set adrift in a small boat out in the North Atlantic, where the sea would decide her fate.

From Duntulm the coast is followed to Ru Bornesketaig; there is a pleasant place to land at Gairbh-sgeir. Paddling around Ru Bornesketaig look out for the cave named Uamh Oir, translating into 'cave of gold'. Legend has it that the smugglers in the area would hide their stolen valuables in this cave. You may not be lucky enough to find any gold as you explore it, but the fantastic basalt columns that surround you will more than make up for it. All that will be left is the final short paddle back to the slipway at Camas Mòr, where an easy landing awaits after an amazing paddle – one that easily lives up to being a 'classic'.

Tides and weather

The majority of this trip takes place in tidal waters and careful planning is required, particularly as the crossings to and from Skye involve crossing the main flow. Making use of the north-east going stream is required initially, timing slack water at Fladda-chùain, and then returning on the south-west going stream, makes this trip possible. Heading out to An t-Iasgair is reasonably straightforward on a simple transit, and then the tide pushes well towards Fladda-chùain. Take care when getting close to the islands as it will start to increase in speed and be of a more easterly

The landing on Fladda-chùain

direction, therefore transits will be required to stay on course. After slack water at the islands, transits will again be required to efficiently arrive in Tulm Bay; there is a large eddy formed by Rubha Hunish making this easier. The return to Camas Mòr is then straightforward from a tidal point of view. Making use of a neap tide is recommended to make this trip easier for those less experienced in tidal waters.

This is a trip to save for settled weather and light winds. Offshore in tidal waters is not a place to be if weather conditions change for the worse!

Additional information

Shipping regularly uses this area; take extreme care on the crossings. There are no amenities at Camas Mòr, however there is a hotel serving food and beer at Duntulm, with an amazing view out over the islands. There is a full range of amenities in nearby Uig.

Duntulm Castle

This impressive site is thought to have had a Pictish fort on it originally, the castle seen today being built in the 14th century. Over the years the castle was the site of many bloody battles and passed between the rival MacLeod and MacDonald clans. By the 17th century the Macdonalds finally gained the upper hand in the area and they remained in the castle until it was abandoned in around 1732.

Ru Bornesketaig and Fladda-chùain

Variations

For a shorter day it is possible to paddle out and back to Fladda-chùain starting from the rocky bay just south of Duntulm Castle. The road is very close and there is enough room to park carefully. The launching can be a bit awkward particularly at lower water, and it has less tidal assistance.

For a longer day leaving Fladda-chùain and heading to Eilean Trodday makes for a great day out. From Trodday the trip can finish at Port Gobhlaig, continue on to Staffin, or return to Camas Mòr depending on tidal timings and preferred distance to paddle. Shuttles may be required and further tidal planning will definitely be needed.

Waterfall south of Stac a' Bhothain

Waternish Point & the Ascrib Islands

No. 28 | Grade C | 40km | OS Sheet 23

Tidal Port	Ullapool
Start	△ Loch Greshornish (NG 335 527)
Finish	◯ Stein (NG 263 563)
HW/LW	HW/LW the Ascrib Islands is around 30 minutes before Ullapool.
Tidal Times	For Loch Greshornish: The outgoing stream starts at about 30 minutes before HW Ullapool. The ingoing stream starts at about 5 hours and 50 minutes after HW Ullapool.
	Off Waternish Point: The SW going stream starts at about 2 hours and 25 minutes after HW Ullapool. The NE going stream starts at about 4 hours before HW Ullapool.
Max Rate Sp	Off Waternish Point 2.5 knots, generally weak elsewhere.
Coastguard	Stornoway, tel. 01851 702013, VHF weather every 3 hours from 0710.

Introduction

This trip takes you to a place that feels as if time has forgotten it; all you will have for company here is the wildlife. Waternish Point offers spectacular waterfalls with sea eagles soaring above

Looking to Waternish Point from the Ascrib Islands

and a remote coastline of cliffs and isolated rocky bays. The Ascrib Islands are a place where you could lose yourself forever; you will be sharing them with puffins and seals, surrounded only by peace and solitude.

Description

This journey is possible as a big day out, but to make the most of the amazing location it is best to take a couple of days over it, camping along the way. The put-in at Loch Greshornish is from a lay-by where the narrow single-track road comes closest to the sea. A short carry down the heathery shoreline leads to the rocky beach. From here a short paddle up the loch leads to the point, passing some very impressive houses. Reaching Greshornish Point a view of what lies ahead unfolds; the Ascrib Islands sitting peacefully in the middle of Loch Snizort, the isolated and craggy coastline of Waternish Point, and the backdrop to all this is the outline of the Outer Hebrides; breath-taking does not do it justice. Do not be tempted to cut across direct to Waternish Point from here, but instead head south down the western side of Greshornish Point. The cliffs down here are a complete surprise and a real hidden gem. Enjoy them down as far as some small caves and then cut across the bay near its head to a natural arch on the other side. This small detour is well worth it, but now it is time to start heading up the Waternish peninsula.

The coastline is steep with cliffs and crags along the way. When the cliffs and crags ease, a small bay is reached backed with forest plantation. Hug the coastline, as you will soon discover one of the most amazing waterfalls on Skye, tumbling down from up high, cascading over rocks and plummeting into the sea. This is also a nesting area for a pair of sea eagles, so spend some time enjoying the waterfall and hopefully admire its guardians soaring above. There is a rocky landing just along from the waterfall to take a break if required. Leaving the eagles to their hunting, continue along the coastline to the small, yet imposing, rocky outcrop of Stac a' Bhothain. There is an easy landing just before this, worth taking a rest as from here the crossing out to the Ascribs begins. A little over half an hour should get you to South Ascrib; the lack of buoys and boat traffic will be apparent. Loch Snizort is a forgotten corner of Skye.

Arriving at the Acribs is a magical experience. The shelter found in the many skerries of the western side ensures a calmness about the place, and the resident seals will be here waiting for you. The area is part of a Special Area of Conservation because of the common seals. Thirty-five percent of Skye's breeding population live on these islands, and these 600 seals make up 1% of the EU population. A small passage midway up the western side of South Ascrib leads to a natural harbour and a well-maintained house built by the island's owner; rarely stayed in however. This is a perfect place to land and spend some time, and if paddling this trip over two days it also makes for the ideal overnight camping spot. There is no water and the ground is a little rough, but the surroundings will more than make up for it. Before continuing the journey with the crossing back

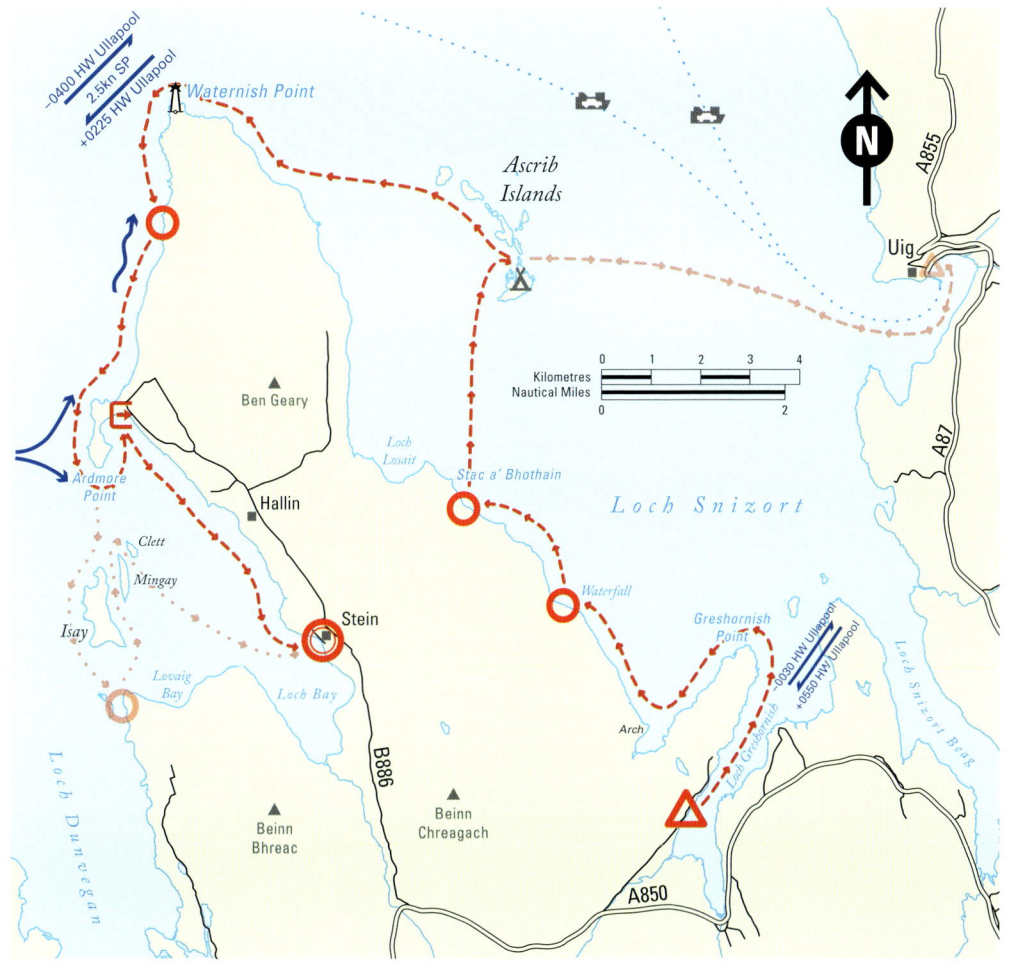

to Waternish Point, take the time to explore these islands. On Eilean Creagach you will see the resident puffins, here they will float in the water alongside you in their dozens. I have not seen more puffins anywhere else on Skye.

Leaving the Ascribs aim for the steep cliffs that lead to Waternish Point. Here the gentle tidal flow may well start to become apparent, as will the headland of Rubha Hunish over the right shoulder, Skye's most northerly point. The light on Waternish Point is nowhere near as impressive as its location, as more of the Hebrides come into view, along with the islands off the north of Skye and the Shiant Islands. Rounding the point the western coastline of Waternish is revealed, no less remote or dramatic than the eastern. Soon the first waterfall will be passed and beyond this are a number of rocky shore landings that can be used. Continuing on towards Ardmore Point, the waterfalls will keep appearing. Dominating the view to the south-west will be the imposing Dunvegan Head, where Skye's highest cliffs tower out of the Minch. At Ardmore Point you will discover the strange rock formations and arches that make up Rogheadh framing the view of Loch Dunvegan and its islands beyond.

All that remains is the last few kilometres along the low-lying coastline to Stein. This marks the end of the peace and solitude with the return to the real world. Luckily this return can involve making use of the pub only a few paces away from the landing at the pier.

Tides and weather

The tide off Waternish Point can flow reasonably fast and is noticeable most of the way from the Ascribs, so it is best to time the trip to have this assisting. On the western side of Waternish Point all the way to Ardmore Point the tide generally runs in a continuous northerly direction due to the eddy and NE going tidal stream. The eddy is never too strong and staying in close ensures it will not cause too much of a problem.

The trip is very remote with no possibility of escape, and also involves open crossings. Any wind or swell from the south-west through to the north will have a big effect on the coastline. Save this trip for a period of light winds and settled weather.

Additional information

There is very limited parking on the single-track road at the put-in, please park considerately here. If the recommended put-in is occupied it is also possible to park/launch a little further on at NG 338 534 but the carry is slightly further to the water. There is a good campsite at Borve (NG 343 525) on the east side of Loch Greshornish. This makes for a good base and if staying here offers an ideal alternative launching spot to start the trip. At Stein there is plenty of parking as well as a perfectly situated pub.

Variations

The Ascrib Islands are worthy of a day trip in their own right. To do this, starting and finishing at Uig (NG 387 638) at the old slipway works well. This then requires a seven-kilometre crossing to the islands.

To extend the described trip at the end, exploring the islands of Isay (Ìosaigh), Mingay, Clett and Lampay along with their coral beaches is recommended on the route back to Stein.

The coral beaches

Loch Dunvegan

No. 29 | **Grade A** | **16km** | **OS Sheet 23**

Tidal Port	Ullapool
Start	△ Dunvegan (NG 245 497)
Finish	○ Stein (NG 263 563)
HW/LW	HW/LW in Loch Dunvegan is around 45 minutes before Ullapool.
Tidal Times	In the loch the direction and the times of the small amount of tidal flow are variable.
Max Rate Sp	South of Isay 0.5 knots in the channel, elsewhere very weak.
Coastguard	Stornoway, tel. 01851 702013, VHF weather every 3 hours from 0710.

Introduction

Loch Dunvegan offers a sea kayaker incredible diversity and a great day in any conditions. There is wildlife, history, geology, beaches and a pub to finish. On a hot summer's day, it is fantastic to linger and enjoy the unique coral beaches. On a day with strong winds, the area is sheltered enough to give an enjoyable paddle when most other venues are too exposed.

Dunvegan Castle

Loch Dunvegan

Description

Setting off from the small seaweed-covered beach you are instantly immersed in the wildlife haven of Gairbh Eilein, overlooked by the impressive Dunvegan Castle. As well as a variety of bird life, you will be paddling amongst the resident common seals. Enjoy your ringside seat view, but try not to disturb them as there are regular seal watching boat trips in this area. If you have time you may want to continue seeking out the wildlife by paddling across to Eilean Dubh before heading northwards up the loch. Camalaig Bay gives a stony beach to land on, and also the opportunity to explore the remains of a broch on the hillside above.

Heading up the coast towards the island of Lampay you will get ever improving views of the majestic Outer Hebrides. On a clear day it will be the islands of North Uist, Harris and Lewis that you will see. At Lampay, the beautiful coral beaches on the east side of the island and opposite on Skye, provide an ideal place to land. The fantastically ornate pieces of white 'coral' that make up this beach are technically algae, but 'algae beach' doesn't quite have the same appeal!

Leaving the beach make the small crossing to the island of Isay (Ìosaigh), its Norse name translates into 'porpoise island'. This is no coincidence and I have had some of my best sightings of porpoise in this area, as well as otters, eagles and a host of birdlife. It is well worth paddling around the west side of Isay and exploring the islands of Mingay and Clett. These islands give more wildlife and some good examples of basalt cliffs. Down the east side of Mingay you will also notice the small disused lime kiln. The crofters would feed shells into the kiln to extract the lime from them, which they used for building and fertilizer. Before leaving the islands take the time to land at the old disused village on Isay's eastern shore.

Massacre on Isay

In the 1800s Isay supported a community of 90 people, with its own fishing station and general store. Today you can explore the ruins of over eighteen cottages and black houses, along with the grand main house. This main house was the scene of a gruesome massacre in the 16th century, when Roderick MacLeod owned it. He wished his grandson to inherit the island, but unfortunately there were two families with first claim to the island. To solve this inheritance problem he invited them all to a big meal, and after eating called the potential inheritors of the island into his room for discussion. As each of the inheritors came for their discussion with MacLeod they were duly murdered, until his grandson was left as the sole inheritor of the island.

The picturesque village of Stein is the finishing point. On the way there it is worth passing the small skerry of Sgeir nam Biast for a final paddle amongst the common seals. On a sunny day you will then be able to sit in the pub garden at Stein and enjoy the sun setting over the Western Isles while reflecting on a great day's paddle.

Tides and weather

This trip can be undertaken at any state of the tide, as the tidal streams within the loch are barely noticeable. The main consideration for this trip is the weather. The route direction described works best with a wind from a southerly direction; if it is from the north consider starting at Stein. In stronger winds the area around Isay is more exposed, and it may be worth considering just paddling out of Dunvegan and remaining in the shelter of the small islands and skerries at its southern end. Here it is protected from the full force of the sea and wind so it is possible to paddle when most other areas will be too rough.

Additional information

Both at Stein and Dunvegan there are good amenities with pubs, hotels and restaurants. If a transport shuttle is not possible with two cars, consider hiring a taxi from Dunvegan to collect you at the pub in Stein.

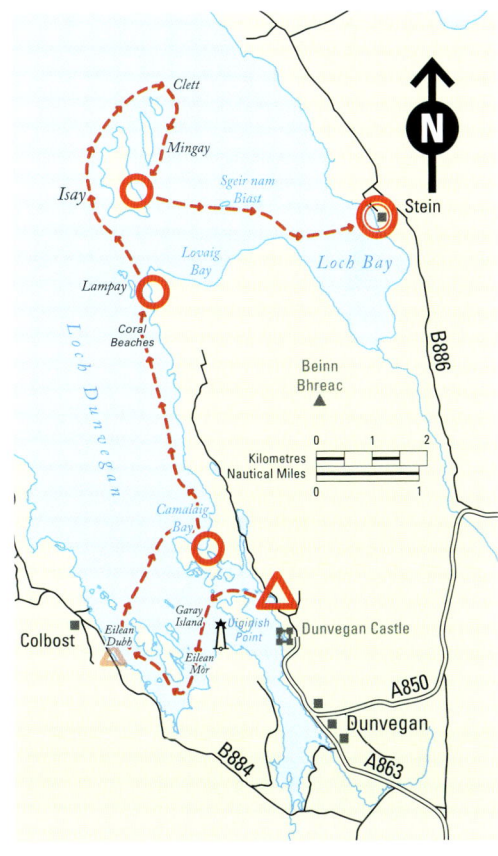

Heading out to Isay, Mingay and Clett

Variations

A trip exploring the islands around the head of Loch Dunvegan starting and finishing at the put-in works well as a shorter day or in very windy conditions.

Starting and finishing at Stein and enjoying the islands and coral beaches from there is a great trip on its own, if a bit more exposed.

Dunvegan Head

No. 30 | **Grade B** | **17km** | **OS Sheet 23**

Tidal Port	Ullapool
Start	△ Colbost (NG 216 487)
Finish	◯ Meanish (NG 154 506)
HW/LW	HW/LW in Loch Dunvegan is around 45 minutes before Ullapool.
Tidal Times	The W side of Dunvegan Head: The NE going stream starts at about 4 hours and 15 minutes before HW Ullapool. The SW going stream starts at about 2 hours after HW Ullapool.
Max Rate Sp	Off the west side of Dunvegan Head 1.5 knots.
Coastguard	Stornoway, tel. 01851 702013, VHF weather every 3 hours from 0710.

Introduction

Dunvegan Head boasts Skye's highest sea cliffs; at over 300 metres they rise out of the Minch and are a sight not to be missed. In the right conditions this headland is accessible to many paddlers and the dramatic location rivals any of Scotland's less accessible mighty headlands. The trip provides a wonderful day out and will leave you with a sore neck from looking up at the imposing cliffs and eagles soaring amongst them.

© Meanish Pier and Dunvegan Head

Dunvegan Head

Description

There is a cleared launch way and reasonable parking in Colbost by the museum and the famous Three Chimneys restaurant. Leaving here you will be able to enjoy the wildlife haven formed by the many small islands at the heart of Loch Dunvegan. If time allows, exploring some of these will have you paddling amongst common seals and plenty of birdlife, as well as enjoying great views of the dramatic Dunvegan Castle.

Leaving the islands and seals behind, the journey makes its way up the east side of Dunvegan Head. This is a coastline of small cliffs and bays, with some impressive houses built to make most of the fantastic location. The small headland of Gob na Hoe is passed and beyond this is a wide bay, known as Galtrigill Bay, with a choice of stony beaches to land on. It is worth taking a rest here as, depending on the sea state, there may not be another opportunity once around Dunvegan Head. While enjoying the views from Galtrigill look for 'Piper's Cave' on the hillside overlooking the bay. The nearby village of Borreraig was once the home of the MacCrimmon piping school, the hereditary pipers of Clan MacLeod. So as not to incur the wrath of the neighbours, the pipers would practise in the nearby sea caves, the one at Galtrigill being the most famous of these. The monument you will have seen above Gob na Hoe is to commemorate these pipers.

Just beyond here the sea arch of Am Famhair marks the approach of Dunvegan Head. Sadly it is not possible to paddle through it. Paddling around the head the view opens up with Waternish Point clear to see and then the Hebrides stretching out along the horizon. Sea conditions may be a bit more lively now and the cliffs will start to rise high above. These cliffs just get bigger and bigger over the next few kilometres, reaching their high point of 313 metres at Biod an Athair.

Dunvegan Castle

There has been a castle on this site in one form or other since AD1200, with the castle seen today dating back to the 14th century. It is the ancestral home of Clan MacLeod and is said to be the oldest residence in Britain continuously occupied by generations of the same family. Considering the many battles fought over the years by the clan, in particular against the MacDonalds, it is a wonder that the castle still stands in such good condition. This could perhaps be attributed to Clan MacLeod's most treasured possession, the Fairy Flag. Legend has it that a clan chief once married a fairy thinking she was mortal, then after a happy twenty years her allotted time with mortals came to an end and she returned to her own people. To make up for his loss the fairies presented him with the silk Fairy Flag, the flag having magical powers when unfurled to save the clan from destruction. The flag can only be used on three occasions. So far the flag has been used twice, at the battle of Glendale in 1490 and Trumpen in 1578, working on both occasions, with the MacLeods overcoming adversity and winning the battles.

Words cannot express how amazing these cliffs are, comparable with the more famous Clò Mòr cliffs of Cape Wrath or St John's Head on Orkney. The cliffs of Dunvegan Head however are far more accessible and less affected by tide and weather. They really should be on every paddlers 'to do' list! Beyond the high point the cliffs continue, unrelenting, all the way to the finish. In calm conditions there are reasonable landing opportunities as the foot of the cliffs are generally stony beaches.

Some final waterfalls mark the end of the main cliffs and time for the short hop across the bay to the finish at Meanish Pier. This provides an easy landing with the backdrop of cliffs to remind of a great day out.

Tides and weather

For such an impressive headland there is surprisingly little tidal movement on this trip. What little there is flows down the west side of the head, and planning the trip to have this assisting is recommended. Although relatively short, the west side of Dunvegan Head is exposed to all the Minch can throw at it, as well as being inescapable. Good weather is essential, ensuring there is little swell around.

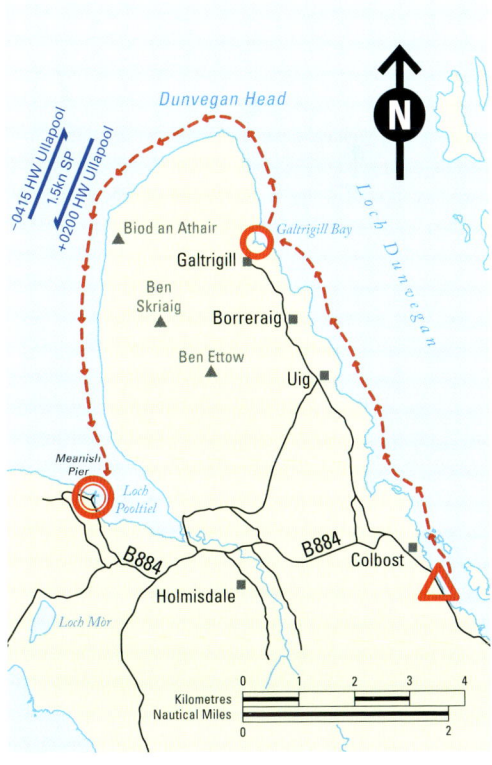

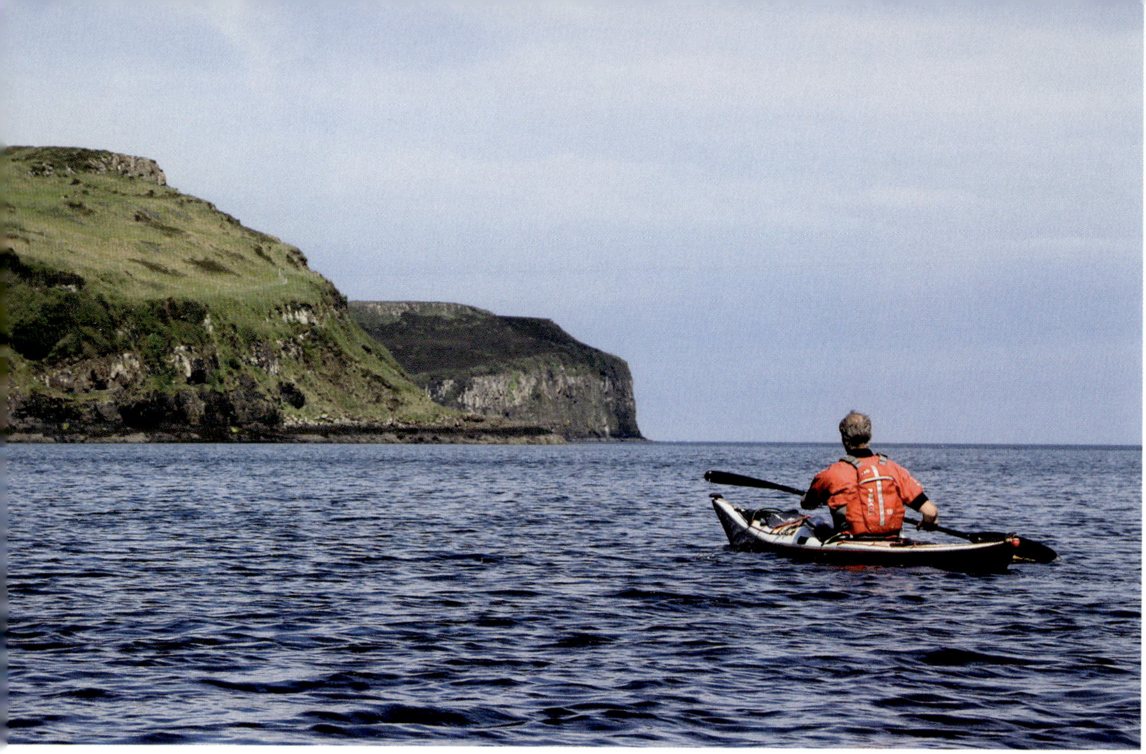

Heading out to Dunvegan Head

30

Dunvegan Head

Additional information

Please park and change considerately at Colbost as it is a popular area for visitors, many staying at the 5-star Three Chimneys. If food at this restaurant is out of your price bracket, then the Red Roof Café in Holmisdale is highly recommended.

Variations

Extending this trip to continue on around Neist Point and into Loch Bracadale arguably offers one of the best two-day trips that Skye has to offer.

Neist Point

No. 31 | Grade C | 32km | OS Sheet 23

Tidal Port Ullapool
Start △ Meanish Pier (NG 154 506)
Finish ○ Camas Bàn (NG 284 413)
HW/LW HW/LW in Loch Bracadale is around 50 minutes before Ullapool.
Tidal Times Off Neist Point: The N going stream runs between 4 hours and 15 minutes before and 2 hours and 10 minutes after HW Ullapool. The SE going eddy in Moonen Bay starts at about 35 minutes before and continues until about 2 hours and 10 minutes after HW Ullapool. The S going stream runs between 2 hours and 10 minutes after and 4 hours and 5 minutes before HW Ullapool. The NW going eddy in Moonen Bay starts at about 5 hours and 35 minutes after and continues until about 4 hours and 5 minutes before HW Ullapool.

Between Neist Point and Loch Bracadale: The NW going stream starts at about 5 hours and 25 minutes after HW Ullapool. The SE going stream starts at about 35 minutes before HW Ullapool.

Max Rate Sp Off Neist Point 3 knots (approx.).
Coastguard Stornoway, tel. 01851 702013, VHF weather every 3 hours from 0710.

Macleod's Maidens and the Cuillins

Neist Point

Introduction

This is a committing journey that takes you a long way from any habitation with only a few landing spots available, and the sea can work itself into a frenzy as the tidal streams are squeezed past Neist Point. This commitment adds to the attraction of kayaking along this stunning section of Skye's western coastline.

Description

Meanish Pier is a dramatic starting place for the journey, with the towering cliffs of Dunvegan Head to the north. This journey takes us south to Neist Point just around the corner, and starting so close to the complicated tidal waters of Neist Point should make it easier to time an arrival at slacker water. Leaving the pier the lighthouse at Neist Point will soon be visible; before it is an imposing rock buttress known as An t-Aigeach (the stallion).

Once round the point it is worth landing at the jetty that was used by the lighthouse keepers, as the next landing place is almost 9km away at Lorgill Bay. The lighthouse was manned until 1989 when it was automated, and the associated living quarters can now be rented for holidays.

At Lorgill Bay a landing should be possible and will provide a welcome break, especially if you didn't stop at Neist Point. The people that once crofted this land back in 1830 were given an ultimatum when the landlord decided that he wanted to clear the land. It was to either get on a ship and be shipped elsewhere, or go to prison. Lorgill Bay is worth considering as a place to stop overnight if you want to make this into a two-day trip.

The next section of coast is full of interest with caves, arches and waterfalls constantly appearing. The Hebrides are ever present long the western horizon and the view south along the west coast of Skye opens up all the time. In the distance the mighty sea stacks of MacLeod's Maidens will tempt you onward. MacLeod's Maidens are found just before Idrigill Point and are named in memory of three female members of the MacLeod family who drowned at sea many years ago. They provide a fitting finish to the exposed west coast, as the trip now turns the corner to follow the western coastline of Loch Bracadale.

A new view opens up on entering Loch Bracadale, with Wiay Island at its entrance, Harlosh and Tarner Islands to the left and the Cuillins of Skye in the background. If you need a break before landfall at Camas Bàn, you might get ashore at Camas na h-Uamha (cave bay). This final section of coastline down to Brandarsaig Bay provides yet more spectacular rock scenery with arches and caves. Don't be tempted to cut across to Harlosh Island too soon and miss out on this great little section of coastline.

Harlosh Island has a wonderful sheltered sandy beach on its north side, which is a great place to relax, before the short paddle to the finish at Camas Bàn.

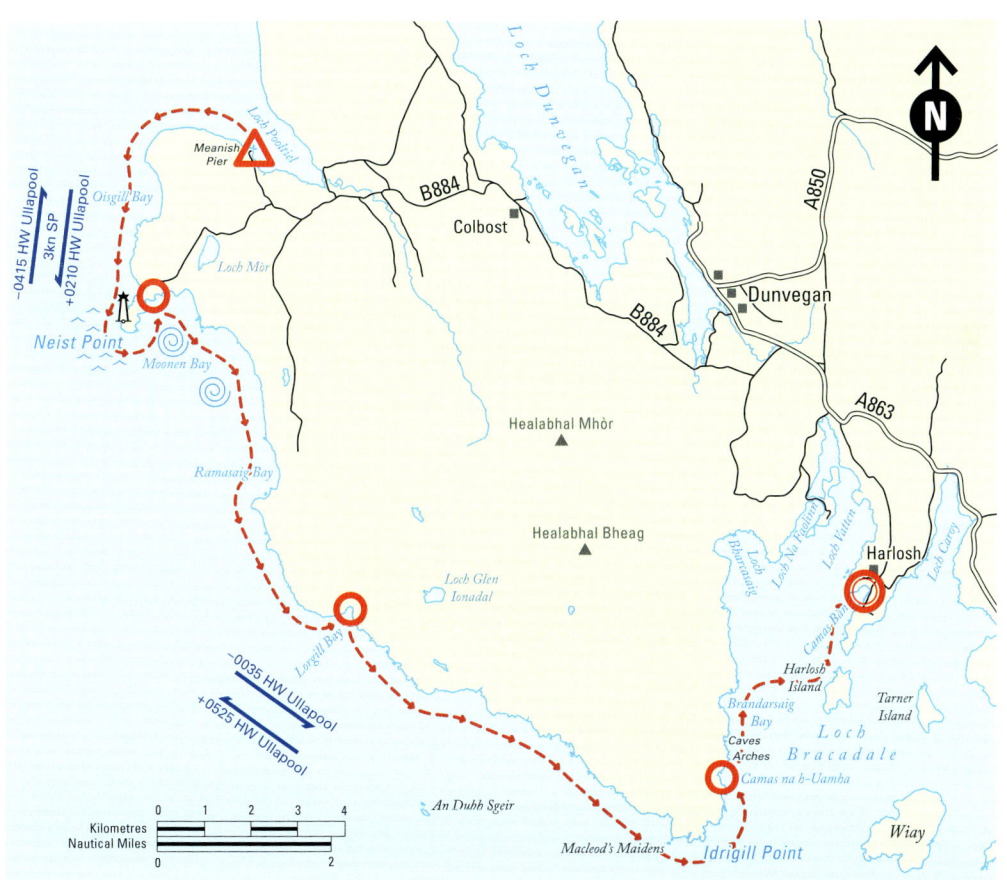

© An t-Aigeach and Neist Point

Tides and weather

Rough water can often form off Neist Point, particularly on the north going stream when a rip can extend for about 3km to the NW of the point on a spring tide. In Moonen Bay the tidal stream runs almost continuously north due to the eddies, however it is easy enough to paddle against them close in to shore. Timing the trip to arrive at Neist Point at slack water and make use of the south/south-east going stream from there works well, thus minimising the eddy effect in Moonen Bay. Neap tides could also be considered.

For this trip settled weather and light winds will be required. Be aware that any swell from the south-west will have a big effect and may make the landing in Lorgill Bay more challenging.

Additional information

There are plenty of amenities in Dunvegan and you could consider making use of a taxi from here for the shuttle at the end of the trip. The Red Roof Café in Holmisdale is highly recommended, this is not far from Meanish Pier. There is limited parking at Camas Bàn so please park considerately.

Variations

Extending the trip by either including Dunvegan Head or exploring Loch Bracadale is highly recommended if time allows. If this is done there are camping possibilities at Lorgill Bay and on Harlosh or Wiay Islands.

Portnalong and the Cuillins

Loch Bracadale

No. 32 | **Grade B** | **20km** | **OS Sheets 23 and 32**

Tidal Port	Ullapool
Start	△ Portnalong (NG 343 358)
Finish	○ Portnalong (NG 343 358)
HW/LW	HW/LW in Loch Bracadale is around 50 minutes before Ullapool.
Tidal Times	In the entrance to Loch Harport: The outgoing stream starts at about 25 minutes before HW Ullapool. The ingoing stream starts at about 5 hours and 35 minutes after HW Ullapool.
	In Loch Bracadale: The tidal streams are unnoticeable.
Max Rate Sp	In the entrance to Loch Harport 1 knot.
Coastguard	Stornoway, tel. 01851 702013, VHF weather every 3 hours from 0710.

Introduction

What Loch Bracadale lacks in tidal streams it more than makes up for in scenery. With the Cuillins on one side and MacLeod's Tables on the other, Skye's most famous mountains overlook you. Add to this the spectacular cliffs and caves of Wiay and this is a great day out.

Wiay's impressive cave

Description

Portnalong is found at the entrance to Loch Harport and is an idyllic place to start. The small light on Ardtreck Point is soon passed and from here Oronsay Island is the first of the Loch Bracadale islands to be visited. At high tide it is possible to paddle on the inside of this island, however going around the outside allows the more impressive cliffs on the north of the island to be enjoyed.

From here head across to Tarner Island. A rocky bay on the south-eastern tip gives a reasonable landing spot with excellent views of the Cuillin mountains. On leaving the bay you can continue on around the island and then across to Harlosh Point. Keep an eye out for wildlife as whales, porpoises and seals have been seen in Loch Bracadale, along with the resident sea eagles circling high above. At the point look out for Piper's Cave, it is not marked on the map but is a cave with much history. It is one to explore on foot as it is not possible to paddle into it.

From the point, an immaculate sandy beach is seen across on Harlosh Island, which makes a perfect stopping place to enjoy the surroundings for a while. On leaving the beach you paddle along the east coast of the island's ragged cliffs with a clear view on to Wiay. From the south-eastern tip of Harlosh a two-kilometre crossing takes you into Camas na Cille on Wiay. This translates into 'church bay' and is the only easy landing spot on the island, other than the odd smaller pebble beach on the west. There is no longer any trace of the church that was once on Wiay, all that can be seen nowadays is the ruins of some houses. The island never housed a great community and it was deserted in 1890 and has had no inhabitants since, other than the wealth of seabirds that make it their home today.

Piper's Cave

Legend has it that the first of the great MacCrimmon pipers found his way into this cave and in its depths met a beautiful woman thought to have been the Fairy Queen. On leaving the Fairy Queen she presented him with a silver chanter to enable him to play 'magical' music, but also requested he promise to return to her at a set time and date in the future. He returned to his home in Borreraig and became not only the greatest piper of his day, but also the most famous there ever was. He and his family became the hereditary pipers of Clan MacLeod. In due course he had to keep his promise and return to the Fairy Queen. Having said goodbye to his family he entered the cave playing his pipes. From above the family followed the sound of his pipes all the way across Skye to the Fairy Bridge; here they heard his magical music for the last time.

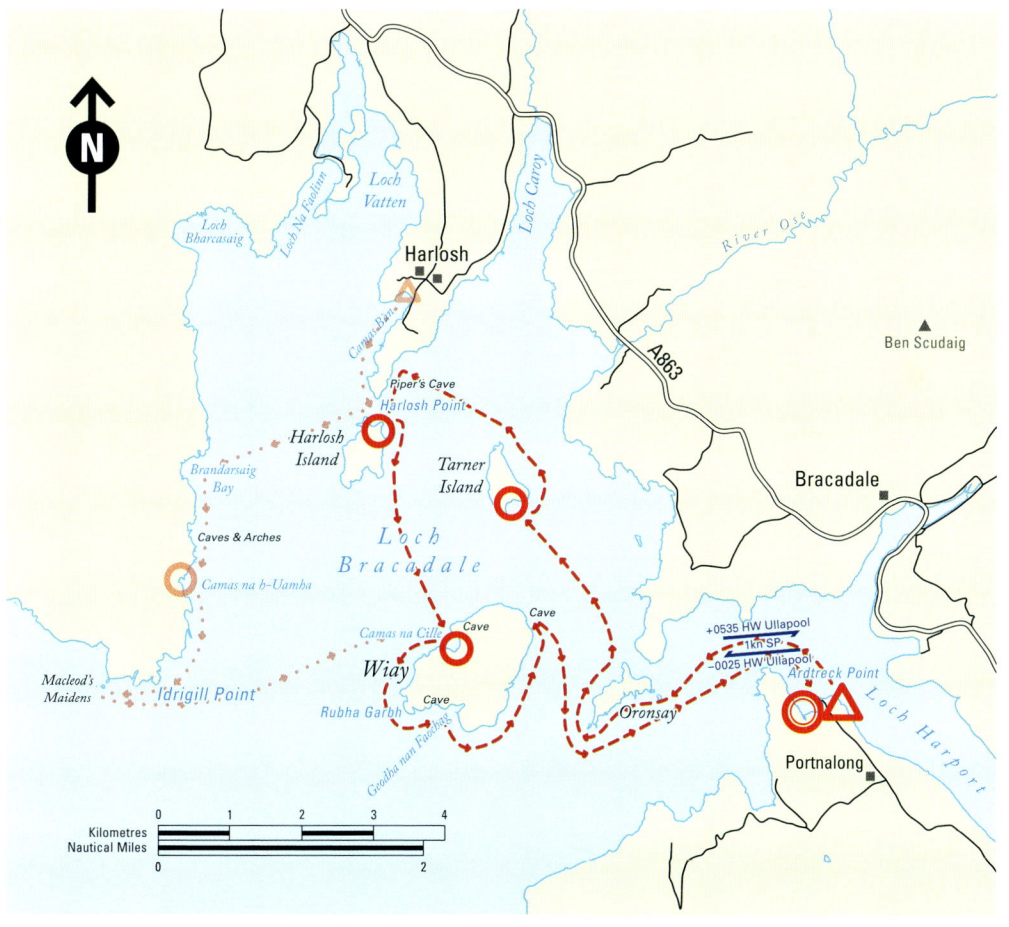

Leaving Camas na Cille, head south to Rubha Garbh and it is here the journey takes on a different feel. The cliffs gradually get steeper, overhang in places, and the sea becomes more exposed to the ocean's weather. From this southern end of the island the sea stacks of MacLeod's Maidens can be seen over to your right as they emerge from behind Idrigill Point. As you paddle round into Geodha nan Faochag the rock architecture will become increasingly more spectacular. There are numerous small inlets, caves and a natural arch to explore, if the sea is calm enough to allow this. Hopefully it will be, because as you pass under the tallest, slightly overhanging cliffs of the island at 59m, you will come across the largest cave of them all. This is a cave to house a family of giants, and upon entering you will feel very insignificant in its dark depths. For this cave alone it is worth waiting for a calm day to paddle around Wiay. On emerging from the cave, Wiay still has a few surprises, with more cliffs and a small natural arch leading on to the north of the island. Take the time to explore this section of coastline before returning to Portnalong to finish.

Tides and weather

There are no noticeable tidal streams within Loch Bracadale, so tidal planning is not required. The loch is very exposed to any wind and swell that comes from the south and west, so reasonable weather conditions are best to make the trip as enjoyable as possible. Off the south of Wiay the sea state can often be considerably rougher than the rest of the trip.

Additional information

In Carbost and Portnalong there are pubs to enjoy, as well as a small shop and visitor centre in Carbost. Talisker whisky distillery is also found in Carbost and is worth a visit.

Variations

Camas Bàn (NG 284 413) provides an alternative start/finish point if the drive to Portnalong is inconvenient. This trip can be made as long or as short as time permits. For a longer trip consider exploring the coastline out to Idrigill Point and the MacLeod's Maidens.

Stac an Tuill, cliffs and waterfalls

Talisker

No. 33	**Grade C**	**30km**	**OS Sheet 32**
Tidal Port	Ullapool
Start	△ Glen Brittle (NG 410 205)
Finish	◯ Portnalong (NG 343 358)
HW/LW	HW/LW in Loch Brittle is around 45 minutes before Ullapool.
Tidal Times	In the entrance to Loch Harport: The outgoing stream starts at about 25 minutes before HW Ullapool. The ingoing stream starts at about 5 hours and 35 minutes after HW Ullapool.
	Along this section of coastline: The SSE going stream starts at about 25 minutes before HW Ullapool. The NNW going stream starts at about 5 hours and 35 minutes after HW Ullapool.
Max Rate Sp	In the entrance to Loch Harport and along this section of coastline 1 knot.
Coastguard	Stornoway, tel. 01851 702013, VHF weather every 3 hours from 0710.

Introduction

This is a wild and remote section of coastline, littered with caves, stacks and waterfalls. The cliff scenery is spectacular from start to finish and it will feel like entering the 'land that time forgot'. Add to this the beautiful beach at Talisker, and the numerous golden and sea eagles that make this coastline their home, and you have yourself an amazing day out.

Another spectacular waterfall

Description

The beach at Glen Brittle that nestles in the heart of the Cuillin mountains is a truly spectacular launching place. While heading along the northern coastline of Loch Brittle you will need regular pauses to take in the scene behind. The coastline quickly steepens and it is highly likely that amongst the grassy and craggy slopes above there will be golden eagles watching you pass. After Loch Brittle the coastline becomes exposed to the expanse of the Minch and the views open up to the cliffs ahead, along with the islands of the Outer Hebrides and Small Isles. The imposing sea stack of Stac an Tuill has a hole through the middle of it forming an arch. Not far beyond this, one of the many impressive waterfalls cascading from above into the sea will be reached at Geodha nan Gobhar; here a cave hides alongside it.

At the entrance to Loch Eynort there is a sheltered stony beach at Sgeiteadh which is worth stopping at, as beyond here the landings are few and far between, particularly if there is any swell. Crossing the loch, the cliffs that continue to rise on the other side will draw you on, and looking into the loch gives views back into the Cuillin mountains. From the entrance of Loch Eynort to Talisker Bay is the most spectacular section of coastline on this trip. Along here there are numerous waterfalls along with caves and arches, many of these being surprisingly hidden. Take the time to savour this section and ensure no nook or cranny is left unexplored. The scale of this coastline, its location and the potential of a sea eagle around every corner make for an awe-inspiring experience. Midway along this section, not far beyond the first impressive arch and hidden waterfall inlet, there is a reasonable landing on a stony beach, if conditions allow.

33

Talisker

A large stack of rock that dries at low tide marks Talisker Point, and from here it is but a few paddle strokes into the beautiful sands of Talisker Bay. This provides a well-earned resting place, however if there is any swell around it may also provide a wet landing! When you reach Rubha Cruinn, look for the channel that cuts through the rocks; it continues for a good few hundred metres and leads beyond the headland.

The cliffs and scenery continue. Here Idrigill Point, the MacLeod's Maidens and Loch Bracadale will all start coming into view. At the entrance to Loch Harport the small light of Ardtreck Point marks the approach to the finish. The cliffs continue unrelenting with caves and waterfalls right to the end. One of these waterfalls tumbles down the cliff face, twisting and turning, forming pools on its way. It is easy to imagine the local fairies and pixies using these cliff face pools to bathe!

After Ardtreck Point you arrive at the small harbour at Portnalong ... the end to a spectacular day out.

Tides and weather

There is very little tidal movement along this section of coastline, so wind and swell should be the main considerations. This entire coastline has very few landings; many of these are affected by swell from the south through to west. Plan this trip on a day with light winds and minimal swell.

Additional information

At Glen Brittle there is a long carry at low tide, a trolley can make this a lot easier. Parking at Glen Brittle can also become busy; arriving early can avoid this. There is a campsite at Glen Brittle but no other amenities. In Portnalong and Carbost there are pubs to enjoy, as well as a small shop, visitor centre and the Talisker whisky distillery in Carbost.

Variations

This trip works well when paddled in either direction. If a shorter day is preferred it is possible to use Loch Eynort (NG 378 262) as an alternative start/finish. This does require a long carry however, and a trolley is recommended. If staying at Glen Brittle, paddling from here to Soay and back is a good day out (see Trip 34).

Loch Scavaig and the Cuillins from Elgol

Loch Scavaig & Soay – 'Cuillin Magic'

No. 34 | Grade B | 30km | OS Sheet 32	
Tidal Port	Ullapool
Start	△ Elgol (NG 516 136)
Finish	○ Elgol (NG 516 136)
HW/LW	HW/LW in Elgol is around 40 minutes before Ullapool.
Tidal Times	In Loch Scavaig: The ingoing stream starts at about 5 hours and 35 minutes after HW Ullapool. The outgoing stream starts at about 25 minutes before HW Ullapool.
	In Soay Sound: The W going stream is continuous.
Max Rate Sp	In Loch Scavaig 0.5 knots. In Soay Sound 1.5 knots.
Coastguard	Stornoway, tel. 01851 702013, VHF weather every 3 hours from 0710.

Introduction

This trip is one of the most iconic on Skye; it is magic – 'Cuillin magic'!

'Cuillin Magic'

Description

Leaving the small fishing village of Elgol it will be impossible not to be lured towards the Cuillin mountains and into Loch Scavaig. These mountains are the most dramatic in the British Isles, forming a 12 mile long, knife-edge ridge that is the aspiration of many a mountaineer. Nestled into the remote and inaccessible eastern side of these great mountains is Loch Coruisk. To view this is a must and it is this trip's first objective.

Paddling up the coastline into Loch Scavaig the bay of Camasunary is soon reached. There is a beautifully-situated bothy on the shores of this bay if time allows for a visit. Further west, the head of Loch Scavaig is split into two lochs, Loch nan Leachd and Loch na Cuilce. While exploring these you will be paddling amongst the guardians of this loch, the numerous common seals. Take time to absorb this dramatic location, it is like no other in Britain. The hut that is visible, with the St Andrew's cross, is used by members of the Scottish Mountaineering Club.

The easiest landing place is at the head of Loch nan Leachd, which at lower tide provides a stunning sandy beach that seems strangely out of place in such mountainous scenery. It is well worth stretching the legs by walking the very short distance up to Loch Coruisk, where the view into the heart of the Cuillins is stunning.

Leave the heart of Loch Scavaig by the western coastline that leads around into Soay Sound. Cross the sound to reach the island of Soay and continue along the northern coastline into the sheltered, and perfectly formed by nature, Soay Harbour. It is at the back of this you will find the factory ruins, once used by the Island of Soay Shark Fisheries.

Shark fishing

Soay Shark Fisheries was set up by the author Gavin Maxwell when he bought the island in 1946. The island was used as a base for the hunting of basking sharks that once regularly frequented these west coast waters. The good news is that their numbers are now increasing again. The factory on the island was used to process the shark oil, although the venture only ran for three years due to the drop in value of shark oil in 1949. 'Tex' Geddes, who was the harpooner from the shark fishing days, owned the island prior to his death.

From the back of the harbour there is a good path leading across the short gap to the bay of Camas nan Gall and the main village on the island. Although sparsely populated these days, this village once housed 158 people at its busiest before the Clearances. On the way to the village you will also pass the 'solar telephone exchange', which was the first of its type in the world and powers nine telephones.

The journey continues on around the island. On the west coast of the island you will be rewarded with fine views out to the 'Small Isles' of Canna, Rum and Eigg. On a calm day they

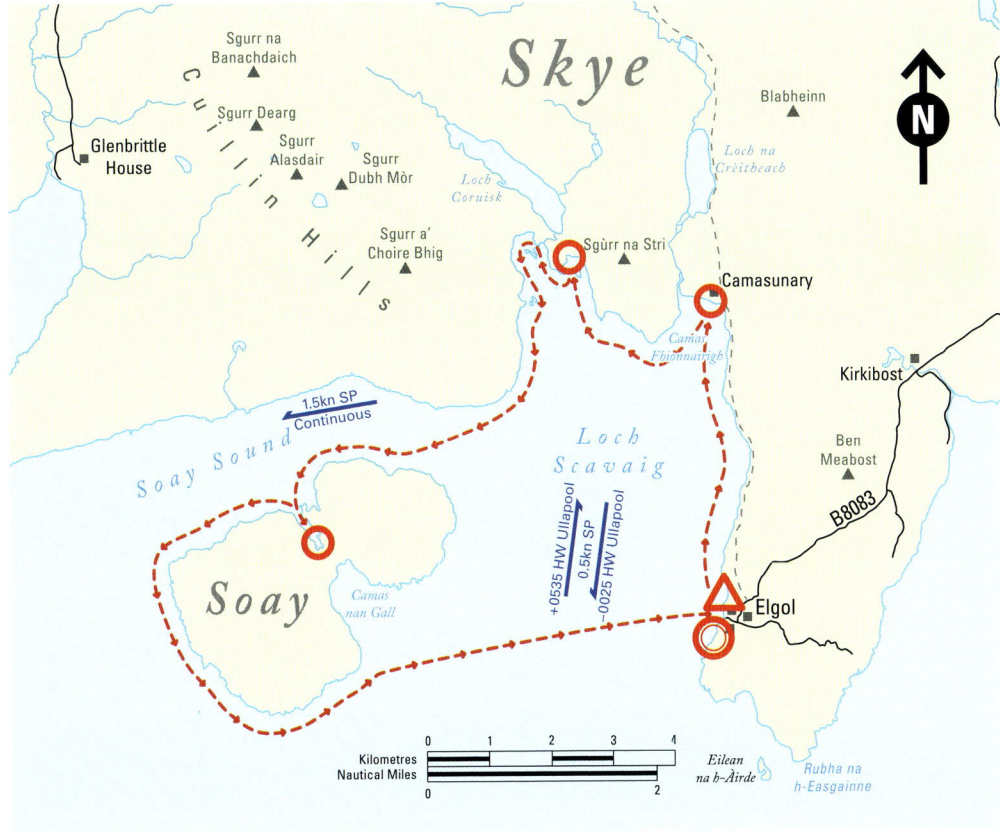

look deceptively close and try to lure you out to them. The island will continue to delight with its wildlife and its small, yet ornately-shaped, sandstone cliffs. Around the southern tip look out for a small cave as well as a 'Saltire' in the cliffs formed by two diagonal intrusions into the parent rock.

On reaching Camas nan Gall it is time to leave Soay and embark on the final crossing back to Elgol, to finish a great day out.

Tides and weather

There is little tidal movement of note in this area, and by visiting Loch Coruisk first it gives the benefit of the small amount of continuous west-flowing tidal stream in Soay Sound. The trip should be planned taking into consideration the wind and swell.

This area generally offers reasonable shelter in mixed weather conditions. There can often be extreme downdraughts and winds rushing down from the Cuillin mountains; these affect Soay Sound the most. The west coast of Soay is also exposed to any westerly swell, which breaks over the numerous small reefs and rocks.

Additional information

Elgol is a very popular place to visit and the road can be very busy. There is plenty of parking but consideration is required. Arriving early is recommended in the holiday season from a traffic and parking point of view. There are public toilets in Elgol and it may be possible to buy an end of trip snack at a tour boat, jetty-side, temporary café. There are regular seal watching boats in this area as well, so try to disturb the seals as little as possible. Gavin Maxwell's book *Harpoon at a Venture* gives further insight into the shark fishing of the west coast of Scotland.

Variations

If time is limited or a shorter distance is preferred, then either just heading in to Loch Coruisk and back, or just going around Soay, is recommended. If it is your only visit to the area, Loch Coruisk is a must, you need to get a taste of its 'magic'!

Cliff scenery near Spar Cave

Strathaird Peninsula & Spar Cave

No. 35	**Grade B**	**11km**	**OS Sheet 32**
Tidal Port	Ullapool
Start	▲ Kilmarie (NG 554 169)
Finish	⭕ Elgol (NG 516 136)
HW/LW	HW/LW in Elgol is around 40 minutes before Ullapool.
Tidal Times	Along the coastline: The N going stream starts at about 5 hours and 35 minutes after HW Ullapool. The S going stream starts at about 25 minutes before HW Ullapool.
Max Rate Sp	Along the coastline 0.5 knots.
Coastguard	Stornoway, tel. 01851 702013, VHF weather every 3 hours from 0710.

Introduction

For a small headland that could be easily overlooked, the quality of the cliffs on this paddle is outstanding. In addition to this, the trip offers a cluster of wildlife-packed skerries with the Small Isles as the backdrop, and the impressive Spar Cave.

Suidhe Biorach and the Cuillins from Eilean na h-Àirde | Donald Macpherson

Description

The start is at Kilmarie where the dead-end road first meets the sea by the river mouth. Leaving the sheltered bay the mighty mountain of Blabheinn will be looking down on you. The coastline starts relatively low-lying with a mixture of steep open slopes and old woodlands. Passing the open wooded bay of Tomb the cliffs slowly start to pick up; at the top of these there are stunted trees overhanging the sea and clinging on precariously. The cliffs rising out of the water consistently marks the approach to the huge entrance canyon of Spar Cave. Don't be tempted to paddle on by. This one is well worth an explore but it will mean landing at the back of the canyon and taking a short walk – head torches advised!

Spar Cave

Spar Cave is an astonishing, cathedral-like structure, it is 50m long and houses marble-like flowstone staircases and huge columns formed by centuries of water dripping through the limestone. It is referred to as one of the natural wonders of Scotland and Sir Walter Scott, who visited it in 1814, described it as Strathaird's 'enchanted cell'. Sadly many of the stalactite formations have long since gone, taken as souvenirs in the Victorian era. Despite this it is still an impressive feature. If you choose to explore it, enter the left-hand entrance, and beyond the muddy start you will discover a steep flowstone staircase. It is not as slippery as it looks, and from the top you access the crystal clear pool found at the end of the cave. From here it is back the same way, or a cold swim!

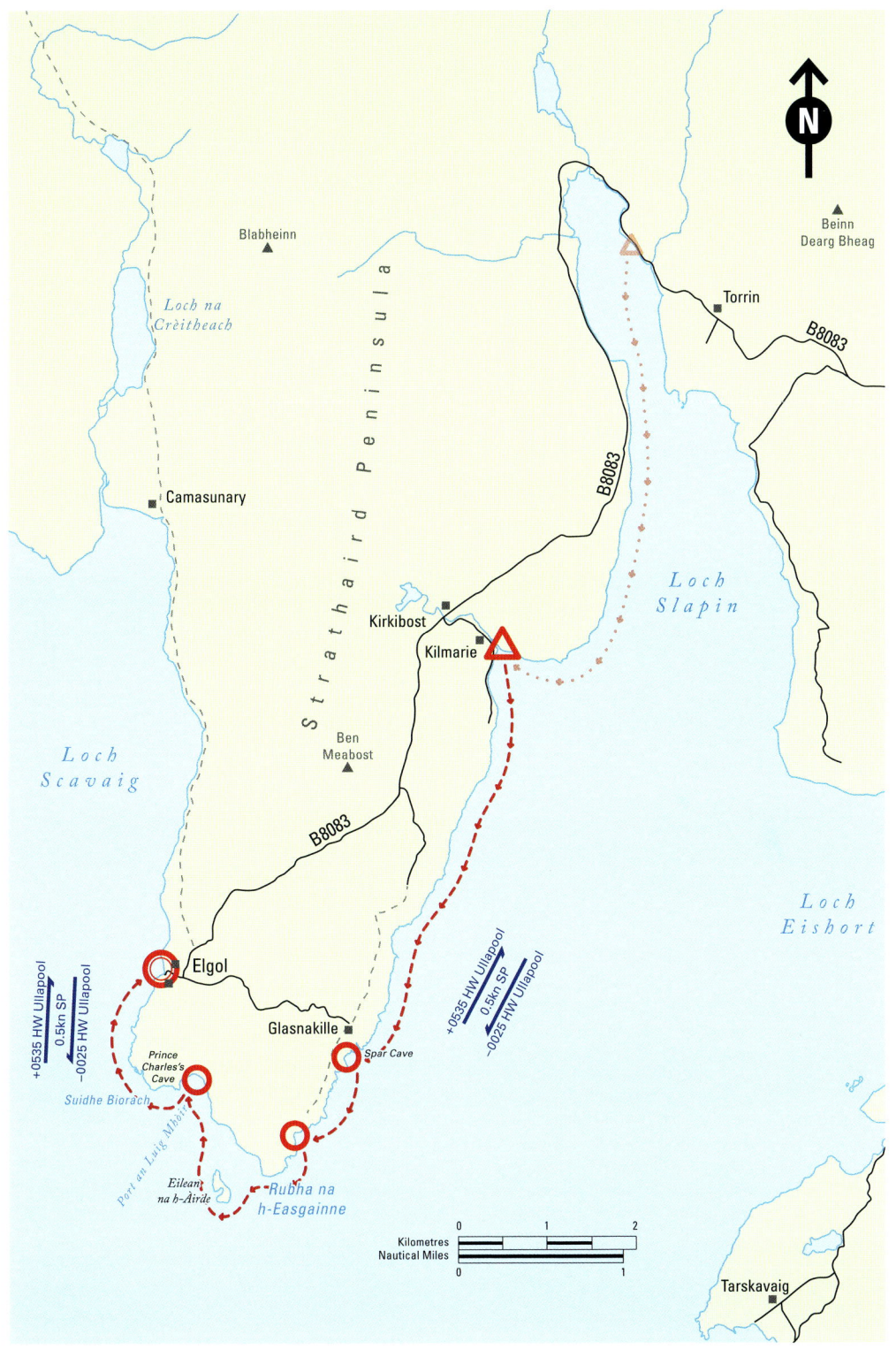

Leaving Spar Cave, the paddle continues along a section of fantastically ornate cliffs leading towards Rubha na h-Easgainne. Having taken the time to enjoy these it is worth considering a stop at the easy to land stony beach just before the headland. Beyond the headland lies a sight that never fails to impress, with the Point of Sleat, Ardnamurchan, Small Isles and Cuillins all coming into view. Head across to explore the small island and skerries of Eilean na h-Àirde; this is a magical place for wildlife, with crystal clear waters and that aforementioned view. There is another possible landing at Port an Luig Mhóir, and not much above sea level just to the west of this is one of Prince Charles's many caves. This was the cave where he spent his last few hours before leaving the islands and heading back to the mainland on the night of 4th July 1746.

As with all good things the best should be saved until last. The cliffs that lead you around the corner into Loch Scavaig are stunning. The rock forms intricate shapes and features, with inlets to explore and cliffs towering above. Don't leave anything undiscovered here; there are some real hidden gems. As if the views could not get better, paddling to the finish at Elgol provides arguably Skye's most iconic view of the Cuillin mountains. Soak it all in as you come to land at the beach near the jetty which marks the finish of a great little trip.

Tides and weather

There is no tidal movement of note in the area; the trip should be planned around wind and swell conditions. The main headland is exposed to south-west winds and swell with a reasonable fetch out to sea. Because of this, in order to make the most of the cliffs and caves, calm seas are recommended.

Additional information

There are no amenities at Kilmarie and limited parking, so please be considerate if leaving cars. Elgol is a very popular place to visit and the road can be very busy; there is plenty of parking but again consideration is required. Arriving early is recommended in the holiday season from a traffic and parking point of view. There are public toilets in Elgol and it may be possible for an end of trip snack at a tour boat, jetty-side, temporary café.

Variations

If wanting shelter from a westerly wind then paddling to Rubha na h-Easgainne and back from Kilmarie works well. To extend the paddle and explore Loch Slapin, starting at the NE corner of the loch (NG 569 215) at one of the stony beaches is recommended. The trip can also be extended by continuing from Elgol into the heart of Loch Scavaig, see Trip 34.

The Cuillins and Rubha Suisnish from Ord

Loch Eishort

No. 36 | **Grade A** | **14km** | **OS Sheet 32**

Tidal Port	Ullapool
Start	△ Ord (NG 616 132)
Finish	◯ Ord (NG 616 132)
HW/LW	HW/LW in Loch Eishort is around 40 minutes before Ullapool.
Tidal Times	In Loch Eishort: The ingoing stream starts at about 5 hours and 35 minutes after HW Ullapool. The outgoing stream starts at about 25 minutes before HW Ullapool.
Max Rate Sp	The streams are generally weak.
Coastguard	Stornoway, tel. 01851 702013, VHF weather every 3 hours from 0710.

Introduction

This is one of Skye's hidden gems, offering skerries, waterfalls, dramatic views, history and a spectacular desert island coral beach. Save this one for a perfect day and discover its hidden treasures for yourself.

© Boreraig

Loch Eishort

Description

Ord is an idyllic place to launch from, with views out across to the Strathaird Peninsula and the Cuillin mountains beyond. On a calm, sunny day launching out from the beach will have your kayak cutting through crystal clear, azure blue waters. The trip heads out across Loch Eishort to the clearance village of Boreraig. Take time to explore the small islands and skerries along the way; here you will find seals, birds and more of that crystal clear seawater. In amongst this tranquillity you will discover one of Skye's most beautiful tiny coral beaches, a magical place. It will be hard to leave this small piece of paradise, but when you eventually do, head across the loch to the obvious waterfall by Boreraig. It provides a great photo opportunity, but head along the coast a little for a better landing place to stretch the legs and explore Boreraig.

Leaving Boreraig behind, head along the dramatic coastline out to Rubha Suisnish. Cliffs and waterfalls will please the eye and if lucky you may well see eagles soaring high. The view from the small headland is worth taking time to enjoy. If it is calm there are a few rocky beaches where you may wish to land, but it is better to head back across Loch Eishort to the bay by Dun Scaith Castle for a break.

You will paddle past the faint remains of an older fort on the small island of Eilean Ruairidh before arriving at the imposing ruins of Dun Scaith Castle. Although very much a ruin the castle is still impressive. There is an easy landing in the bay behind the castle and from here it is possible to walk out to it. The wooden drawbridge which was used to access the castle has long since rotted away, so to enter the castle these days is sadly not possible without some challenging scrambling.

Leaving the castle and its legends behind a final section of coast is all that remains to finish back at the beach at Ord.

Boreraig, the clearance village

In 1853 the tranquillity that surrounded the village of Boreraig was lost forever as the people were forcibly cleared from their homes to make way for sheep. Lord MacDonald instructed his agents to clear the village, and in doing so they burned many of the houses. Stories tell how the wailing of the families could be heard far and wide as they were forced off the land. With twenty-two households and over one hundred men, women and children, the spectacle of the clearance is unimaginable. Many of the families from the village emigrated to distant shores, some not making it on the fever-ridden ships. Take the time to walk around Boreraig today and reflect on this sad time in history. If walking the path look out for the large, single slab of rock that forms a bridge over the stream. A giant of a man called 'Knock-knees', who lived in the village before it was cleared, reputedly laid it down single-handedly.

Tides and weather

There is no tidal movement of note in this area; the trip should be planned taking into consideration the wind and swell. If there is anything from the south-west it will create a sea state to be wary of as there is a fair fetch funnelling into the loch. At low water there is a reasonable carry to the water at Ord, a trolley can make this easier.

Legends of Dun Scaith Castle

Clan MacDonald used the castle until the early 17th century. However, long before this the castle was the source of many legends. It is said that the Scottish warrior woman and martial arts teacher Scáthach the Shadow lived in the castle.

It is said she trained many warriors, and according to Irish mythology the heroic warrior Cúchulainn was trained at Dun Scaith.

The coral beaches near Eilean Dubh

Additional information

There are no facilities at Ord and although there is a fair amount of parking, please be considerate to the small local community.

Variations

The small section of coastline from Dun Scaith Castle to Tarskavaig offers some interesting cliffs and a cave. If time and energy allow it is worth considering adding this on to the trip.

The Point of Sleat, Rum in the background

Point of Sleat

No. 37 | Grade B | 25km | OS Sheets 32 and 33

Tidal Port	Ullapool
Start	△ Tarskavaig (NG 587 087)
Finish	○ Armadale (NG 637 037)
HW/LW	HW/LW at Armadale is around 40 minutes before Ullapool.
Tidal Times	Off the Point of Sleat: The NE and NW going stream starts at about 5 hours and 35 minutes after HW Ullapool. The SSE and SW going stream starts at about 25 minutes before HW Ullapool.
Max Rate Sp	Off the Point of Sleat 2 knots.
Coastguard	Stornoway, tel. 01851 702013, VHF weather every 3 hours from 0710.

Introduction

The Point of Sleat marks the southern extremity of Skye and offers a distinctly remote coastline, with interesting cliffs, an amazing beach, and stunning views across to the Cuillins of Skye and out to the Small Isles. There is a constant feeling of solitude while paddling along these shores.

181

Camas Daraich

Description

Tarskavaig Bay is an ideal launch spot, being a sandy beach with views across to the jagged mountains of the Cuillins of Skye. On leaving here the view changes but does not lessen; it is now the equally spectacular mountains on the island of Rum that dominate the view. The coastline here is constantly interesting, with low-lying cliffs – keep an eye out for otters as you go.

The inlet of Inver Dalavil is guarded by skerries upon which seals may be hauled out. If you venture into the beach at the back, you will have a chance to land and stretch your legs. Here you will find the remains of the crofters' houses, where once people worked hard to make a living from this beautiful place. The remote coastline continues with the occasional stony beach or stream cascading its way down into the sea.

Just before the small headland of Acairseid an Rubha you will see a beach at the back of a wide bay; however before landing, explore further and discover the hidden inlet with a natural harbour just beyond this. A track finishes here and there is a gorgeous little house overlooking this hidden gem. Beyond here the cliffs rise in grandeur, marking the approach to the point. Rum looks temptingly close, and alongside this Canna, Eigg and then the Ardnamurchan Peninsula add to the spectacular vista. The Point of Sleat itself lies on a lower-lying extension to the cliffy promontory, and although its setting is dramatic, the modern small light and the point itself are a little lost in the surroundings. Continue on to find the incredible beach at Camas Daraich. This has got to be the best beach on Skye, as you paddle in on a sunny day it will feel more like the Caribbean than the Northern Highlands. This is perhaps the highlight of the trip, so take the time to land on the beach and take it all in. From the beach there is a path out to the point, so if you wish to see the views again from a higher vantage point this is possible.

The seal-maidens of Port na Fagaich

Just along from Ardvasar is tiny Port na Fagaich or Bay of the Forsaken Ones. Standing just offshore from here can be seen a number of large upright stones. Legend has it that one moonlit night local fishermen became enchanted by a number of beautiful seal-maidens swimming in the sea here. The fishermen each married one of these seal-maidens and they lived happily for a year. At the end of the year the sea called to the maidens and they had no choice but to return. The fishermen entered the sea and held on to their wives trying to prevent them from leaving. In doing this they were turned into the great stones. Seal-maidens never forget and it is said that on a moonlit night you can see each maiden waiting by her own stone.

On leaving the beach paddle towards the small headland of Leir Mhaodail where the views up into the Sound of Sleat start to open up. While paddling this final section to Armadale keep an eye out for dolphins and other marine mammals, as where the tide splits off the point provides a good feeding area. There have been many accounts of dolphins keeping paddlers company in this area.

It is possible to land at Port a' Chùil and below Tormore on this last section. Approaching the finish, the mainland mountains of Knoydart will dominate the vista. The entrances to both Loch Nevis and Loch Hourn are visible, these marking where the sea enters into the heart of these hills. In Armadale, be mindful of the Mallaig ferry as you land on the beach in the bay to finish. All that is left now will be an ice cream at the convenient little café at the ferry terminal.

The hidden inlet at Acairseid an Rubha

Tides and weather

Either side of the Point of Sleat the tide is weak, with the only noticeable tide being where it splits off the point. Arriving here at slack water works well, using the outgoing tide to arrive and ingoing to continue on to the finish. If this is not possible the tidal movement is not so strong as to cause too much of a problem. Wind and swell need to be the main consideration as this is a very exposed and inescapable headland. South through to westerly wind and swell will have the most effect.

Additional information

There are no amenities at Tarskavaig, and although there is a reasonable amount of parking please be considerate to the small local community. At Armadale there is a café, tourist shops and a pub just down the road in Ardvasar. The walk out to the Point of Sleat is worth considering; this starts from the road head at Aird of Sleat and is signposted. At low tide Tarskavaig dries out a long way, so plan to launch at higher water or consider a trolley.

Variations

If the wind is from either the east or west and too strong to make the entire trip comfortable, paddling out and back along the sheltered side is recommended. On the east side this would give a stopping point at the beach, and on the west at the natural harbour. From either of these it is possible to walk out to the light.

Otter Haven, Kylerhea | Donald Macpherson

Kyle Rhea

No. 38	**Grade B**	**23km**	**OS Sheet 33**
Tidal Port	Ullapool
Start	△ Isleornsay (NG 703 125)
Finish	○ Kyleakin (NG 752 264)
HW/LW	HW/LW at Isleornsay is around 50 minutes before Ullapool.
Tidal Times	In Kyle Rhea: The S going stream starts at about 15 minutes before HW Ullapool. The N going stream starts at about 5 hours and 45 minutes after HW Ullapool.
Max Rate Sp	Off the Sandaig Islands 2 knots. In Kyle Rhea 8 knots.
Coastguard	Stornoway, tel. 01851 702013, VHF weather every 3 hours from 0710.

Introduction

This trip leaves the picturesque natural harbour of Isleornsay and heads to the heart of the Sound of Sleat, where the sea is squeezed through the natural cleft of Kyle Rhea. Fast tidal streams speed you on your way to a finish overlooked by the dramatic Skye Bridge.

Kyleakin and Caisteal Maol

Kyle Rhea

Description

With its hotel, pub and idyllic setting it may be difficult to tear yourself away from the starting point of Isleornsay. The tidal island of Ornsay forms this perfect natural harbour. Its stone piers were built by 1820, yet the MacDonalds who owned this part of Skye were using it long before. In the 1800s it also was the place from where many locals left their homes to start new lives by emigrating. In 1837 the *William Nicol* sailed to Sydney from Isleornsay with 322 passengers including 70 families from Sleat. It was reported that so many people wanted to emigrate, the ship did not have room for everyone.

Leaving the peaceful natural harbour, take a moment to enjoy the view of the Ornsay lighthouse, first lit in 1857, with the vast backdrop of the Sound of Sleat to the south. Across the sound you will be looking into the dramatic Loch Hourn, the Gaelic name means 'hell' in English. The small light marking the beautiful Sandaig Islands to the north of this should also be visible.

Depending on weather conditions and preference there is a choice of routes up to Kyle Rhea. The remote north shore offers the most direct line with occasional small cliffs and stony beaches. If taking this route there is a pleasant landing at Port Aslaig part way along, or near the few houses at the hamlet of Kylerhea before the tidal waters pick up and whisk you onwards. The recommended route, if time and weather allow, is the short open crossing to the Sandaig Islands. This small cluster of islands are arguably the 'jewel in the crown' of the Sound of Sleat, with an abundance of wildlife and an immaculate sandy beach surrounded by azure blue coloured waters. The extra effort to paddle across to these islands on the route to Kyle Rhea will be well rewarded.

Kyle Rhea's tidal waters and ferry

Daring cattle drovers

While you are whisked along by the tide, spare a thought for the poor cattle that were made to swim across the 534 metres of treacherous waters from Skye to the mainland. Although the drovers timed it at slack water it is still no easy swim. Having survived this they were then herded on down the drovers' road to Kinloch Hourn on the route to the Scottish Lowlands. This involved yet another swim across the narrows in Loch Hourn – they certainly bred the highland cattle tough in those days!

Kyle Rhea

From the Sandaig Islands, following the thickly-forested south coast will lead to the village of Glenelg. In the era of the Jacobite risings this remote village housed one of four military barracks in the Highlands. The steep and dramatic single track road that links Glenelg to the rest of the world was originally built by General George Wade as part of his impressive road network that spanned the Highlands. This village provides a tempting lunch spot, particularly with its fine pub. Be sure not to get carried away and miss the tide through Kyle Rhea!

The fast tidal waters racing through the narrow gap that forms Kyle Rhea are undoubtedly the main focus of this trip. With its boils, eddies and confused waters it will no doubt entertain, however with the tide running in this direction there will be little in the way of waves or rough water. Look out for (and make sure you avoid) the ferry that operates in the summer months. This small six-car ferry is the last turntable ferry in operation, and watching it navigate the fast tidal waters will help you understand where the term 'ferry glide' came from!

Cliff scenery near Port Aslaig

The Leopard Man

The Leopard Man of Skye was a former soldier called Tom Leppard, once considered by the Guinness Book of Records to be the world's most tattooed man. He was said to have spent £5,500 on his extensive body tattoos that covered 99.2% of his body in a leopard-like way. He lived on the shores of Loch na Bèiste until 2008, when at age 73 he moved to the more convenient location of Broadford. Although changing location at this ripe old age he certainly did not change his spots!

If you are comfortable negotiating the eddies, it is well worth paddling in close to the west shore of Kyle Rhea to the area known as Otter Haven. With a little bit of luck, this is a great spot to see these amazing creatures as they enjoy feeding in these tidal waters.

'Popping' out from the narrows you could be excused for feeling like a cork leaving a bottle of champagne. Make sure you hang a left for the final part of the journey to Kyleakin. On the south shore of Loch na Bèiste see if you can find the Leopard Man's now abandoned bothy.

As you approach Kyleakin, look out for the 15th century building of Caisteal Maol, which was the site of fortifications long before this. The Viking King Haakon IV is said to have assembled his fleet of longships at this castle before his defeat at the Battle of Largs in 1263, which ended Norse domination of the west of Scotland. The name Kyleakin is thought to come from this link with the Viking king, meaning 'Haakon's kyle'.

At Kyleakin the landing spot is at the stony beach beyond the pier with perfect views of the Skye Bridge to finish off a great trip. There is a large car park behind the beach, along with handy pubs and cafés!

Tides and weather

There is a small amount of tide off the Sandaig Islands and although there is tidal movement in Kyle Akin this does not affect the end of the trip if finishing at the beach and staying close in to shore. Kyle Rhea itself is the main tidal consideration and careful planning is required to ensure the tide is going with you at a speed appropriate for the group. Neap tides and/or slacker water should be considered for the less experienced, as well as staying in the main flow away from the eddies. On the north going tidal stream there will be eddies and confused water, however rough water and waves are not generally found. If deciding to paddle Kyle Rhea on a south going stream, then care should be taken if there is a south-westerly wind as this can produce waves and rough water at the south end.

Additional information

There is plenty of parking along with pubs and/or cafés at the start and finish of this trip. It is possible to start/finish the trip at Kylerhea where the ferry lands, however if doing this please drop off kayaks with consideration to the ferry traffic and park up the hill out of the way.

Variations

The trip can be paddled in either direction. For a shorter trip that doesn't involve going through Kyle Rhea, paddling across to the Sandaig Islands and back from Isleornsay is a spectacular day out in its own right. If you just wish to play in the tidal waters, launching at Kylerhea works well.

Sound of Sleat to Ardnamurchan

Introduction

From the justifiably famous Eilean Donan Castle in the north to the gateway to the North West Highlands that is Ardnamurchan Point in the south, this coastline provides some of the North West's more sheltered water options. Lochs Hourn and Nevis provide day or multi-day trip options, their waters leading deep into the heart of the inaccessibly-remote Knoydart mountains. Loch Duich, with its famous castle, and Loch Ailort, with a fine bothy, are also surrounded by impressive mountains.

When it comes to beaches Morar and Arisaig, with their countless skerries and wildlife in abundance, are hard to top. Eilean Shona and Ardnamurchan Point have their fair share of hidden gems. As well as its beaches, Ardnamurchan Point has one of the finest lighthouses of the North West, fitting for the dramatic headland that is Britain's most westerly point. From all of these fine locations the views out to sea of either the Small Isles or Skye provide a panorama that will never be tired of.

Whether it be the bustling tourist villages of Mallaig or Arisaig, or the village of Inverie that is only accessible by boat, this area will provide a warm welcome. Food, drink and accommodation will be easy to find, with much of the produce coming from local waters.

Tides and weather

Other than Ardnamurchan Point, most of the trips in this area take place in the comparatively sheltered confines of the sounds and lochs. Apart from the odd small section of exposed coastline, swell is not an issue. Shelter can also often be found from the wind; however many of the lochs are notorious for vicious downdraughts from the surrounding mountains.

Tidal streams are fairly negligible in this area, usually only found in the narrows of the lochs as they empty and fill. Without the added effect of wind and swell, these areas often only provide flow to contend with without any unduly rough water. Although relatively sheltered it should still be noted that many of the venues are very inaccessible so, if a kayaker was to get caught out by bad weather, escape may not be easy.

Ardnamurchan Point is the obvious exception to all of the above. Although it does not have particularly strong tidal streams, it is very exposed to any swell and wind.

Ardnamurchan Point – gateway to the NW highlands

Eilean Donan Castle and Loch Duich

Loch Duich & Eilean Donan Castle

No. 39	**Grade A** | **17km** | **OS Sheet 33**
Tidal Port	Ullapool
Start	△ Reraig (NG 813 272)
Finish	○ Kintail Lodge Hotel (NG 936 196)
HW/LW	HW/LW in Loch Duich is around 25 minutes before Ullapool.
Tidal Times	At the entrance to Loch Duich: The ingoing stream starts at about 6 hours after HW Ullapool. The outgoing stream starts at about 20 minutes before HW Ullapool.
Max Rate 3p	The streams are generally weak, not exceeding 0.5 knots. In the narrow, shallow entrance to Loch Long they are appreciable, up to approximately 4 knots.
Coastguard	Stornoway, tel. 01851 702013, VHF weather every 3 hours from 0710.

Introduction

Eilean Donan Castle is perhaps the most iconic and well-known of all the Scottish castles. Approaching it by sea kayak and paddling around its impressive structure gives a great vantage point. Add to this the impressive mountain scenery of Kintail and you have a very worthwhile trip.

Eilean Donan Castle

39 Loch Duich & Eilean Donan Castle

Description

The viewpoint marked on the map at Reraig has plenty of parking and a slipway to launch from. Entering Loch Alsh you will have views into the narrow tidal passage of Kyle Rhea that leads to the south and west coasts of Skye, as well up to the Skye Bridge and beyond into the Inner Sound. This journey heads in the other direction, leading into the mainland mountains of Kintail. Heading off this way may feel like the 'short straw' as the other two options look far more dramatic, however just around the corner all will change. The journey starts gently, heading towards the entrance to Loch Duich, with the low-lying, grassy island of Glas Eilean barely above sea level. Beyond this, the narrows that mark the entrance to Loch Duich can be seen. Take the time to look over your shoulder and enjoy the dramatic backdrop of the distant Cuillin mountains.

Entering the narrows by their southern shore you paddle by some some tranquil wooded bays and on to the small white house and stone jetty at Totaig. The views into the Kintail mountains open up now and the impressive Eilean Donan Castle is clear to see. Head across the loch to the castle and take the time to paddle around it and marvel at its structure. At high tide it is possible to circumnavigate the castle, which sits on a small rocky island, paddling under the bridge that links it to the mainland.

Leaving the castle behind, the long expanse of Loch Duich leads towards the heart of the Kintail mountains. To better enjoy the peace of the loch it is worth paddling on the western shore away from the main road that follows the eastern shore. Despite the road the loch has a special feel about it, surrounded as it is by these grand mountains. The western shore is a succession of quiet rocky beaches with occasional isolated houses, and there are plenty of places to stop along the way if a rest is required. The trip finishes as the loch finishes, the Kintail mountains finally preventing it encroaching any further inland. There is an old pier next to the Kintail Lodge Hotel, with easy parking and an ideal landing spot.

Eilean Donan Castle

This castle is one of the most iconic images of Scotland and is recognised all around the world. Its use in many films over the years has added to its notoriety, in particular the films *Highlander* and *James Bond – The World is Not Enough*. It is now one of Scotland's most visited tourist attractions; seeing it by kayak is a great way to avoid the crowds!

The castle has been built and rebuilt at least four times over the years. The first fortification was built in the mid 13th century and the current castle was finished in 1932. Eilean Donan had lain in ruins for the best part of two hundred years prior to the current castle being built. Government ships destroyed it in 1719 due to the Clan MacKenzie's support of the Jacobite rebellion at the time. In 1911 Lieutenant Colonel John MacRae-Gilstrap bought the island and preceded to restore the castle to its former glory; it took him twenty years of hard toil.

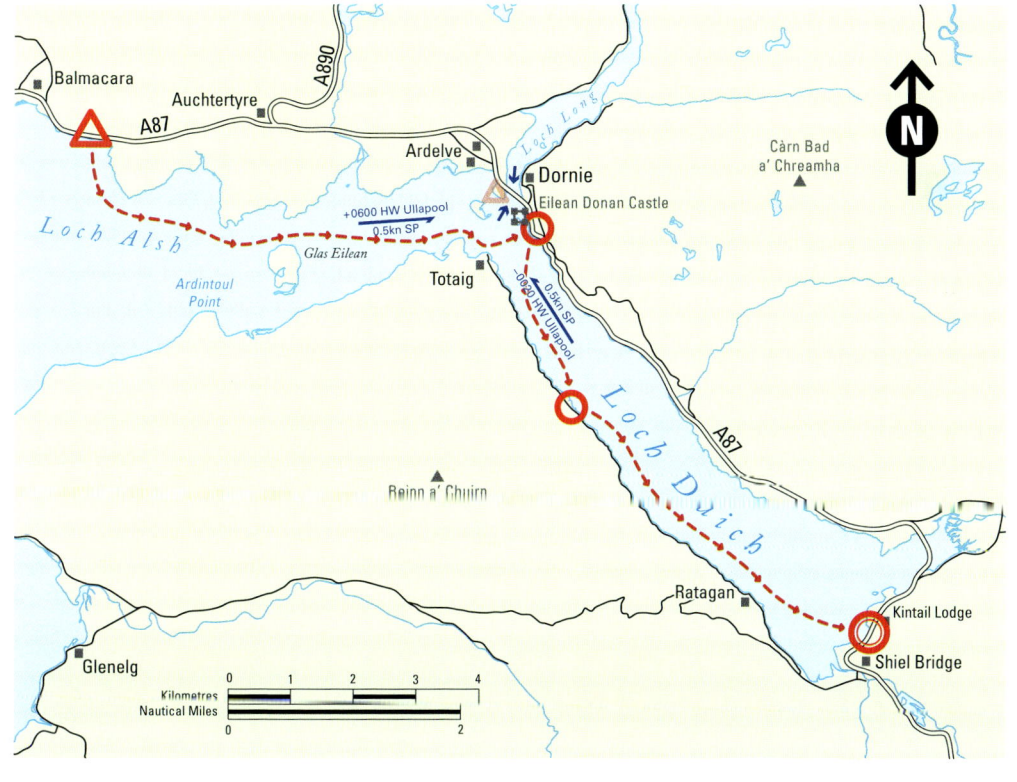

Totaig and the mountains of Kintail

Tides and weather

This is a relatively sheltered location with minimal tides to consider. The strongest tidal movement is found (particularly on the outgoing tide) where Loch Long enters Loch Duich, by Eilean Donan Castle. However, it is easy to avoid or ferry glide as required. To make use of the small amount of tidal flow there is, planning the trip on an ingoing tide is preferable but certainly not essential.

On windy days downdraughts and localised winds from the mountains will need to be considered in Loch Duich. The effects of these winds will be easy to see from the road prior to putting on.

Additional information

There are plenty of local amenities as well as pubs at Reraig and also at Dornie, next to Eilean Donan Castle at the entrance to Loch Long. There are no amenities at the finish; however just up the road at Shiel Bridge there are toilets and a shop.

Variations

There is an alternative start/finish point at the entrance to Loch Long (NG 879 262) opposite Eilean Donan Castle, which has plenty of parking as well as toilets. Starting here and doing a circular paddle taking in the castle and the views down Loch Duich makes for a great short trip, or offers a good alternative on a windy day.

Loch Hourn from Arnisdale

Loch Hourn

No. 40	**Grade A** **36km** **OS Sheet 33**
Tidal Port	Ullapool
Start	△ Arnisdale (NG 846 102)
Finish	◯ Arnisdale (NG 846 102)
HW/LW	HW/LW at Arnisdale is around 1 hour and 10 minutes before Ullapool.
Tidal Times	In Loch Hourn: The ingoing stream starts at about 6 hours after HW Ullapool. The outgoing stream starts at about 10 minutes before HW Ullapool.
Max Rate Sp	At the Caolas Mòr narrows 3 knots, generally weak elsewhere.
Coastguard	Stornoway, tel. 01851 702013, VHF weather every 3 hours from 0710.

Introduction

Although the Gaelic name translates as 'hell', Loch Hourn is far from it. Starting with open views out to the Cuillins of Skye the loch leads into the heart of the mountains with the Knoydart Munros towering overhead. With remote, small islands and plenty of wildlife, this is a great place to while away some time exploring. Whether it be for a half-day paddle or multiple days, Loch Hourn has plenty to offer.

Barrisdale Bay from Fraoch Eilean

Loch Hourn

40

Description

Squeezed between the towering flanks of the Munro (mountain over 3,000 feet) Beinn Sgritheall and the loch shore, Arnisdale is an idyllic starting point. The drive to this remote village is an adventure in itself and on arriving it feels like the kind of place where time stands still. To do Loch Hourn justice it is well worth packing the camping gear and taking a few days to get to know this special place. If this does not suit however, there are plenty of other options, with half-day or day trips from Arnisdale.

Paddling off from the stony foreshore of Arnisdale village you will see the impressive large white Arnisdale House, built in 1898 by Valentine Fleming, father of author Ian Fleming who wrote the James Bond books. The journey now heads towards the heart of Loch Hourn. Passing the small islet of Sgeir Leathan where there will be plenty of terns noisily filling the sky, keep an eye out for porpoises that are often seen on mirror calm days. At this point your eye will be drawn into Barrisdale Bay; however ensure you keep to the north shore as the narrow entrance to the inner loch is hiding around the corner.

A small cluster of wooded islands marks the start of the narrows and the inner loch. It is in this area that the tidal movement will be noticed as the water squeezes through this narrow passage. The scenery is dramatic while paddling into the heart of the mountains. The tiny narrows of Caolas Mòr is a great place to stretch the legs and watch the tide flow by, and is a good camping spot.

Beyond here lies the hidden heart of the loch. Along the shores are renovated crofts used by those wanting to escape it all, the only access being by boat. It is certainly worthwhile heading for the island of Eilean Mhogh-sgeir, where you will find the seals and birdlife that make this amazing place their home. Kinloch Hourn marks the end of the loch, and if you paddle all the way to here do not expect anything other than peace and solitude, it is a truly isolated spot.

On the way back along the southern shore you come to Barrisdale Bay. This is a popular camping spot with the estate providing some facilities and accommodation for walkers and kayakers alike. The beach here dries to over a kilometre at low tide, so you need to time it carefully or use the landing spot by Fraoch Eilean.

Continuing on from Barrisdale, stay on the south side of the loch as far as a great landing spot and possible camping at Rubha an Daraich, just beyond a steep rocky headland. Here the views are dramatically different as you overlook the expanse of the Sound of Sleat across to the mighty Cuillin mountains. From here cut across to a group of islands not to be missed, its biggest called Eilean Ràrsaidh. This cluster of islands provides sheltered waters and refuge for a host of wildlife including seals, otters and numerous birds. It is easy to while away a fair bit of time here, soaking in the natural surroundings before paddling the last few kilometres back to Arnisdale.

The cattle drovers

On route you will have noticed the well-made path that starts on the north shore and then continues on the south beyond the narrows. This forms the old drovers' road that the cattle herders once used; having swum their beasts across Kyle Rhea they herded them to Kinloch Hourn. To do this they had to swim once more, this time across the narrows of Loch Hourn. These tough herders and cattle were on route to the Scottish Lowlands. These days you will just see walkers making their way into Barrisdale on the drovers' road on the south side of the loch, Barrisdale being a popular starting point for walking in the Knoydart mountains.

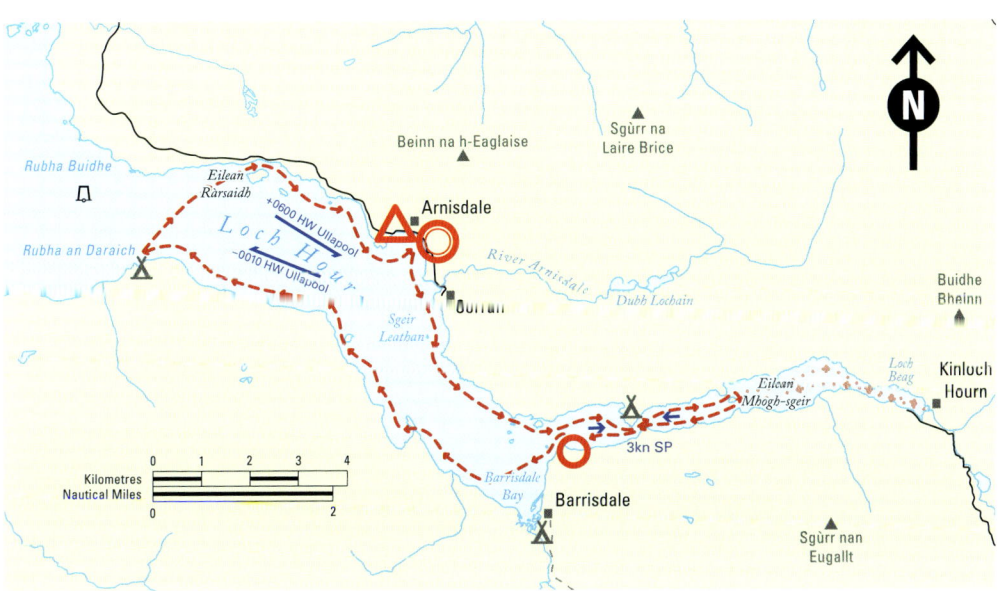

Leaving Arnisdale

Tides and weather

The only noticeable tidal flow is in the narrows around Caolas Mòr. Although best to plan to have them assisting the journey, they are short-lived and it is easy to use the eddies to paddle against them. Although Loch Hourn is sheltered from the stronger winds care should be taken, particularly in the inner loch, of strong downdraughts and localised gusts. These have been known to lift the surface water high into the air. Strong southerly winds making these conditions more likely.

Additional information

There are no facilities at Arnisdale, however at the end of the road Corran offers toilets, local information about the area and its history, and a unique tea shop. Glenelg (on the route to Arnisdale) provides a range of amenities and a fine pub.

Variations

There are endless variations for paddling in Loch Hourn, making it an ideal location to meet a range of aspirations or weather conditions. The trip described would be best done over two days camping along the route. A great day trip is up through the narrows to Eilean Mhogh-sgeir and back, and a shorter day or half-day trip is up to the beautiful islands around Eilean Ràrsaidh.

The head of Loch Nevis

Loch Nevis

No. 41	**Grade B**	**48km**	**OS Sheets 33 and 40**
Tidal Port	Ullapool
Start	△ Mallaig (NM 678 968)
Finish	○ Mallaig (NM 678 968)
HW/LW	HW/LW at Mallaig is around 50 minutes before Ullapool.
Tidal Times	At the entrance to Loch Nevis: The ingoing stream starts at about 5 hours and 15 minutes after HW Ullapool. The outgoing stream starts at about 1 hour and 5 minutes before HW Ullapool.
Max Rate Sp	At the entrance to Loch Nevis 0.5 knots. In the Inner Narrows 3 knots.
Coastguard	Stornoway, tel. 01851 702013. VHF weather every 3 hours from 0710.

Introduction

Loch Nevis cuts its way into the heart of Knoydart, often referred to as 'Britain's last wilderness'. To spend time exploring the loch, surrounded by mountains, wildlife and solitude, is a magical experience. One possible translation of Nevis is 'heaven' and no doubt you will feel you have

◎ Leaving Mallaig

Loch Nevis

arrived when you get there. To do Loch Nevis justice and fully appreciate all that it offers, it is best to do this trip over a couple of days, camping at the head of the loch nestled amongst a backdrop of remote mountains. If time does not allow there are plenty of options of shorter day trips to get a taste of 'heaven'.

Description

The launching point is in the busy fishing port of Mallaig. Here the hustle and bustle of boats, ferries and tourists is a far cry from what awaits. The trip starts by following the south coast of the loch, the village of Inverie will be visible in the distance with the mountains dominating the surroundings. The boats and people of Mallaig will soon be forgotten as the rugged coastline leads towards where the loch turns in a southerly direction. Just before this there is a good landing spot in the bay behind Eilean Giubhais, with golden sands at low tide. As the loch turns south the remoteness of the setting builds, the mountains tower increasingly overhead and the view behind out to the Sound of Sleat and distant Cuillin mountains disappears.

Soon the tiny, remote settlement of Easter Stoul appears; nestled in amongst the rugged backdrop of mountains it seems an unlikely place to live. This is one of quite a few small, isolated settlements and houses found within Loch Nevis. They are mostly used as holiday houses, enabling people to make Loch Nevis their home for a while. A small local ferry services some of the tiny settlements; the rest can only be accessed by private boat, or kayak!

After Stoul a surprise waits at the outdoor centre/bunkhouse owned by Tom McClean at Ardintigh – look for the whale beached upon the shore! Beyond this is the once busy fishing community of Tarbet. Its name refers to a portage or isthmus, in this case the one between Loch Nevis and Loch Morar. This small bay provides another opportunity to stop, its entrance being overlooked by perhaps the grandest of all Loch Nevis houses.

Hiding around the corner from Tarbet are the narrows of Kylesknoydart, the passage into the inner sanctuary of Loch Nevis. A lone tree stands defiant overlooking these narrows; it is a wonder it has stood the test of time with the strong winds that must funnel up the loch. Passing through the narrows some tidal movement will be noticeable and hopefully it will be helping you on your way into the heart of Knoydart. This inner sanctuary is a truly special place and one to savour. As you paddle up to the head of the loch and Camusrory, the pointed peak of Sgùrr na Ciche dominates the view. Along from the grand house at Camusrory is an open bothy shown on the map as 'Sourlies'. As well as this as an option for the night there is good camping outside the bothy or next to Eilean Tioram. This along with an abundance of fresh mussels makes for a perfect place to break the journey and spend the night.

Having spent a night in 'heaven' you will no doubt feel refreshed and ready to explore the rest of what Loch Nevis has to offer. Head back out through Kylesknoydart and then follow the northern coastline of the loch that leads to Inverie. Just beyond the Kyles look out for the remains of a small concrete landing point. On the hillside above lies a clear zigzag path leading to the Knoydart mica mine. The mine was only worked for a few years during World War II when the supplies from India were disrupted; Knoydart was one of the few sources of mica in Britain. The mica was used for the Spitfire windscreens, and it can still be found up at the mine if you have the time to explore.

The rugged coastline continues on to the tranquil bay of Inverie, a perfect place to take a well-earned rest. Inverie is the only village on the peninsula of Knoydart and is only accessible by boat.

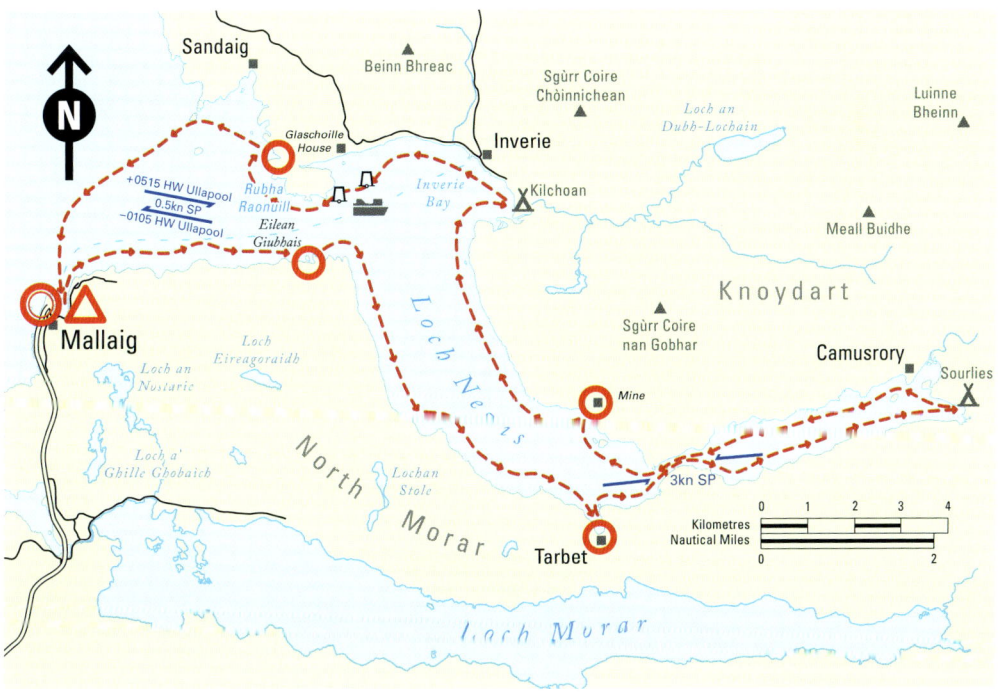

The village has a campsite, bunkhouse, accommodation and a post office, but most importantly it has the well known pub The Old Forge. It is Britain's remotest pub and is a great source of good food and beer, as well as music and hospitality.

When you eventually manage to leave Inverie and The Old Forge, head on around Rubha Raonuill and into Sandaig Bay. On Rubha Raonuill 'Our Lady of Loch Nevis', a huge statue of the Madonna, stands with open arms to welcome sailors into the loch. (The statue was erected by the local Catholic community.) Just offshore from this is a unique marker for shipping with a cross on top of it. On the eastern side of this bay you will discover some truly amazing beaches, so if you still don't think you have been to 'heaven' you will now! These beaches catch the afternoon and evening sun perfectly. The view out from them across the Sound of Sleat to Skye is one to savour – the tent might be coming out again!

All too soon it is time to head back to Mallaig, and as you pass Glas Eilean on the way look out for seals hauled up on the rocks. Take care with the ferries and other water users as you paddle back into Mallaig. Ensure you take the time to enjoy the final views into Loch Nevis as you have now been to heaven and back again!

Tides and weather

There is minimal tidal movement in the loch other than at Kylesknoydart; if possible plan the trip to have tidal assistance through this narrow gap. If this is not possible then you can paddle against the tide using eddies. At the head of the loch at low water it dries for up to a kilometre, so if planning to camp it is worth timing launching and landing around higher water.

Although comparatively sheltered from the wind and completely protected from any swell, Loch Nevis still demands respect. Surrounded by mountains the winds can funnel and the loch is big enough to produce a reasonable sea state, particularly where it is more open to the Sound of Sleat.

Additional information

There is a variety of accommodation available, from bunkhouse through to luxury holiday homes, at many of the tiny settlements within Loch Nevis. Many of these offer ferry services that could include the transportation of kayaks. There is a full range of amenities in Mallaig and a limited range at Inverie. The campsite at Inverie is situated at Long Beach (NM 774 993) where there are basic facilities and an honesty box for camp fees. The main ferry to Inverie is usually happy to transport kayaks though it is worth booking in advance for this. Leave cars in the long stay car parks in Mallaig that are clearly signposted.

Variations

There are many variations and different camp options to that described here. Two noteworthy variations would be a day trip from Mallaig to Inverie, returning via the sandy beaches found in Sandaig Bay; or for the adventurous a trip up Loch Morar (start point NM 707 929) to South Tarbet Bay, portaging across to Tarbet Loch Nevis, and returning to Mallaig. Using the campsite at Inverie as a base also works well, with the pub a short walk away and a ferry option to return if the weather is unfavourable.

Sandaig Islands

Sound of Sleat

No. 42	**Grade B**	**50km**	**OS Sheets 32, 33 and 40**
Tidal Port	Ullapool
Start	△ Mallaig (NM 678 968)
Finish	◯ Mallaig (NM 678 968)
HW/LW	HW/LW at Mallaig is around 50 minutes before Ullapool.
Tidal Times	In the Sound of Sleat: The NE going stream starts at about 5 hours and 35 minutes after HW Ullapool. The SW going stream starts at about 25 minutes before HW Ullapool.
Max Rate Sp	In the Sound of Sleat 1 knot. Off the Sandaig Islands 2 knots.
Coastguard	Stornoway, tel. 01851 702013, VHF weather every 3 hours from 0710.

Introduction

Exploring the Sound of Sleat you will discover remote coastlines, isolated crofts, picturesque villages, wildlife aplenty and a cluster of perfect islands in azure waters. An inescapable eastern coastline to complement an inhabited western, along with some small crossings, gives the perfect blend for an ideal couple of days paddling.

Ornsay lighthouse

Description

The starting point, Mallaig, is a busy port with a combination of tourist craft, ferries and fishing vessels. In the 1960s it was one of the busiest herring ports in Europe and to this day is one of the main west coast fishing ports. Leaving the hustle and bustle of Mallaig behind head across the entrance of Loch Nevis to the small peninsula with Eilean Dearg at its point. As tempting as exploring Loch Nevis will be, save it for another day and head on up the remote eastern coastline of the Sound of Sleat.

The coastline starts with small cliffs to complement the grand views up the Sound, with the Cuillin mountains of Skye a distant backdrop. After passing the site of a small fort, Dùn Bàn, you will discover the isolated houses of Doune. Only accessible by boat, like so many of the houses on this coastline, these provide luxurious holiday accommodation for those wishing to get away from it all. Beyond this is the old fishing settlement of Airor, situated at the road head of what has got to be one of Britain's most isolated and little-used roads. Enjoy the fantastic wildlife found on Airor Island and the incredible white sandy beach at its north-eastern end. Up to the entrance to Loch Hourn the coastline is low-lying with stony beaches. Another nice sandy stopping point can be found opposite Eilean Shamadalain – look out for the remains of the chapel here.

Arriving at Rubha Àrd Slisneach provides more landings and a potential camp spot, but our trip heads across Loch Hourn and on up to the Sandaig Islands. Dramatic views will unfold as it becomes possible to look into Loch Hourn; like Loch Nevis it cuts deeply into high mountains. At the small archipelago that makes up the Sandaig Islands you will have arrived at arguably the

'Ring of Bright Water'

Gavin Maxwell wrote his autobiographical account of his time with the otters at Sandaig, bringing fame to this remote area. The book is called *Ring of Bright Water* and he called this beautiful area that was his home Camusfearna. The house he lived in no longer remains as it was burnt down, and his famous otter 'Edal' sadly perished in the same fire. Maxwell's times at Camusfearna ended with this, but look for the memorial stone that marks where his writing table once stood and is now the resting place of his ashes.

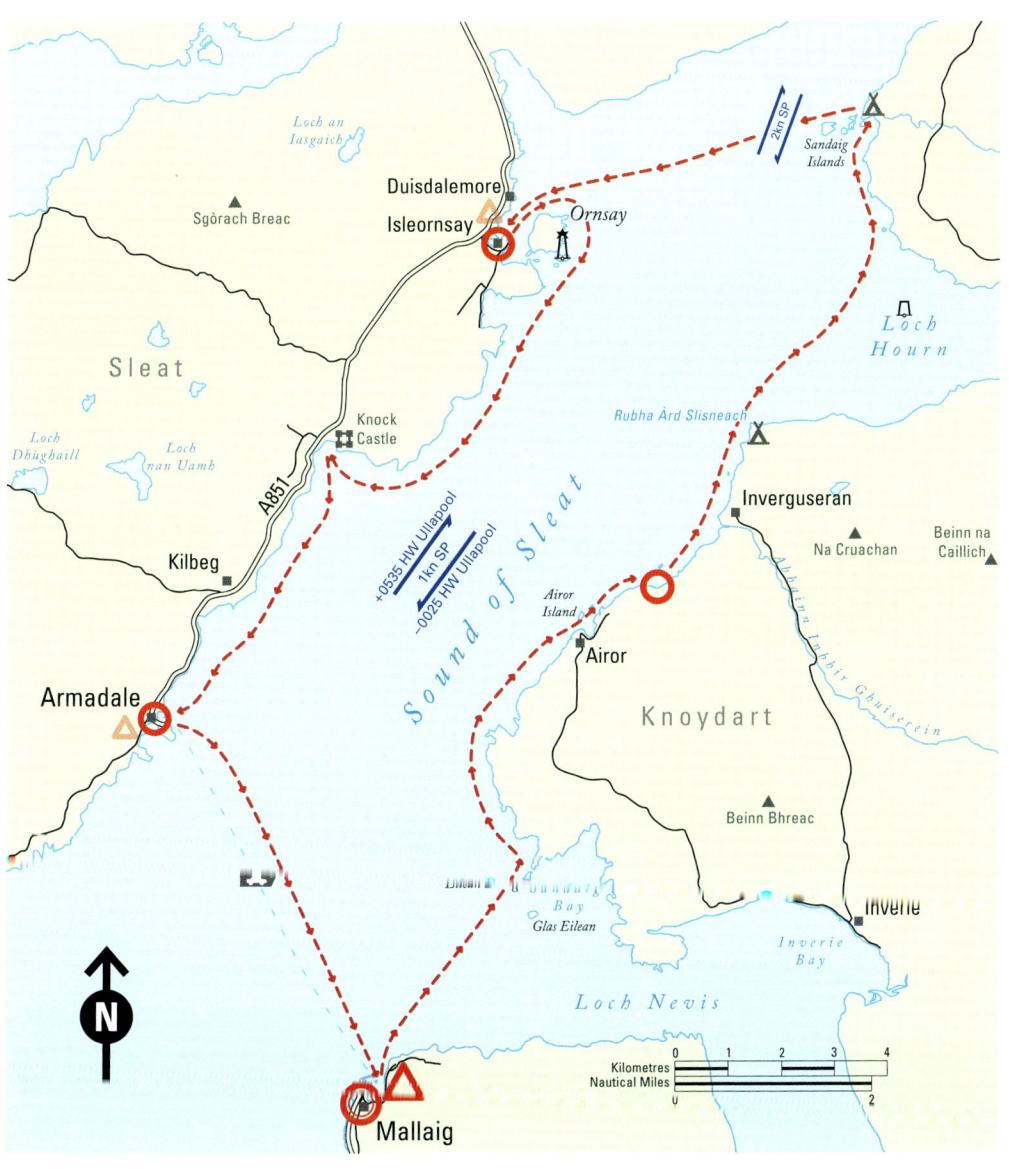

'jewel in the crown' of the Sound of Sleat. The islands provide shelter for wildlife and kayakers alike, along with a stunning beach and a perfect camp spot on the eastern-most island. It is worth visiting the shell beach on the mainland just across from this island.

Leaving the Sandaig Islands it is time for a short crossing to the western coastline of the Sound of Sleat, heading for the picturesque village of Isleornsay. Situated in a beautiful natural harbour it has a welcoming pub a few paces from the shore for a deserved coffee or other refreshments. The journey heads south from here, passing Ornsay lighthouse, built in 1857 by David and Thomas Stevenson. The low-lying coastline takes you past the village and small bay of Camus Croise and then on to Knock Bay, overlooked by a castle.

Continuing on to Armadale you pass the impressive buildings of the Gaelic college, Sabhal Mòr Ostaig, along with a few small beaches and stopping points. Armadale is the terminal for the Mallaig ferry and also marks the end of the journey down the western coastline of the Sound of Sleat. There is a beach to land, along with a handy café for ice creams or hot snacks. If the weather is good, all that is left is the crossing back to Mallaig.

Tides and weather

There are no tidal flows of note on this trip, however if possible time the trip to make use of the gentle in/outgoing tide within the Sound. Any wind or swell from the south-west will funnel up the Sound and can give rise to quite challenging seas.

Additional information

If the conditions, energy levels or time do not suit the final crossing from Armadale to Mallaig, it is possible to carry sea kayaks onto the ferry and get a lift back! Leave cars in the long stay car parks in Mallaig that are clearly signposted.

Variations

For a shorter day trip, consider a paddle out to the Sandaig Islands from Isleornsay. This in itself is an amazing trip and will not disappoint. From Mallaig, heading up to Airor and back, perhaps taking in the sandy beaches in Sandaig Bay is another great day out.

The Green Lady of the Castle

The castle was known as either Knock or Camus Castle. Originally built by the Clan MacLeod and later captured by Clan MacDonald it was the site of many a feud between the two rival clans. The Green Lady, a ghost that appears happy if good news is to come and weeping if it is bad, reputedly haunts the castle. Hopefully she will be smiling down on you as you pass.

Arisaig skerries with Rum behind

Morar & Arisaig

No. 43 | Grade A | 18km | OS Sheet 40

Tidal Port	Ullapool
Start	△ Morar (NM 677 920 or NM 681 922)
Finish	○ Arisaig (NM 659 859)
HW/LW	HW/LW at Arisaig is around 40 minutes before Ullapool.
Tidal Times	In Loch nan Ceall: The ingoing stream starts at about 5 hours and 45 minutes after HW Ullapool. The outgoing stream starts at about 50 minutes before HW Ullapool.
Max Rate Sp	In the North and South Channels of Loch nan Ceall 1–2 knots.
Coastguard	Stornoway, tel. 01851 702013, VHF weather every 3 hours from 0710.

Introduction

The white sands of Morar are an idyllic start to a trip that is dominated by spectacular beaches with expansive views across to the mountains of Skye and Rum. The maze of skerries that guards the entrance to Arisaig are a wildlife haven and a sea kayakers' paradise, the shallow azure blue waters a unique and sheltered place to explore.

River Morar meets the sea

Description

The preferred launching place is by the road with just a short carry across the immaculate beach to the estuary of the River Morar. At low water it may be easier to launch from the back road to Morar where the river cascades into the tidal estuary; there is a track down to the water and a parking bay nearby. Once afloat, take the time to explore where the river cascades down under the main road bridge before heading out of the shallow waters of the Morar estuary to the seaward coastline.

At the coast the views open up in dramatic fashion, the Point of Sleat across the water with the Cuillin mountains of Skye behind. The islands of Rum and Eigg stand out, with their own mountains rising out of the sea. Heading south along the coast there are numerous white sandy beaches and rocky skerries to explore. For the film buffs the sands of Camusdarach will be familiar, as a good deal of the filming for *Local Hero* was done here. You will be spoilt for choice for places to stop and have a rest, each beach being as spectacular as the last and all providing easy landings and stunning views.

On reaching Gortenachullish there maybe an option to paddle through the narrow shallow channel that separates the mainland from Eilean Ighe. This is a hidden and unlikely way through into Loch nan Ceall and well worth exploring if possible. If the tide is not high enough then the maze of skerries that guard the entrance to Loch nan Ceall are approached by paddling around Eilean Ighe. It is worth allowing plenty of time to explore the skerries, with Luinga Mhòr and Luinga Bheag being the two largest. As the tide rises or falls skerries, many with their own sandy beaches, will disappear or appear. Within the heart of the skerries the water is sheltered and shallow, crystal clear, and turquoise in colour. Here you will find a treasure trove of wildlife;

plenty of seals along with a wide variety of wading birds. Paddling in amongst all of this will feel more like the Caribbean on a sunny day than north-west Scotland; it really is a magical place and one to be fully savoured. When the time comes, head into Loch nan Ceall that leads to Arisaig, situated at its head. Arisaig is a popular place for boats and yachts so while paddling there keep to the edge of the loch and out of the shipping channels that are clearly marked with green and red poles and buoys. The village is a busy place in the summer, much visited by tourists and sea kayakers alike. When landing here, consider using the area where the stream enters the loch just south of the village. This provides plenty of parking and is more considerate than trying to land in the main village. At low water you may want to consider one of the alternative landing/launching sites that do not require such a carry (see Variations). Once ashore, Arisaig has a choice of cafés or pubs where you can sit in the sun and enjoy some well earned refreshments while reflecting on a great day's paddle.

Tides and weather

The coastline from Morar to the Arisaig skerries is fairly exposed to any wind or swell so reasonable conditions are needed to paddle this section. Loch nan Ceall and the skerries provide a lot of shelter in most weather conditions, and therefore can be paddled even if the more exposed coastline is not appropriate. The main tidal streams are found in the North and South Channels of Loch nan Ceall. Ideally plan for these tidal streams to be assisting you, but this is not essential and it is easy to avoid them by staying in close to the skerries. Tidal flow may also be noticed going in and out of Morar, this can also be paddled against if necessary.

Additional information

Public toilets can be found at a car park just along the minor road from the put-in at Morar. Arisaig has a full range of amenities including cafés, a pub and a shop as well as public toilets. Arisaig is a busy tourist destination and is becoming increasingly popular for sea kayakers, all of which is putting a demand on the village. When visiting the area, with its small roads and limited parking areas, please be courteous when driving and considerate when parking to ensure a continued good welcome from the local community.

Variations

For a shorter, less exposed trip, just paddling in Loch nan Ceall and exploring the skerries is well recommended. There is a range of options for launching, all of which require a bit of a carry at low water; please try not to overcrowd any given launch site. The alternative launch sites are: Rhue (NM 627 852 or NM 629 854), small bay with private landing pontoon (NM 638 853), bay at NM 648 846 (high water only) or at Gortenachullish (NM 642 877). The trip can also be extended by starting in Mallaig (NM 677 968), five kilometres up the coast from Morar.

The remote northern coastline of the Sound of Arisaig

Sound of Arisaig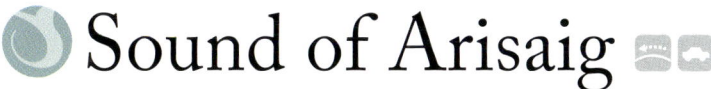

No. 44 | Grade B | 17km | OS Sheet 40

Tidal Port	Ullapool
Start	▲ Rhue (NM 627 852)
Finish	⭕ Head of Loch nan Uamh (NM 727 843)
HW/LW	HW/LW in the Sound of Arisaig is around 50 minutes before Ullapool.
Tidal Times	For the South Channel, Loch nan Ceall: The ingoing stream starts at about 5 hours and 45 minutes after HW Ullapool. The outgoing stream starts at about 50 minutes before HW Ullapool.
	For the Sound of Arisaig: The ingoing stream starts at about 5 hours and 30 minutes after HW Ullapool. The outgoing stream starts at about 50 minutes before HW Ullapool.
Max Rate Sp	In the South Channel 2 knots. Along the Sound of Arisaig 0.5 knots.
Coastguard	Stornoway, tel. 01851 702013, VHF weather every 3 hours from 0710.

Introduction

The Sound of Arisaig is a magical place and its remote northern coastline leaves you with a wonderful sense of isolation. Sandy beaches, islands and wildlife set amongst a backdrop of the Small Isles out to sea and mountains inland ensure a fine day out.

213

Leaving Rhue: Eigg and Rum in the distance

Description

The road head at Rhue is as scenic a put-on as anyone could ask for. It looks out over the Arisaig skerries with their numerous white sand beaches to a wonderful view that includes the Cuillins mountains of Skye, and the islands of Rum and Eigg. Head across the South Channel and weave your way through some of the skerries and their incredible beaches on the route to Rubh Arisaig. You will no doubt be kept company by some of the many common seals that make this wonderful place their home. Passing the low-lying headland of Rubh Arisaig, the trip heads into the Sound of Arisaig. Away from the shelter of the skerries the sea state may be a bit more lively, but soon you will come to the fine beach at Port nam Murrach, nestled in a perfect little sheltered bay. While paddling in here the water will be crystal clear with the silver sands clearly visible below.

The journey leads us on to the obvious small rocky island of Eilean a' Ghaill. Here there are the remains of a small, vitrified fort (vitrification being where the stone walls are exposed to extreme heat from fire to melt/fuse them for increased strength). Yet another stunning beach looks out to this island – another great spot to land and while away some time. Alternatively head out to the rocky skerries of Eilean an t-Snidhe, which act as natural sentries for the entrance to the Sound of Arisaig. Here there is often a great deal of wildlife. Heading on into the sound the beaches end; however the coastline still offers plenty of interest. Just before the Borrowdale Islands, check out the unique little bothy perched on a rocky outcrop overlooking Camas Ghaoideil. A bouldery landing and a bit of easy scrambling will gain access to this amazing lookout, please respect it and leave it for others to enjoy.

The Prince's Cairn

In 1745 Charles Edward Stuart sailed from France to Scotland to begin his efforts to claim the throne of Britain for his father, James Francis Edward Stuart. He first set foot on mainland Scotland in Loch nan Uamh on the 25th July 1745 and from here his army of Jacobites grew as they marched south. The Jacobite forces fought successfully until their final battle on Culloden Moor on 16th April 1776. Here they were defeated, suffering 2,000 deaths compared to the 50 of the British Army. Prince Charles fled, seeking refuge in numerous caves throughout the Highlands and Hebrides, all the time trying to escape back to France. Eventually on 20th September 1746 the French frigate *L'Heureux* sailed out of Loch nan Uamh with the prince on board; he was never to see Scotland again. The Prince's Cairn marks the spot he left.

The Borrowdale Islands guard the entrance to the northern inner loch of the Sound of Arisaig, Loch Nan Uamh (the southern one being Loch Ailort). There is plenty of wildlife to see while exploring the islands before the last part of the journey into the 'Loch of the Caves', Loch nan Uamh. This loch has strong connections to 'Bonnie Prince Charles' and the Jacobites he led.

A final cluster of islands marks the finish at the head of the loch. Look out for a small bay on the north side just before the loch ends. There is a short carry up a grass track to the road.

Tides and weather

The tidal flows are not strong enough to require much consideration on this trip. In the South Channel, where they flow fastest, they are easily paddled against by using eddies formed by Arisaig

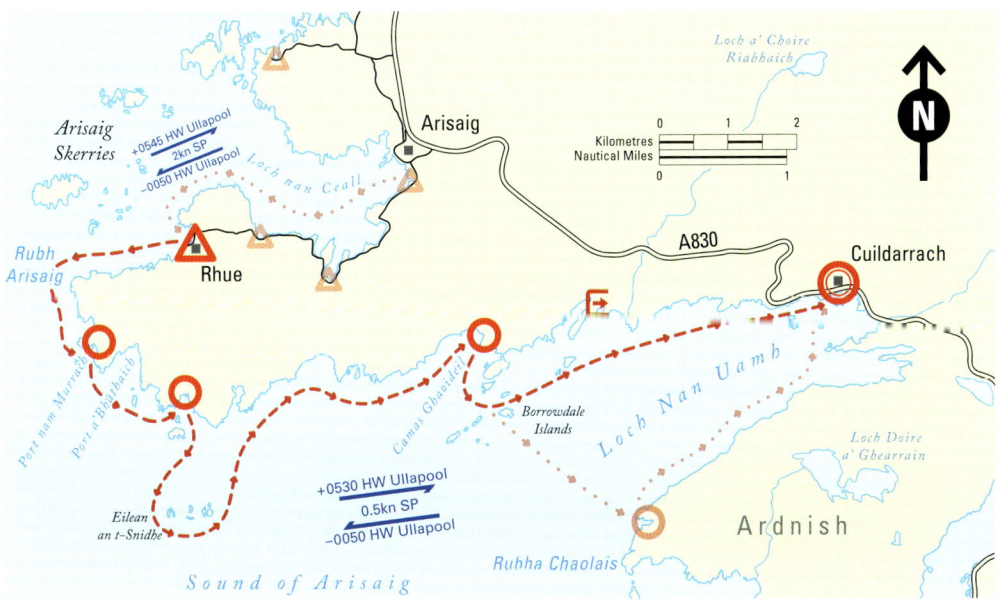

skerries and close in to shore. The trip is exposed to wind and swell from the south and west, and should therefore be planned taking this into consideration. Even though it is only a short trip, the north shore of the Sound of Arisaig is inescapable, so good conditions are recommended.

Additional information

There is limited parking at Rhue and the single-track road is well used; please drive and park courteously. There is a full range of amenities in Arisaig.

Variations

There are additional launch sites if you wish to extend the trip or if parking is tight at the road head. These are: Rhue (NM 629 854), small bay with private landing pontoon (NM 638 853), bay at NM 648 846 (high water only), Gortenachullish (NM 642 877) or in Arisaig just south of the village where the stream enters the loch (NM 659 859).

From the Borrowdale Islands it is possible to cross the entrance of Loch nan Uamh to Port a t-Sluichd. Here an old cleared village is found and the remote southern coastline of the loch makes for a good route to the finish at the head of the loch. There is limited parking by the edge of the road at the finish, so please consider leaving cars parked at the Prince's Cairn where there is plenty of parking.

Eilean nan Gobhar from Peanmeanach

Loch Ailort

No. 45 | Grade A | 12km | OS Sheet 40

Tidal Port	Ullapool
Start	△ Lay-by (NM 738 793)
Finish	◯ Lay-by (NM 738 793)
HW/LW	HW/LW in Loch Ailort is around 50 minutes before Ullapool.
Tidal Times	For Loch Ailort: The ingoing stream starts at about 5 hours and 30 minutes after HW Ullapool. The outgoing stream starts at about 50 minutes before HW Ullapool.
Max Rate Sp	In the narrowest sections of the loch 2–3 knots, weak elsewhere.
Coastguard	Stornoway, tel. 01851 702013, VHF weather every 3 hours from 0710.

Introduction

Whether you are looking for long or short days out on the water, Loch Ailort will guarantee stunning views, sandy beaches, beautiful islands and wildlife to keep you company. No matter how many times you visit, it will always leave you wanting to come back for more.

© Immaculate sandy beach near Rubha Chaclais

Description

At the pebbly beach across from Eilean Buidhe, a short carry from the road launches you into the heart of Loch Ailort. In the distance, beyond the islands of Loch Ailort, there are tantalising glimpses of the Sound of Arisaig and islands of Eigg and Rum.

Start the trip by heading across to the northern shore of the loch. Here you can make your way between the islands and explore the sheltered bays; keep an eye out for seals, otters and herons as you go. A tight cluster of small islands, including Eilean nam Bairneach, guards the way to the outer part of the loch and the narrow channels often have a little bit of tidal flow through them.

As the loch opens out the sea state may liven up a bit, but the islands around Eilean nan Gobhar will still provide protection from the worst of any swell. The northern coastline leads around to Peanmeanach, and passing behind a small island takes you into sheltered and crystal clear waters as you approach the bay. This is a good landing spot. Take a walk up to the Mountain Bothies Association bothy which provides some welcome shelter if the weather is poor, or a place for the night if you decide to spend more time in this beautiful place. From here continue along the northern shore as one of the highlights of the trip awaits, an immaculate sandy beach with a view to die for! This is situated just before Rubha Chaolais and it is worth planning to spend some time here. Crystal clear, azure blue waters will lead you in, white sand will greet you and a view out of Loch Ailort to the Sound of Arisaig and the Small Isles will be the reward.

A group of islands cut across the loch from here and mark the boundary between Loch Ailort and the Sound of Arisaig. On the outside of these islands you will find cliffs and skerries, as well as swell and exposure. In the right conditions this is fantastic; if too rough however the inside of the islands offers protection. On Eilean nan Gobhar there are the remains of a vitrified fort visible on its summit. You can land on a stony beach on the east side and find an overgrown path up to the fort and island summit. Here you will see the vitrified walls, fused by extreme heat in the building to make them stronger to repel attack. In addition to this you will have the best viewpoint of Loch Ailort, the Sound of Arisaig and the Small Isles, a fantastic panorama and one not to be missed.

On leaving the island head towards the impressive house found at Roshven, then follow the southern coast of the loch back to where the trip started. This gives great views of the mountains that overlook the loch, as well as of the waterfalls tumbling down off them. There are further places to land if required, as well as wildlife for company and islands for interest. There could well be some tidal flow in the narrows leading back into Loch Ailort, hopefully this will help whisk you home at the end of this great little trip.

Tides and weather

In the narrows between the islands there can be flows up to 2–3 knots and if possible timing to have this assisting is recommended. If this is not possible then the flow is short-lived and eddies can be used to paddle against it. On spring tides with associated wind, small tidal races can form in these narrows, with eddies of reasonable strength. Loch Ailort offers a lot of shelter and will

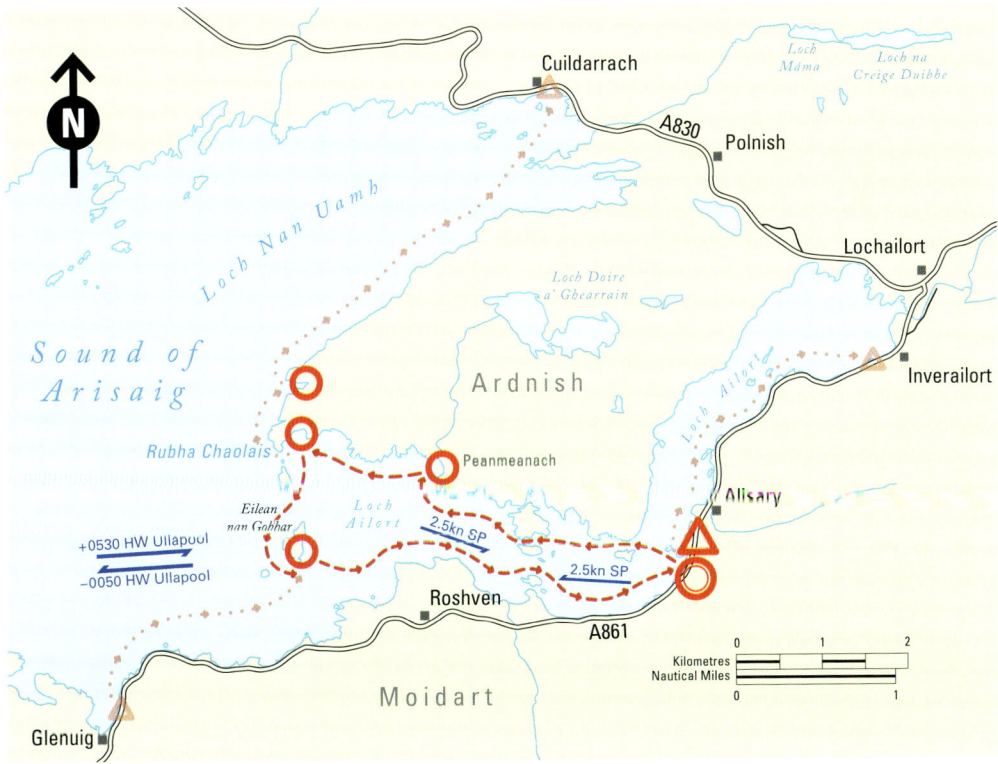

Looking into Loch Ailort and Roshven

Loch Ailort

work in most conditions, however if the wind is very strong from the east or south beware of strong downdraughts off the mountains. These have been known to pick the water up off the loch and spiral it high into the air!

Additional information

There is a welcoming pub at Glenuig to enjoy at the end of the trip, which also offers bunkhouse accommodation. When parking please be considerate to other users of the area.

Variations

There are many variations to this trip, most of them obvious from the map. For a longer trip, starting at Glenuig jetty (NM 673 776) and paddling to the jetty at the head of Loch Ailort (NM 759 814) works well, particularly if there is a westerly wind at your back the whole way! The trip can also be extended by continuing on to the head of Loch nan Uamh (NM 727 843) or along the north shore of the Sound of Arisaig to the village of Arisaig. These may work well over two days making use of the bothy or one of the amazing camp spots overlooking a sandy beach. A vehicle shuttle will be required.

Castle Tioram

Eilean Shona & Castle Tioram

No. 46 | **Grade B** | **25km** | **OS Sheet 40**

Tidal Port	Ullapool
Start	△ Glenuig (NM 674 776)
Finish	◯ Glenuig (NM 674 776)
HW/LW	HW/LW in Loch Moidart is around 50 minutes before Ullapool.
Tidal Times	In the Sound of Arisaig: The W going stream starts at about 50 minutes before HW Ullapool. The E going stream starts at about 5 hours and 30 minutes after HW Ullapool.
	In the N and S Channels of Loch Moidart: The ingoing stream starts at about 5 hours and 30 minutes after HW Ullapool. The outgoing stream starts at about 50 minutes before HW Ullapool.
Max Rate Sp	In the channels 2 knots.
Coastguard	Stornoway, tel. 01851 702013, VHF weather every 3 hours from 0710.

A perfect beach with Eilean Shona beh.ind

Introduction

This is a very varied trip, with an exposed rugged coastline, some incredible beaches and views out across the Small Isles. Contrast this with sheltered waters of an inland sea loch surrounded by ancient woodlands, a dramatic castle and plenty of wildlife, and you have the ingredients for a great day out.

Description

After leaving the slipway at Glenuig, Samalaman Island with its sandy beaches and bay will be the first point of call. The island dries at very low water, however when you can paddle between it and the mainland there are shallow, crystal clear waters with golden sands below. A rocky coastline continues with plenty of good rock hopping opportunities all the way to the old crofting village of Smirisary. Here there are many well-maintained holiday houses, an idyllic place to escape for a while – surprisingly though there is no easy landing here. On the mainland opposite Eilean Collie you will find what has to be one of the best beaches of the west coast, a hidden gem. Land here and spend some time taking in the views, silver sands and turquoise waters.

The towering hillside that forms the north-west corner of Eilean Shona dominates the view, and marks the narrow entrance to the island's North Channel. After the open views and often lively ocean just paddled, the calm and enclosed tranquillity of the North Channel is quite a contrast. The open and rough hillsides are replaced with mature old trees, and at its narrowest part the ford that provides low water access to the island can be seen. Look out for the old schoolhouse on the northern shore of the island before the narrows. The island was once home to many families, working hard to make a living by crofting. The heavily wooded shores islands of Loch Moidart lead you to Castle Tioram. Landing here allows for a rest as well as a chance to explore the island and its castle.

From the castle, head out of the South Channel back to the open seas. On the south-west corner of Eilean Shona there are a couple of islands that hide another fantastic beach behind them. The outer coast of the island is in stark contrast to the rest of the island, with a steep, rugged hillside towering high above the sea. Following this coastline will lead you back to the amazing beach opposite Eilean Collie, perhaps time for one more stop before heading back to Glenuig. A visit to the ideally-situated Glenuig Inn for some welcome refreshments makes a great end to a great day out.

Tides and weather

The outer coastline of this trip is very exposed to wind and swell. If the swell or wind is too much, consider one of the more sheltered variations suggested.

To paddle around Eilean Shona tidal planning is essential, as the narrows of the North Channel dry out at the ford. The trip needs to be timed so that about an hour either side of low water is avoided. Ideally make use of the ingoing tidal flow to paddle down the North Channel, thus ensuring higher water at the narrows, and then use the outgoing flow to assist while leaving the South Channel.

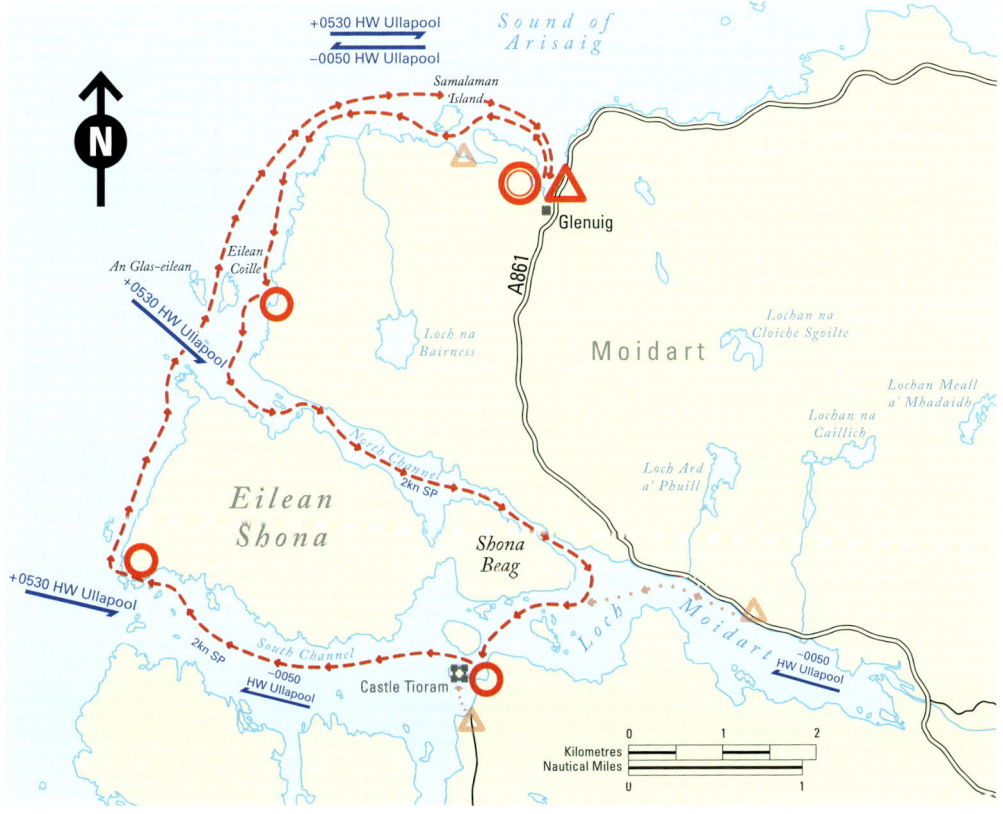

Additional information

Glenuig jetty is used regularly by the local fishermen, so please park considerately. If it is busy here there is an alternative launch place opposite Samalaman Island (NM 663 777). At Glenuig there is a small shop. The Glenuig Inn offers accommodation as well as fine food and drink; they are very sea kayak-friendly with knowledge of the local area.

Variations

For a more sheltered trip, putting on at Castle Tioram (NM 664 720) works well and allows the sheltered South and North Channels, as well as Loch Moidart, to be explored. It is also possible to put in on the north side of Loch Moidart at an old slipway that is in poor repair (NM 688 733). There is limited verge-side parking here, so please be considerate when leaving vehicles.

Castle Tioram

Castle Tioram (pronounced 'chee-rum') means 'dry castle', as the island on which it is built dries out at most states of the tide. There has been a castle on the island since the 13th century and it is the traditional seat of Clan MacDonald of Clan Ranald. Government forces seized the castle in around 1692 when the then Clan Chief joined the Jacobite court in France. The government then stationed a small garrison at the castle until the Jacobite uprising in 1715. At this point the Clan Chief returned and recaptured his castle, however he decided to torch it to keep it out of the hands of his enemies; it has been unoccupied ever since. Nowadays it is in a sorry state of repair, with warning signs advising you to keep out because of the risk of bits of it falling down. It seems a sad end to such a finely positioned castle.

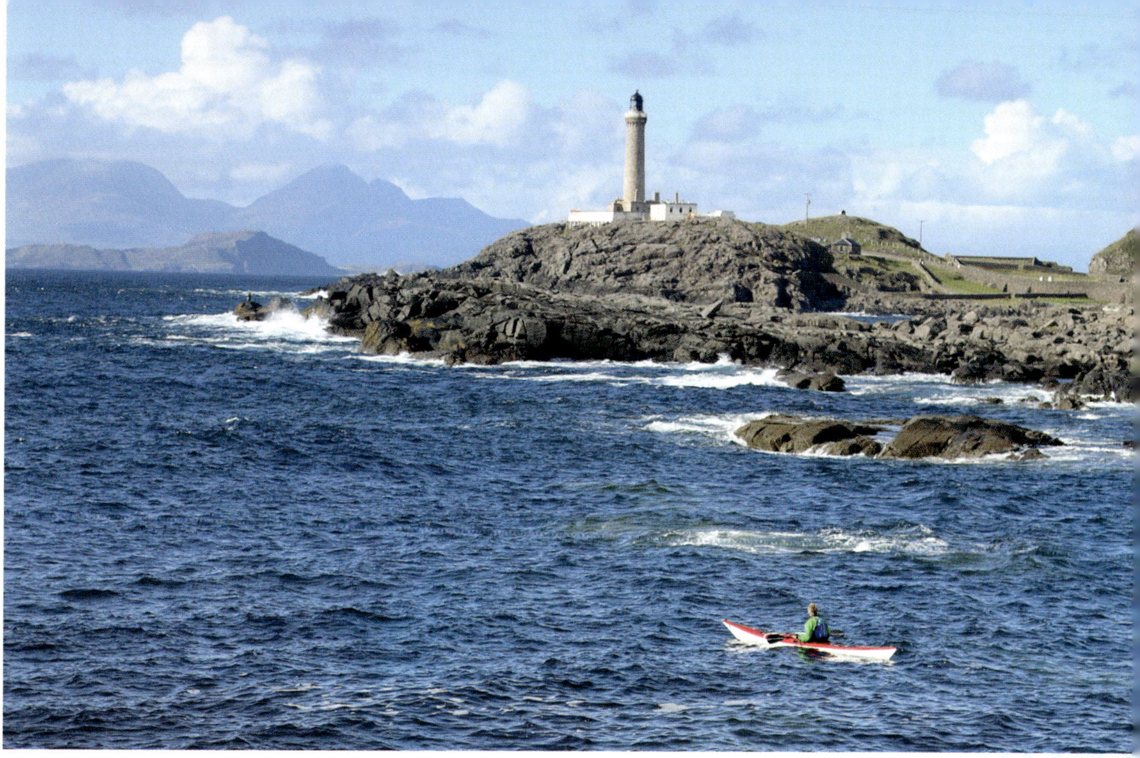

Ardnamurchan Point, Muck and Rum behind

Ardnamurchan Point

No. 47 | **Grade C** | **62km** | **OS Sheets 40 and 47**

Tidal Port	Oban
Start	△ Salen – Camas Torsa (NM 681 631)
Finish	○ Ardtoe (NM 627 707)
HW/LW	HW/LW at Salen is around 10 minutes after Oban.
Tidal Times	In Loch Sunart: The outgoing tidal stream starts at about 1 hour and 30 minutes after HW Oban. The ingoing tidal stream starts at about 5 hours before HW Oban.
	Off Ardnamurchan Point: The NE going stream starts about 5 hours and 25 minutes before HW Oban. The SW going stream starts about 1 hour after HW Oban.
Max Rate Sp	Off Ardnamurchan Point 1.5 knots. In Loch Sunart 0.5 knots.
Coastguard	Stornoway, tel. 01851 702013, VHF weather every 3 hours from 0710.

Introduction

This headland is the most westerly point on the British mainland. For those who sail, it marks a change between southern waters with many sheltered anchorages and a coastline that is altogether more dramatic.

Impressive cliffs heading towards Ardnamurchan Point

Starting at Salen and finishing at Ardtoe allows the entire peninsula to be paddled in all its variety. The route is usually paddled over two or three days. There are some great campsites and the shuttle to finish is minimal.

Description

The jetty at Salen is often busy and offers little parking. The Forestry Commission parking area at Camas Torsa, 1.5km further down the road, has plenty of parking and an easy carry to the water. Leaving here, the wooded shores of Loch Sunart lead to Glenborrodale that overlooks the enticing group of islands of Carna, Risga and Oronsay. Otters are often seen along this section of coastline and there will be plenty of herons flying around in their almost prehistoric way. There are some impressive 'grand design' new-build houses to marvel at as you approach Glenborrodale, recognisable by its stately castle. Originally built in 1901 for the diamond magnate Mr C. D. Rudd, the castle now forms part of Ardnamurchan estates. Along the coastline there are plenty of places to pull ashore for a rest, all generally on low-angled stony beaches.

The impressive headland of Rubha Àird Shlignich marks a change from the sheltered wooded loch to a more exposed rugged coastline. Sea eagles are often seen off this headland. The coastline continues to rise steeply out of the sea and Maclean's Nose forms a wild and impressive headland. From here the Isle of Mull is easily seen. At Kilchoan be sure to take a rest, as if the sea is rough off Ardnamurchan Point it will be the only opportunity for a while.

From Kilchoan the steep coastline and cliffs are unrelenting, the view out to sea dominated by the island of Coll. This section of coastline is as dramatic as you would hope for Britain's most westerly point. Midway along this dramatic section of coastline is the small island of Eilean nan Seachd Seisrichean. Behind this there is a south-facing bay where it is often possible to land. Before long the point and the impressive lighthouse come into view. There is a fantastic landing spot and campsite at Port Mìn.

After the lighthouse there are plentiful bays all offering beautiful sandy beaches and places to land. The beach on the east side of Rubha an Dùin Bhàin is a fine campsite. Beyond here a section of impressive cliffs provide plenty of interest to Fascadale and Port Bàn. After this, lower-lying cliffs lead to the finish at Ardtoe, with plenty of places to stop all along this coastline.

Arriving at Ardtoe the view is dominated by the expanse of sandy beaches that line the coastline as well as the inland mountains towering high beyond. The little beach found at the road head provides the perfect finish and is a very short walk to the convenient car park.

Ardnamurchan Lighthouse

The 36 metre granite tower soars 55 metres above the rocks, and was built in 1849 using granite from the Island of Mull. It was designed by Alan Stevenson, uncle of Robert Louis Stevenson, whose family designed most of Scotland's lighthouses over a period of 150 years. It is the only lighthouse in the world designed in an 'Egyptian' style.

The former lighthouse keepers' cottages and outbuildings have been managed by the Ardnamurchan Lighthouse Trust since 1996. They are open now as a visitor centre.

Tides and weather

Ardnamurchan Point itself is exposed to all swell and wind directions and therefore good conditions need to be planned for to carry out this trip. Do not be lulled into a false sense of security if the sea is calm at Ardtoe or Salen, the point itself is a very different place.

There is minimal tidal flow on the north or south sides of the peninsula. Within Loch Sunart, in the narrows around the islands at Glenborrodale, some tidal movement may be detected, so if possible plan to make use of this. Off Ardnamurchan Point itself there is not as much flow as you would expect off a major headland, however if possible plan to make use of the tidal flow, and be aware of the eddies that can form either side of the point.

Additional information

At Salen there is a shop at the jetty but at Camas Torsa there are no amenities. At Ardtoe, where a small fee is requested for parking, there is a tap with fresh water, however no other amenities. There is a small, basic campsite/caravan park at Ardtoe. At the village of Acharacle that is passed on the shuttle there are public toilets and a well-stocked shop.

Variations

For a short day out, paddling around Ardnamurchan Point starting/finishing at Kilchoan (NM 480 636) and Portuairk (NM 438 683) works well. There is limited parking at Portuairk so please park considerately. It is also possible to start the trip at Glenborrodale, where the road comes close to the sea a few kilometres west of the village.

Portuairk is also a good place to set off from for a day trip out to the Isle of Muck, about 11km to the north.

The Small Isles

Introduction

The Small Isles consist of the islands of Rum, Eigg, Muck and Canna, with Sanday linked to Canna at low tide by a causeway. They are accessed by a 12–16km open water crossing from the mainland or the Island of Skye, or alternatively by making use of the ferry service from Mallaig. If using the ferry you can walk on, either carrying your kayak or ideally making use of a trolley, paying a small fee for the kayak as well as the foot passenger fare.

The islands are a magical place to spend some time, with each one having its own distinct character. Rum, the largest, is diamond shaped and some would say the 'jewel in the crown' of the islands. Renowned for its wildlife, particularly the white-tailed sea eagles and Manx shearwaters, it has a rich and somewhat eccentric human history along with exposed coastline with soaring cliffs, immaculate sandy beaches and a couple of ideally-situated mountain bothies to make use of. Eigg has its distinctive mountain, An Sgùrr, a 'singing' beach, plenty of exposed and remote coastlines and a unique community that owns the island and lives in a self-sufficient, sustainable way. Muck is the smallest of the islands, and has an intimate and friendly feel about it. With some rugged coastlines and sheltered bays it is small enough to get to know well, particularly the friendly café. Canna and Sanday are also small and welcoming. The most westerly and therefore remotest of the Small Isles, with a wild and exposed west and north coast, they have an 'out there' feel about them.

Tides and weather

All of the islands have exposed and committing sections of coastlines, in particular on their western sides. These coastlines are fully exposed to the swell and wind; therefore require careful planning and good weather to enjoy. That said, being islands they also all have their sheltered coastlines, so if the weather does change there is always a sheltered side to be found. Sheltered from the prevailing winds, each of the islands has their own pier with associated ferry service, so escape in poor weather is usually possible.

Off the east and west coasts of all the islands there will be tidal movement to be considered, this also found in some of the sounds separating the islands. With some of this tidal movement flowing up to four knots, tidal knowledge is required to safely enjoy these islands.

Arriving on Eigg (the easy way!)

The Sgùrr of Eigg

Eigg & Muck

No. 48 | Grade C | 42/72km | OS Sheets 39 and 40

Tidal Port	Ullapool
Start	△ Eigg Pier/Rhue (NM 485 838/NM 627 852)
Finish	○ Eigg Pier/Rhue (NM 485 838/NM 627 852)
HW/LW	HW/LW at Eigg is around 40 minutes before Ullapool.
Tidal Times	In Loch nan Ceall: The ingoing stream starts at about 5 hours and 45 minutes after HW Ullapool. The outgoing steam starts at about 50 minutes before HW Ullapool.
	Between Eigg and the mainland: The N going stream starts at about 6 hours after HW Ullapool. The S going stream starts at about 10 minutes before HW Ullapool.
	Around Eigg and Muck: The N going stream starts at about 6 hours after HW Ullapool. The S going stream starts at about HW Ullapool.
Max Rate Sp	Off the east coast of Eigg 4 knots. Off the east and west coasts of Muck 4 knots. In the Sound of Eigg 3 knots. Between Eigg and the mainland 1 knot. In the North and South channels of Loch nan Ceall 1–2 knots.
Coastguard	Stornoway, tel. 01851 702013, VHF weather every 3 hours from 0710.

Rum from Camas Sgiotaig, the 'singing sands'

Eigg & Muck

Introduction

Eigg and Muck are the southernmost of the Small Isles. Both are home to vibrant, small communities that offer a warm welcome, and the seas that surround them are home to whales and marine life. This is a journey that will leave long-lasting memories. You can either paddle out to Eigg or use the regular ferry service.

Description

For the paddle out to Eigg, starting at Rhue in Loch nan Ceall is ideal. Leaving here there is a mass of skerries to negotiate, these are a wildlife oasis with golden sands all around. From the skerries there is a 12km open crossing that takes you across to Eigg. With the imposing Sgùrr of Eigg leading you on and the views of Ardnamurchan Point, Skye, Rum and Muck, there is plenty to keep you occupied. There are regular sightings of whales in this area, so keep an eye and ear out for these fantastic creatures of the ocean. Head for the sandy beach at Poll nam Partan below the old ruined fort, south of Kildonan, as your first landing spot on Eigg. If you are stretching your legs after the crossing you may wish to visit the old Celtic cross-slab and ruined church at Kildonan. It is said that St Donan set up a monastery here with 52 of his monks, who in 617 AD were all murdered by the local Pictish queen who apparently had a disliking for missionaries.

If the crossing out to Eigg does not suit due to conditions, time constraints or personal preference, it is easy to take the regular ferry service from Mallaig out to Eigg. You can just walk on with your kayak and then launch at Eigg Pier where the ferry lands, just south of Poll nam Partan.

Island buy-out

In 1997 the island was bought by the Isle of Eigg Heritage Trust, a partnership between the residents of the island, the Highland Council and the Scottish Wildlife Trust. The residents bought the island for £1.75 million, aided by a £1 million gift from an anonymous donor. It led the way in the land reform movement throughout Scotland. In effect, the islanders could own and run their own island. Since this time the island's population has grown by 24% and even more notable is the fact the island has the first completely wind, water and sun-powered electricity grid in the world.

Eigg's southern coastline, overlooked by the Sgùrr of Eigg

The trip heads up the remote east coast to the northern tip of Eigg. If you have time you may wish to stop and explore Eilean Thuilm for fossils that have been found in the rocks of this area. Continuing on around the next headland you will start to get a feel for the more rugged west coast of Eigg as you reach the fantastic beach of Camas Sgiotaig. This is also known as the 'singing sands' as the dry grains of quartz drone underfoot or sing when the wind blows across them. The area of grass behind the beach makes for a fantastic campsite, with a wonderful view northwestward to Rum. It is worth spending the night here to watch the sun set behind the mountains of Rum and then watch the early morning light bathe these shapely mountains the next day.

Surf can often come into this beach, so there is every chance of an early morning wake up shower when leaving to continue the journey. As you cross the Bay of Laig you will reach the most exposed, yet spectacular, part of the trip. This bit of coastline down to the south of Eigg is fully exposed to the westerly seas, has no landings, and is lined by steep cliffs along the entire route. If conditions allow there will be a chance to explore the odd cave and go in amongst the cliffs to enjoy the varied birdlife that uses this part of Eigg for their summer home. On reaching the southern coastline, Muck will be beckoning, and the sandy beach at Gallanach is the place to head for, an idyllic place to relax and enjoy.

From the sandy beaches, head out around the west coast of Muck to savour the wildness of this island while heading for the next easy landing place at Port Mòr. Muck in Gaelic translates into the 'Isle of Pigs', which could have come from the fact that porpoises were known as sea pigs and are often seen in these waters. Port Mòr is the main centre for Muck and is where the small school is situated, along with a café for the weary paddler. It is possible to camp here or, once fuelled up from the café, make the crossing back to Eigg. Aim for Galmisdale where you will find somewhere to camp if required, or be in situ ready for the ferry.

Eigg's exposed west coast

Massacre Cave

Before leaving Galmisdale you might want to walk and find the caves of Uamh Fhraing. It is here in 1577 that 195 Eigg islanders hid from the MacLeods of Skye. The MacLeods were on the island to retaliate after some of them had been sent back to Skye castrated after being caught raping some MacDonald girls on Eigg. The MacLeods found the cave and, in trying to smoke them out, suffocated the 195 islanders. For this reason the cave is known as 'Massacre Cave'.

Whether paddling back to Loch nan Ceall or taking the ferry back to Mallaig, this trip will leave you filled with memories of a great journey. It is with tired bodies, yet fulfilled souls, that you will reach the mainland.

Tides and weather

Due to the long crossings and/or exposed coastlines with few landings, good weather is required to complete this trip. If the weather changes, shelter is never too far away amongst the islands. The west coast of Eigg and the mainland crossing are the most weather dependent sections.

There are relatively strong tidal streams running around much of the islands and these will need to be taken into consideration when planning the trip. Timings will be fairly critical to ensure these are paddled with, as opposed to against. When crossing the tide on the route to and from Muck, careful use of transits will be required to ensure an efficient crossing.

Eigg's south-western coastline with Rum behind

There is a small amount of tide in the North and South Channels of Loch nan Ceall, but this is easy to paddle against if necessary. On the main crossing to Eigg the tidal streams are fairly insignificant.

Additional information

There is a full range of amenities in both Arisaig and Mallaig. For details about the ferries to and from Eigg and Muck from Mallaig go to: www.calmac.co.uk; consider using a kayak trolley to make life easy! There are limited amenities on the islands, however there is a shop at the Eigg Pier with toilets, showers, café and craft shop, as well as a café and craft shop in Port Mòr on Muck.

There are additional launch sites to Rhue if parking is tight at the road head, these are as follows: Rhue (NM 629 854), small bay with private landing pontoon (NM 638 853), bay at NM 648 846 (high water only), Gortenachullish (NM 642 877) or in Arisaig just south of the village where the stream enters the loch (NM 659 859).

Variations

If weather or time dictates it is possible to get the ferry back to Mallaig from Muck, thus avoiding the need to cross back to Eigg. You may also want to consider spending more time out exploring the Small Isles and visiting Rum and maybe Canna. For further information on this see Trips 49 and 50.

Camping at Harris

Rum

No. 49	**Grade C** **50/86km** **OS Sheets 32 and 39**
Tidal Port	Ullapool
Start	▲ Kinloch/Elgol (NM 413 992/NG 515 136)
Finish	◯ Kinloch/Elgol (NM 413 992/NG 515 136)
HW/LW	HW/LW at Kinloch is around 50 minutes before Ullapool.
Tidal Times	Along the SE and SW coasts of Rum: The N going stream starts at about 5 hours and 50 minutes after HW Ullapool. The S going stream starts at about 10 minutes before HW Ullapool.
	In the Sound of Canna: The NE going stream starts at about 6 hours after HW Ullapool. The SW going stream starts at about HW Ullapool.
Max Rate Sp	Off the SE and SW coasts of Rum 3 knots. In the Sound of Canna 1.5 knots.
Coastguard	Stornoway, tel. 01851 702013, VHF weather every 3 hours from 0710.

Introduction

This is an outstanding trip that has everything a sea kayaker could ask for: fantastic cliffs, towering mountains, sandy beaches and plentiful wildlife. There is a real sense of remoteness on

237

49 Rum

the committing coastlines and the crossing out to the island. The passing whales and sea eagles will be your only company for much of this trip. You can either paddle out to Rum or use the regular ferry service.

Description

Starting at Elgol on the Isle of Skye involves a 16km crossing out to the Isle of Rum, a task not to be undertaken lightly. Ideally this crossing will be on a calm day, this being the case it will provide a good chance of seeing the whales and porpoises often seen in this area. The impressive mountains of Rum will gradually draw nearer and the beach just south of Rubha Shamhnan Insir provides a perfect place to aim for. This has a fantastic beach to relax on after the crossing; ideal to enjoy your first taste of Rum.

Alternatively the ferry from Mallaig will take you and your kayak to the pier at Kinloch. This lies eight kilometres south of Rubha Shamhnan Insir and provides a fine paddle with a few extra beaches. Rubha Shamhnan Insir offers an amazing camp spot to relax and enjoy this magical place.

The north coast of Rum is the next destination, with fine views of Skye to the north. You will soon arrive at the beach at Kilmory, a huge expanse of sand, with a smaller white sandy beach at its eastern end. Continuing along the north coast the most westerly of the Small Isles, Canna, starts to dominate the view and the hidden bay of Guirdil will be reached. This bay is home to a mountain bothy, open for all to use and perfect to spend a night in, however it does not provide ideal launching or landing at low water.

Leaving Guirdil, ensure you are well rested and fed. The west coast of the island is next and this is long and committing, with few landing opportunities. The only company you will have along here are the towering cliffs above, the lively seas below and perhaps one of Rum's many sea eagles keeping a watchful eye on your progress.

Wreck Bay's name tells the story; it needs to be a calm day to land here. The stony beach at Harris is the best spot on the west coast, but this may still have surf to deal with. This is a beautiful location looking up to the mountains, overlooked by an unlikely Greek temple. This is the mausoleum that houses the tombs of the eccentric previous owner of Rum, George Bullough, his father, and his wife. Harris provides another good camping venue. Beyond here the west coast

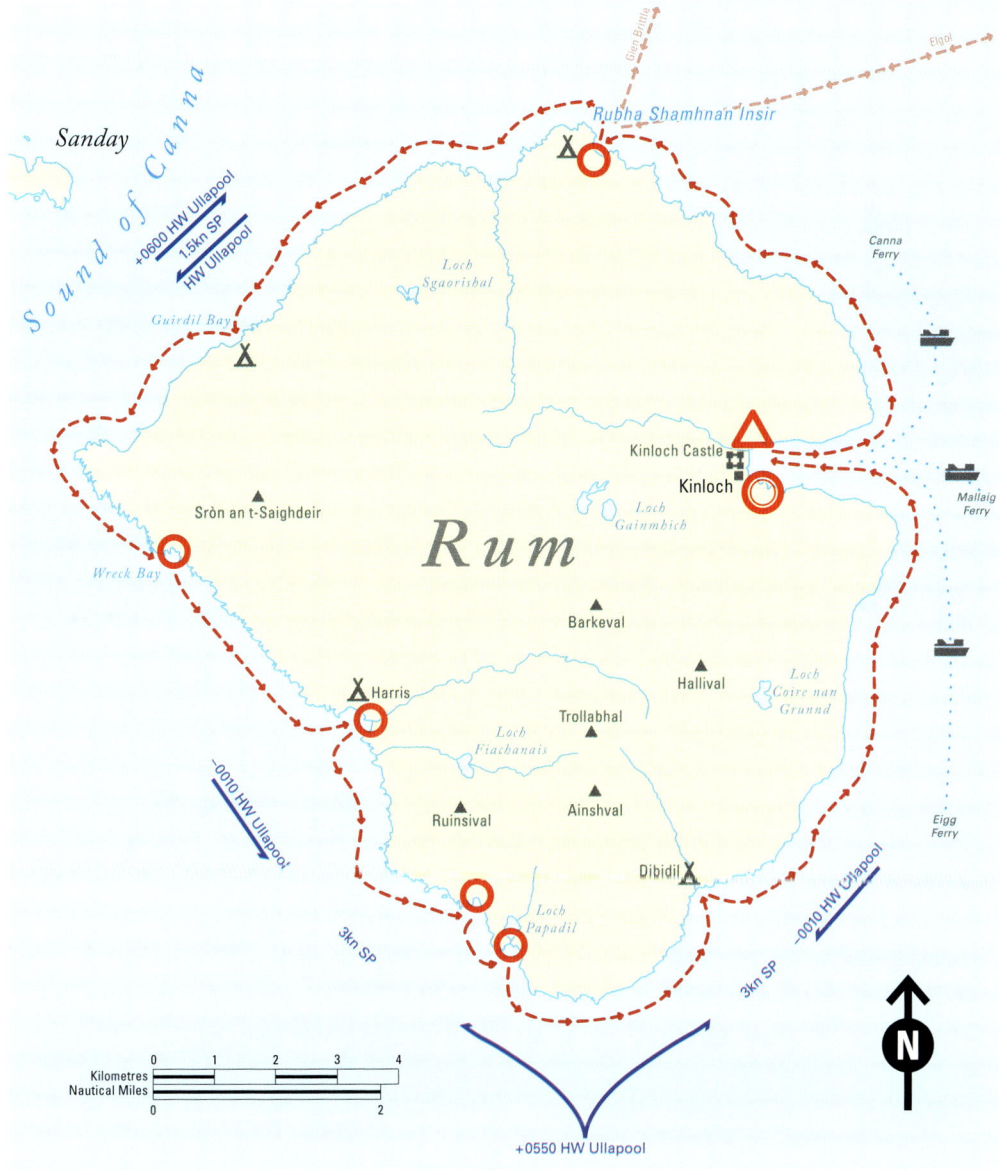

George Bullough's mausoleum at Harris

continues in a similar dramatic fashion, and on calmer days you can land at Inbhir Ghil and Loch Papadil. At Loch Papadil there is a perfectly-situated inland loch where George Bullough built a lodge for his wife Lady Monica Bullough. Unfortunately she did not like it and it is now a ruin.

On the east coast the sea will be calmer, with views of the islands of Eigg and Muck. At Dibidil there is another mountain bothy that provides a place to stay for the night not far from the coast. Continue up the east coast to the tree-lined shores of Loch Scresort. The main settlement on the island and pier is found at the head of this loch at Kinloch. It is a very small community, but 2009 saw the start of a phased transfer of land and assets in and around the village from the island's owners Scottish Natural Heritage to the Isle of Rum Community Trust. If time allows, take the time to visit, or at least go and see, the incredible Kinloch Castle.

The ferry back to Mallaig departs from the pier at Kinloch. If you are paddling back to Elgol the long crossing will start just up the coastline. Whatever the chosen route off, the island will no doubt leave some magical memories to be savoured for a long time to come.

Tides and weather

Due to the committing nature of this trip, a period of settled weather will be required to make it possible. The crossing and the west coast are exposed to the wind and swell and this should be considered carefully in the planning. Off the southern and western coasts of Rum and the Sound of Canna the tidal streams can run up to 3 knots, and with opposing wind this can provide rougher conditions. When planning the trip these tides need to be taken into consideration to ensure they are aiding the journey as opposed to making it difficult. On the crossing from Skye there is negligible tidal movement and any wind will have a far greater effect.

The remote west coast of Rum

Kinloch Castle

This castle was built in 1902 by George Bullough, whose family owned the island from 1888 until 1957 when they sold it to the Nature Conservancy Council for £26,000. Having inherited the island from his father, George Bullough built the castle after sailing around the world. Money was no object to him and he imported a workforce and materials from all over the UK. The finished castle is a sight to behold and in its day housed air conditioning in the billiard hall, a Victorian jacuzzi bath, birds of paradise in the conservatory, and live turtles and alligators in heated tanks! George Bullough's guests were brought to Mallaig by private train, taken by steam yacht to the island where they were met by Albion motorcars, which he kept on the island. The island's current owners do not have quite the same funds so sadly the castle is gradually falling into disrepair.

Additional information

At Elgol there are public toilets and at Mallaig there is a full range of amenities. If catching the ferry to the island from Mallaig, times and information can be found at www.calmac.co.uk; consider using a kayak trolley to make life easy! On the island there is a well-provisioned shop, post office and in the summer a small café, all found at Kinloch.

Crossing the Sound of Rum

Variations

This trip works very well combined with Canna and Sanday if time allows. If a longer period is possible then Eigg and Muck can also be visited. See Trips 48 and 50 for further information. By using the ferry it is possible to start on Rum but finish on any of the islands and catch the ferry back to Mallaig; this can provide plenty of flexibility to maximise time out on the islands. Starting from Glen Brittle (NG 409 205) on Skye also works, giving a slightly shorter crossing.

Rum's sea eagles and Manx shearwaters

In 1912 white-tailed sea eagles were exterminated on Rum, and not long after this they became extinct in Scotland. In 1975 a programme was launched to reintroduce sea eagles to Scotland, and this started on Rum. Young eagles were brought from Norway and released into the wild, within ten years 82 young eagles had been released. The reintroduction was a great success and now we are lucky enough to marvel at the many breeding pairs of sea eagles around the Scottish coastline, with Rum still being home to many.

Rum is also home to the graceful Manx shearwater, seen flying effortlessly at speed close to the sea, with its wing tips practically touching the water. These birds spend their winters off Brazil and return to Rum every summer to breed in underground burrows high up in the island's mountains. With a breeding colony of 70,000 it is one of the largest in the world.

Canna and Sanday with Rum in the background

Canna & Sanday

No. 50	**Grade C** 25/66km **OS Sheets 32 and 39**
Tidal Port	Ullapool
Start	△ Canna Harbour/Glen Brittle (NG 278 051/NG 409 205)
Finish	○ Canna Harbour/Glen Brittle (NG 278 051/NG 409 205)
HW/LW	HW/LW at Canna is around 50 minutes before Ullapool.
Tidal Times	In the Sound of Canna: The NE going stream starts at about 6 hours after HW Ullapool. The SW going stream starts at about HW Ullapool.
	Off the west coast of Canna: The N going stream starts at about 6 hours and 15 minutes after HW Ullapool. The S going stream starts at about 15 minutes after HW Ullapool.
Max Rate Sp	Off the east coast of Sanday 4–5 knots. Off the west coast of Canna 2.5 knots. In the Sound of Canna 1.5 knots.
Coastguard	Stornoway, tel. 01851 702013, VHF weather every 3 hours from 0710.

Introduction

Canna is the most western of the Small Isles and has a remote and 'out there' feel about it. The north and west coasts offer committing paddling with views across to the Outer Hebrides,

Dùn Mòr on Sanday, Canna behind

Canna & Sanday

whereas the south coast harbours the island's tiny village and more sheltered water. Sanday is joined to Canna by a bridge, and combined they make for a great trip away from it all with only wildlife for company. You can either paddle out to Canna or use the regular ferry service.

Description

The beach at Glen Brittle of Skye is the starting point for the paddle out to Canna and Sanday. The headland of Rubha an Dùnain is reached after 5km, and it may be worth stretching the legs here because it is another 16km of open water to Canna. The long, open crossing will give some prospective of how 'out there' Canna is. Aim for the pier on the island's south-eastern corner, as this provides shelter and a place to rest when landing after the crossing.

The ferry from Mallaig arrives at this pier, and this is the alternative way to get out and explore Canna and Sanday, carrying your kayak on board the ferry. Whichever way you arrive, it is worth taking the time stretch the legs and visit the small community built up along the short road that leads to the pier. Here you will find the café and small community shop, ideal for some refreshments before paddling around the island.

From the pier paddle across the natural harbour to Sanday. Heading around the east coast of the island some rougher water may be encountered as this is where some of the fastest tidal waters are found. On the southern coast of Sanday there is plenty of interest with rock hopping and geos along the way, as well as some great caves to explore. Look out for the impressive puffin colony on Dùn Mòr as you paddle past. Continue around Sanday until the bridge that joins it with Canna is seen, just before this is a fantastic beach to stop on and enjoy. It is a good camp site too. On Sanday you will see the school which, depending on how many children are living on the island at the time, may or may not be open. There is also a new arts centre in the former St Edwards Chapel.

Along the south side of Canna you come to another stunning sandy beach in Tarbert Bay, another good stopping place or campsite. From here the western tip of Canna is soon reached. While paddling around this you will get a fantastic sense of remoteness, with dramatic cliffs and distant views to the Outer Hebrides to the north and west. Ten kilometres to the south-west you may also see the impressive lighthouse that sits on the tiny island of Oigh-sgeir or Hyskeir. The light was established in 1904, and in 1997 it was the last lighthouse in Scotland to become automated. It was here that the livestock from Canna used to be taken for summer grazing; this must have been quite a challenge! The north coast of Canna is stunning, with plenty of wildlife and a dramatic coastline soaring out of an often-lively ocean. Just past Sgeir nan Sgarbh (NG 220 060) there is a sandy beach known as Garrisdale where it is often possible to land; a great place to take in the scenery as well as a fantastic camping spot. Look out for golden eagles often seen in this area, and the larger sea eagles usually seen on the higher cliffs further along the north coast. The coastline continues in dramatic fashion for the entire length of the northern edge of Canna, another possible landing at Camas Thairbearnais on a calm day being the only respite from impressive cliffs and caves.

Grey seals will be regular companions as you paddle, along with the numerous sea birds flying noisily overhead. At Iorcail there is sea stack to marvel at that nestles below the tallest and most

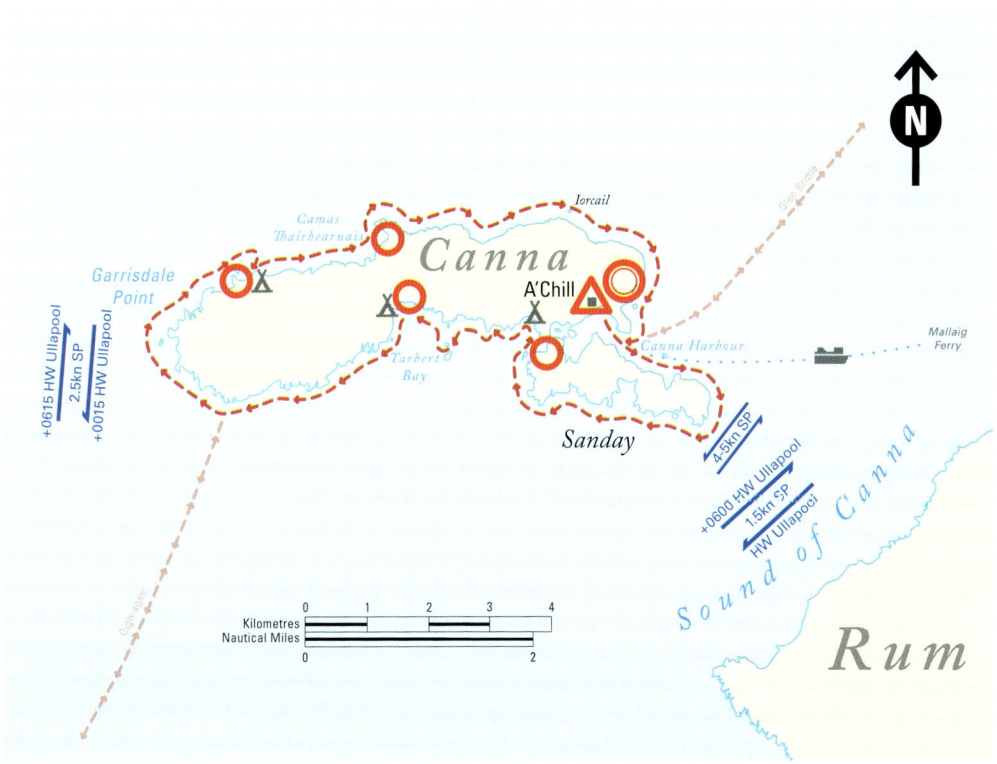

© Camping at Garrisdale

spectacular cliffs along this coastline. Just beyond this be sure to look out for An t-Each, where you will find the home of the many puffins you may well have already seen on the trip, their nests in the burrows of this exposed little outcrop. From here a short paddle will see you back into the sheltered harbour of Canna, and an opportunity to land and take a rest. If catching the ferry back then perhaps some time in the café may be available – if undertaking the long crossing back to Skye, then maybe it is better to get started!

Call for families for Canna

In 2006 the National Trust for Scotland who own and manage Canna decided to invite two families to rent properties on the island, in an effort to attract new skills and spirit to the island community. The invitation was mainly aimed at people with 'skills in building, plumbing and gardening'. The call was global and over 400 responses were received, from places as varied as Germany, Sweden and India. In 2007 a 'new' family arrived on the island and in 2008 another family followed, both with the required 'skills' to support and enhance the community. The community has now formed the Isle of Canna Community Development Trust, which provides a mechanism for future economic growth in tandem with the conservation and preservation of the island's environment.

Canna's north coast

Tides and weather

Canna and Sanday are exposed to wind and swell from all directions, with much of the coastline offering very little in the way of shelte. This is a trip to save for fine weather only.

Off the east coast of Sanday the tidal stream can run pretty fast and although short-lived with eddies either side, it is still worth planning to take advantage of the tidal streams. Off the west coast of Canna there are also some tidal streams to consider, so plan to make use of them if possible. On the crossing out to Canna the tidal streams are negligible; it will be the wind that will affect maintaining an efficient course.

Additional information

There are no amenities at Glen Brittle, and at low water it can be quite a walk to the sea (a trolley and/or making use of the river can assist). At Mallaig there is a full range of amenities. For the ferry to the island, times and information can be found at www.calmac.co.uk; consider using a kayak trolley to make life easy! On Canna there is a tap at the pier as well as a café and small shop. The island also offers a great campsite, with pods and caravans available to rent as well. Although not immediately next to the water, the owners will pick you up from your kayaks if required; information can be found at www.cannacampsite.com. Showers and toilets are also available at the farm (NG 270 053), showers operating with a £1 coin.

Canna's most impressive cliffs and the sea stack Iorcail

Variations

This trip works very well combined with Rum if time allows. If a longer period is possible Eigg and Muck can also be visited. See Trips 48 and 49 for further information. By using the ferry, it is possible to start on Canna but finish on any of the islands and catch the ferry back to Mallaig; this can provide plenty of flexibility to maximise time out on the islands.

A trip out to the tiny island of Oigh-sgeir or Hyskeir (NM 156 962) is also recommended if the conditions are appropriate for the 10km crossing. There is landing on the island in most conditions and the impressive lighthouse will guide you there!

Appendix A – HM Coastguard and Emergency Services

In UK waters, HM Coastguard coordinates rescues and emergency services. They also broadcast weather forecasts and inform water users about potential hazards in their area. They monitor VHF channel 16 and you should use this channel to make initial contact; you will then be directed to a working channel. Note the times here are for UT. During the UK summer months remember to add 1 hour.

All of the trips in this guide fall within the area covered by Stornoway HM Coastguard station:

HMCG	Area	Telephone	Weather announced on CH16 (UTC)
Stornoway	Cape Wrath to Mull of Galloway	01851 702013	0110, 0410, 0710, 1010, 1310, 1610, 1910, 2210

Appendix B – Weather Information

The weather is the most discussed topic within the communities that make up the UK coastline, and this is especially true on the north-west coast of Scotland which is affected by a wide range of weather conditions. The Met Office (www.metoffice.gov.uk) was founded in 1854 to provide information about the weather to marine communities. It was not until 1922 that forecasts were first broadcast by BBC radio, a tradition that still remains today.

The Met Office website provides detailed predictions for the weather all over the UK, but if you are away from a computer or phone with web access then there are several other ways of obtaining a reliable weather forecast.

RADIO

BBC RADIO 4 (92.5–94.6 FM AND 198 LW)

  0048 – Shipping and inshore waters forecast, coastal station reports

  0520 – Shipping and inshore waters forecast, coastal station reports

BBC RADIO SCOTLAND (92–95 FM AND 810 MW)

  1904 (Mon – Fri) – Outdoor conditions, including inshore waters forecast

  0704 (Sat and Sun) – Outdoor conditions, including inshore waters forecast

  2204/2004 (Sat/Sun) Outdoor conditions, including inshore waters forecast

WEB

Met Office – www.metoffice.gov.uk

BBC Weather – www.bbc.co.uk/weather

XC Weather – www.xcweather.co.uk

Windfinder (includes swell forecast) – www.windfinder.com

Magic Seaweed (surf forecasts) – www.magicseaweed.com

Appendix C – Mean Tidal Ranges

Tidal Port	Mean Spring Range (metres)	Mean Neap Range (metres)
Dover	6.0	3.2
Ullapool	4.5	1.8
Oban	3.3	1.1

Appendix D – Glossary of Gaelic Words

Before the advent of maps and charts the Scottish fishermen navigated the waters by local knowledge. To help them with this they would descriptively name many of the coastal features. This way they could describe to each other where they went or how to get there. When translating the Gaelic names around the coastline you will learn a lot about the area from these very descriptive names. The fishermen only fished a relatively small area near to their crofts, and therefore would just name all the features in that area. The next area's fishermen would then name the features in their area likewise. As a result you will see lots of repetition in the Gaelic names as, for example, each area would have its own 'black rock'. Here is a list of some of the more common Gaelic names you will find while kayaking the Scottish coastline. A lot of the original mapmakers would have been non-Gaelic speaking, which is why you'll find variations of spelling. To make matters more complicated, 'local' names, particularly for wildlife, can vary from area to area!

COASTAL FEATURES

Acairseid	Anchorage
Aiseag	Ferry
Ard or Aird	Promontory or Height
Bàgh	Bay
Bodha	Rock over which waves break
Bogha	Arch
Cabhsair	Causeway
Cala	Port
Camus	Bay/Inlet
Caol or Caolas	Narrows or Kyle/Firth/Strait
Carraig	Rock/Cliff
Ceann	Headland/Point
Cladach	Shore/Stony Beach
Cleit	Rocky Ridge
Coire	Whirlpool
Cuan	Ocean
Eilean	Island
Geò or Geodha	Chasm/Rift

Innis	Island or Meadow/Pasture
Long	Ship
Mol	Shingly Beach
Maol	Promontory
Muir/Mara	Sea/of the sea
Oitir	Sandbank
Port	Harbour
Poll	Fishing Bank
Rinn or Roinn	Point or Promontory
Rubha, Rubh or Ru	Point/Headland
Sgeir	Skerry/Reef
Sròn	Nose/Point
Sruth	Current
Taobh	Coast
Traigh	Tidal Beach
Uamh	Cave

LAND FEATURES

Abhainn	River
Aill	Steep river bank
Allt	Stream
Aonach	Moor/Plain/a desert place
Bàrr	Top/Summit
Bealach	Pass
Beinn	Mountain
Bidean	Pinnacle
Bruthach	Steep Place/Brae
Bun	River Mouth/Source/Root/Base
Caisteal	Castle
Cill or Ceall	Church or Burial Place
Clach	Stone
Clais	Ditch
Cnap	Hillock
Coille	Wood/Forest
Creag	Crag/Cliff
Dùn	Fortress/Castle
Eas or Easan	Waterfall
Fraoch	Heather
Glac	Hollow
Inbhir	River Mouth
Linn	Pool
Meall	Rounded Hill/Mound
Ord	Steep Hill
Sgùrr	Large Conical Hill
Slochd	Hollow
Tigh	House

Glossary of Gaelic Words

COMMON DESCRIPTIONS FOR THESE FEATURES

Àrd	High
Bàn	Pale/White
Beag or Bheag	Small
Buidhe	Yellow
Dearg	Red
Dubh	Black/Dark
Domhain	Deep
Donn	Brown
Fada	Long
Garbh	Rough/Thick
Geal	White
Geàrr	Short
Glas	Pale/Grey
Gorm	Green/Blue
Liath	Grey/Blue
Mòr or Mhòr	Big/Large
Naomh	Saint
Ruabh	Red/Brown
Uaine	Green

WILD LIFE

An Leumadair	Dolphin
Buthaid	Puffin
Caora	Sheep
Coinneanach	Rabbit
Cù	Dog
Eun-mara	Seabird
Faoileag	Black Headed Gull
Gille-Brìghde	Oyster Catcher
Gobhar	Goat
Iasg	Fish
Iolaire	Eagle
Madadh	Wolf/Dog
Muc-mhara	Whale (pig of the sea)
Puthag	Porpoise
Ròn	Seal
Sgarbh	Cormorant
Sùlaire	Gannet
Trilleachan	Sandpiper

Thanks to Anne Martin for technical comment.

Appendix E – Trip Planning Route Card – Users' Guide

The trip planning route card is designed to be used in conjunction with the information supplied in each route chapter in the book. In addition to this you will also require a set of relevant tide timetables. If the blank route card is photocopied, all the information for your route to be paddled can be worked out on it. This way it will help you plan your paddle as effectively as possible, and then allow you to have all the information you need on a handy piece of paper. This can be displayed in your map case on your kayak for easy reference. To help you use the card please refer to the following example and guidelines:

Trip Name & Number	*Rubha Hunish*		
Page Number	*127*	VHF Weather	*0710, 1010, 1310, 1610*
Date	*10th August 2017*	Weather Forecast	*Fair, visibility good, wind W F2-3*
Coastguard Contact	*Stornoway, 01851 702013*		

- Fill in the name, number and page of your chosen trip for easy future reference.
- When choosing the date of the trip, check in the chapter's 'Tide & Weather' section as to whether it will need specific tides that will dictate the date.
- Obtain a weather forecast using information supplied in Appendix B.
- Coastguard contacts can be found in the introductory info for each trip and in Appendix A.

TIDAL INFORMATION

Tidal Port		Mean Sp Range	4.5m	Local Port			
Ullapool		Mean Np Range	1.8m	*Duntulm*			

Tidal Port Tide Times (UT)	Height in Metres	Tidal Range in Metres	HW/LW	+1 Hr for BST?	Local Port HW/LW Time Difference	Local Port HW/LW	Sp or Np Tides
0018	0.8	4.3	LW	0118	-0030	0048	*Sp*
0620	5.1	4.3	HW	0720	-0030	0650	*Sp*
1241	0.8	4.7	LW	1341	-0030	1311	*Sp*
1834	5.5		HW	1934	-0030	1904	*Sp*

- Identify Tidal Port from the chapter introductory information.
- Identify Mean Spring and Neap Ranges from tide timetable or see Appendix C. These will help identify Spring or Neap Tides and Estimated Maximum Speed.
- Local Port is also found in the chapter introductory information.
- Obtain the Tidal Port Times and Height in Metres from your tide timetables. Usually four times and heights, but occasionally three.
- To work out the Tidal Range in Metres subtract the LW heights from the HW heights.

- Add 1 Hr for BST? Add an hour to your Tidal Port Times if you are in British Summer Time.
- The Local Port HW/LW Time Difference can be found in the chapter introduction.
- To work out Sp or Np Tides compare your Tidal Range to the Mean Sp and Np Ranges.

TIDAL STREAM TIMES

Location	Direction of Tidal Stream	Tidal Stream Time Diff.	Tidal Port HW (BST?)	Tidal Stream Start Time	Tidal Rate	Est. Max Speed
Eilean Trodday	W	+0225	0720	0945	2.5kn	2.5kn
	E	-0400	1934	1534		

Location	Direction of Tidal Stream	Tidal Stream Time Diff.	Tidal Port HW (BST?)	Tidal Stream Start Time	Tidal Rate	Est. Max Speed
Rubha Hunish	SW	+0210	0720	0930	3kn	3kn
	NE	-0430	1934	1504		

Location	Direction of Tidal Stream	Tidal Stream Time Diff.	Tidal Port HW (BST?)	Tidal Stream Start Time	Tidal Rate	Est. Max Speed

- Use the Location as indicated in the chapter introductory and tidal information.
- For the Direction of Tidal Stream there are generally four periods of tidal movement every 24 hours. Direction for the Tidal Stream Start Time soonest after 0000 hours in the first box.
- The Tidal Stream Time Difference is found in the chapter introductory and tidal information.
- Tidal Port HW can be transposed from above converting to BST if appropriate.
- The Tidal Stream Start Time is worked out by subtracting/adding the Tidal Stream Difference from/to the Tidal Port HW time.
- Tidal Rate is the average spring speed for the tidal stream, found in the chapter introduction.
- Estimate Maximum Speed based on whether it is Spring, Neap or in between tides.
- If it is Springs use the speed given in the chapter's introductory and tidal information.

- On Neap Tides halve this spring rate.
- When in between springs and neaps use the average of the spring and neap speeds.
- Note that speeds given are average spring rates. If paddling on a spring tide look to see if your Tidal Range in Metres is bigger or smaller than the Mean Sp Range. If it is bigger the speeds will be faster than average spring rates given.

ROUTE PLAN

	Location	Notes	ETA	ETD
Start	Staffin			0930
1st	Kilmaluag Bay	Rocky beach by old salmon fishery	1130	1230
2nd	Rubha Hunish	Small landing east side of headland, need to round headland before tide changes at 1504	1400	1430
Finish	Duntulm	Rocky landing, beware of surf if there is swell	1530	

- When choosing Locations for the Route Plan use places that have tidal importance and where you may want to stop.
- When working out ETD (Estimated Time of Departure) or ETA (Estimated Time of Arrival) enter key times which need to be met for the best use of tidal stream first, as recommended in Tide & Weather. Work out other times around these.
- To work out the times an average paddling speed of 6km/h or 3 knots can be used. This can be adjusted to suit your needs, or time added for coastal exploration if desired.

Please feel free to photocopy the blank Trip Planning Route Card on the page overleaf.
An A4 downloadable version is available on our website.
For this and other resources go to www.pesdapress.com, follow the links to the Scottish Sea Kayaking page and look for the download symbol in the right-hand column.

www.pesdapress.com

Trip Planning Route Card

TIDAL INFORMATION

Trip Name & Number		
Page Number	VHF Weather	
Date	Weather Forecast	
Coastguard Contact		

| Tidal Port | | Mean Sp Range | | Local Port | |
| | | Mean Np Range | | | |

Tidal Port Tide Times (UT)	Height in Metres	Tidal Range in Metres	HW/LW	+1 Hr for BST?	Local Port HW/LW Time Difference	Local Port HW/LW	Sp or Np Tides

TIDAL STREAM TIMES

Location	Direction of Tidal Stream	Tidal Stream Time Diff.	Tidal Port HW (BST?)	Tidal Stream Start Time	Tidal Rate	Est. Max Speed

Location	Direction of Tidal Stream	Tidal Stream Time Diff.	Tidal Port HW (BST?)	Tidal Stream Start Time	Tidal Rate	Est. Max Speed

Location	Direction of Tidal Stream	Tidal Stream Time Diff.	Tidal Port HW (BST?)	Tidal Stream Start Time	Tidal Rate	Est. Max Speed

ROUTE PLAN

	Location	Notes	ETA	ETD
Start				
1st				
2nd				
3rd				
4th				
5th				
Finish				

Index of Place Names

A

Acairseid an Rubha 182
Acairseid Eilean a' Chlèirich 62
Acairseid Mhòr 121
A'Chailleach 17
Acharacle 228
Achiltibuie 56, 57, 58, 59, 60, 64
Achmelvich 49, 50, 52
Achmelvich Bay 51
Achmore 73
Achnahaird 53
Achnahaird Bay 54
Acrib Islands 147
Àird 96, 98
Aird of Sleat 184
Airor 206, 208
Airor Island 206
Altandhu 56
Am Bodach 17
Am Buachaille 16
Am Famhair 154
An Dùn 91
An Garbh-eilean 18
Annat peninsula 71, 73
An Sgùrr 229
An t-Aigeach 158
An t-Each 246
Anthrax 77
An t-Iasgair 134, 140
Applecross 69, 97, 100, 102, 104, 106
Applecross Inn 102
Applecross peninsula 97, 98, 103
Arctic convoys 83, 88
Ardarroch 97, 100, 101, 102
Ardban 100
Ardintigh 202
Ardmair 65, 66, 68
Ardmore Point 23, 148
Ardnamurchan 191
Ardnamurchan Lighthouse 227
Ardnamurchan Lighthouse Trust 227
Ardnamurchan Point 191, 225, 226, 228
Ardtoe 225, 226, 227, 228
Ardtreck Point 162, 168
Ardvasar 183, 184
Arisaig 191, 209, 212, 216, 220, 236
Arisaig skerries 214, 215
Armadale 181, 183, 184, 208
Arnisdale 197, 198, 199, 200
Arnisdale House 198
Arnish 120, 122
Ascrib Islands 145, 146, 148
Aultbea 79, 82, 84

B

Badachro 92
Badachro Bay 90
Badachro Inn 90, 92
Badcall Bay 30
Badenscaille burial ground 62
Badenscallie 61, 63, 64
Badentarbat Bay 58
Badluarach 71, 73
Badluarach jetty 64, 72, 73
Bàgh Leathann 30
Balnakeil 20
Balnakeil Bay 15, 19
Barrisdale Bay 199
Battle of Largs 189
Bay of Culkein 48
Bay of Laig 234
Bay of Stoer 47, 48
Bay of the Forsaken Ones 183
Bealach na Bà 100, 101, 104
Bearreraig Bay 125, 126
Beinn Sgritheall 198
Ben Mor Coigach 66, 73
Ben Stack 23
Big Sand 85, 86, 88, 91
Biod an Athair 154
Black Islands 107, 109
Black Isles 69
black rabbits 134, 141
Bogha Mòr 26
Bonnie Prince Charles 215
Boreraig 178, 179
Borreraig 154
Borrowdale Islands 214, 215, 216
Borve 148
Bothies, mountain 38
Bottle Island 62, 73
Brandarsaig Bay 159
Bridge Cottage café, The 88
Broadford 115, 117, 118
Brochel 121
Brochel Castle 120
Brothers Point 126
Bullough, George 239, 240, 241
Bullough, Lady Monica 240

C

Cailleach Head 71, 72, 73, 76
Caisteal Maol 189
Caledonian MacBrayne Ferries 138
Calum's Road 120, 121, 122
Camalaig Bay 150
Camas a' Chruthaich 76
Camas Allt Eoin Thòmais 88
Camas Bàn 157, 159, 160, 164
Camas Coille 54
Camas Daraich 182
Camas Eilean Ghlais 55
Camas Ghaoideil 214
Camas Mòr 86, 134, 137, 138, 139, 140, 142, 143, 144
Camas na Cille 162, 164
Camas na Geadaig 116
Camas na h-Annait 105
Camas na h-Uamha 159
Camas nan Gall 171, 172
Camas Sgiotaig 234
Camas Thairbearnais 245
Camas Torsa 225, 226, 228
Camasunary 170
Camus Bàn 117
Camus Castle 208
Camus Croise 208
Camusdarach 210
Camusfearna 207
Camus na Ruthaig 72
Camusrory 203
Camusteel 106
Canna 229, 236, 238, 242, 243, 244, 245, 246, 247
Canna Harbour 243
Caolas Mòr 103, 105, 198, 200
Caolas Scalpay 113, 115
Caol Fladda 121
Caol Mòr 119, 120
Caol Rona 121
Cape Wrath 15, 16, 17, 18, 19, 20
Cape Wrath lighthouse 18
Carbost 164, 168
Càrn Dearg 73
Càrn nan Sgeir 62, 73
Castle Tioram 221, 223, 224
cattle drovers 188, 199
Charles, Prince 176, 215
Charlestown 89, 90, 91, 92
Church Cave 121
Churchton Bay 116
Clach nan Ràmh 129
Clachtoll 45, 47, 48
Clashnessie 39, 40, 43, 45, 46, 48
Clearances, the 91, 171, 179
Cleats, the 140
Clett Island 148, 150
Clò Kearvaig, Stack 15, 18
Clò Mòr 16, 18
Cluas Deas 45
Cnoc a' Mhoil Bhàin 40
Cocoa Mountain 20
Coillegillie 100
Colbost 153, 154, 156
Columba 1400 centre 131
Corran 200
Corran a' Chinn Uachdaraich 116
Cove 88
Craig 92, 96
Creag na h-Eiginn 128
Crowlin Islands 100, 102, 103, 104, 118
Cúchulainn 179
Culloden Moor, Battle of 215

D

Darling, Dr Fraser 64
Diabaig 96
diatomite 125
Dibidil 240
divers (birds) 73
dolphins 141, 183
Donan, St 232
Dornie 196
Doune 206
Drumbeg 43
Duartmorc Point 32
Dùn Bàn 206
Dun Caan 120
Duncraig Castle 108
Dundonnell 73
Dùn Mòr 244
Dun Scaith Castle 178, 180
Duntulm 127, 131, 143
Duntulm Castle 130, 142, 143, 144
Dunvegan 111, 149, 151, 160
Dunvegan Castle 150, 154, 155
Dunvegan Head 153, 154, 155, 160
dynamite 125

E

eagles, golden 166
Eas a' Chual Aluinn 36
Easter Stoul 202
East Loch Tarbert 137
Eddrachillis Bay 39, 41
Eigg 229, 231, 232, 234, 235, 236, 242, 248
Eigg Pier 231, 236
Eilean a' Chait 108
Eilean a' Chait lighthouse 108
Eilean a' Chaoil 95
Eilean a' Ghaill 214
Eilean a' Ghamhna 42
Eilean an Ròin Beag 15, 20
Eilean an Ròin Mòr 20
Eilean an Taighe 136
Eilean an t-Snidhe 214
Eilean Bàn 109, 114, 118
Eilean Beag 104
Eilean Beag light 105
Eilean Buidhe 218
Eilean Collie 222
Eilean Creagach 148
Eilean Dearg 206
Eilean Donan Castle 191, 193, 194, 195, 196
Eilean Dubh 22, 62, 63, 73, 150
Eilean Fada Mòr 58
Eilean Fladday 121
Eilean Flodigarry 128
Eilean Giubhais 202
Eilean Horrisdale 90
Eilean Ighe 210
Eilean Meadhanach 104
Eilean Mhogh-sgeir 198, 200
Eilean Mhuire 136
Eilean Mòr 98, 104, 105
Eilean Mòr a' Bhàigh 137
Eilean Mullagrach 59, 60
Eilean na h-Àirde 176
Eilean nam Bairneach 218
Eilean nan Gobhar 218, 219
Eilean nan Seachd Seisrichean 227
Eilean Ràrsaidh 199, 200
Eilean Ruairidh 178
Eilean Shamadalain 206
Eilean Shona 221, 222
Eilean Thuilm 234
Eilean Tigh 121
Eilean Tioram 203
Eilean Trodday 127, 129, 130, 131, 132, 144
Elgol 169, 170, 172, 173, 176, 237, 238, 240, 241
Erbusaig Bay 109
Eyre Point 120

F

Fairy Flag, the 155
Faochag Bay 55
Fascadale 227
Fèith an Fheòir 73
Firemore 88
Fladda-chùain 132, 133, 134, 139, 140, 141, 142, 144
Fleming, Ian 198
Fleming, Valentine 198
Flodigarry Cliffs 129
Fraoch Eilean 199

G

Gaeilavore Island 140
Gaineamh Smo 88
Gairbh Eilein 150
Gairbh-sgeir 142
Gairloch 69, 88, 91, 92
Gallanach 234
Galmisdale 234, 235
Galta Mòr 136
Galtrigill Bay 154
Garbh Eilean 136
Garrisdale 245
Gearran Island 134
Geddes, 'Tex' 171
Geodha an Leth-roinn 46
Geodha nan Faochag 164
Geodha nan Gobhar 166
Geodha na Seamraig 18
Gille Brighde Café and Restaurant 96
Glas Eilean 194, 204
Glas Leac 22
Glas-leac Mòr 59, 60
Glenborrodale 226, 228
Glen Brittle 165, 166, 168, 242, 243, 244, 247
Glencoul Thrust 34
Glenelg 188
Glenuig 220, 221, 222, 224
Glenuig Inn, The 224
Glenuig jetty 220, 224
Gob a' Gheodha 82
Gob na Hoe 154
Gortenachullish 210, 212, 216, 236
Great Escape 100
'Great Stack of Handa' 27
Green Lady of the Castle, the 208
Greenstone Point 79, 80, 82, 84
Greshornish Point 146
Gruinard 69
Gruinard Bay 75, 76, 78
Gruinard Island 69, 75, 76, 77, 78
guillemots 27
Guirdil 238, 239

H

Haakon IV, Viking King 189
Hallaig 120
Halls, Monty 100
Hamish Macbeth 108
Handa Island 23, 25, 26, 28
Handa, Queen of 27
Harlosh Island 159, 162
Harlosh Point 162
Harpoon at a Venture 172
Harris, Rum 239
Hermit's Castle 52
Highlander 195
Holm Island 124, 125
Horse Island 62, 63
Hyskeir 248
Hyskeir lighthouse 245

I

Idrigill Point 164
Inbhir Ghil 240
Inner Sound 100
Inside Passage, The 113, 114
Inveralligin 95, 96
Inverarish 116, 122
Inver Dalavil 182
Inverie 191, 203, 204
Inver Tote 125
Iorcail 245
Isay Island 148, 150, 151
Island Years 64
Isle Martin 65, 66, 67
Isle of Canna Community Development Trust 246
Isle of Eigg Heritage Trust 233
Isle of Ewe 82, 84
Isle of Lewis 136
Isle of Lewis and Harris 136
Isle of Muck 228
Isle of Rum Community Trust 240
Isleornsay 185, 186, 190, 208
Isle Risto 59
Isle Ristol 55, 60

J

Jacobites, the 188, 195, 215, 224
James Bond – The World is Not Enough 195

K

Kearvaig Bay 18
Kerrachar 42
Kerrachar Bay 41
Kerrachar Man 42
Kilchoan 226, 228
Kildonan 232
Kilmaluag Bay 129
Kilmarie 173, 174, 176
Kilmory 238
Kilt Rock 111, 123, 126
Kinloch 237, 238, 240, 241
Kinlochbervie 15, 16, 20, 21, 22, 24
Kinloch Castle 240, 241
Kinloch Hourn 199
Kintail 193
Kintail Lodge Hotel 193, 195
Kirkaig Point 50
Kishorn Islands 100, 102, 110
Kishorn Seafood Bar 102
Knock Bay 208
Knock Castle 208
Knoydart 203
Kyleakin 113, 115, 117, 185, 187, 189, 190
Kyle Akin 106, 107, 113, 190
Kyle of Durness 19
Kyle of Lochalsh 69, 104, 106, 107, 109, 110
Kylerhea 186, 190
Kyle Rhea 111, 185, 186, 188, 189, 190
Kylesknoydart 203, 204
Kylesku 29, 32, 33, 36, 39, 44
Kylesku Bridge 29, 32, 35, 39, 42
Kylesku Hotel 32, 36, 37, 43, 44

L

Laide 73, 75, 76, 77, 78
Lampay Island 148, 150
Laxford Bay 21
Leac Innis nan Gobhar 76
Leac Mhòr 80
Leac Tressirnish 125
Leir Mhaodail 183
Leopard Man, The 189
Leppard, Tom 189
Lewisian Gneiss 22, 28, 30, 50, 121
L'Heureux 215
Little Loch Broom 71, 72, 73
Little Minch 133
Local Hero 210
Loch a' Chàirn Bhàin 32, 41, 43
Loch Ailort 191, 215, 217, 218, 219, 220
Loch Alsh 194
Loch an Ròin 22
Loch Beag 36

Loch Bracadale 156, 159, 160, 161, 162, 164
Loch Brittle 165, 166
Loch Broom 65, 67, 71, 73
Loch Ceann na Sàile 22
Loch Clash 16, 22
Loch Coruisk 170, 172
Loch Diabaig 95, 96
Loch Duich 191, 193, 194, 196
Loch Dunvegan 111, 149, 152, 154
Loch Eishort 111, 177, 178
Loch Ewe 69, 79, 80, 82, 83, 84, 85, 86, 88
Loch Eynort 166, 168
Loch Gairloch 89, 90
Loch Glencoul 33, 35, 36
Loch Glendhu 33, 34, 35
Loch Greshornish 145, 146, 148
Loch Harport 162, 165, 168
Loch Hourn 191, 197, 198, 200
Loch Inchard 22
Lochinver 37, 49, 50, 51, 52
Loch Inver 49, 50, 52
Lochinver Larder 52
Loch Kishorn 100
Loch Laxford 21, 23, 24
Loch Moidart 221, 223, 224
Loch Morar 203, 204
Loch na Bèiste 189
Loch na Cuilce 170
Loch nan Ceall 210, 212, 231, 232, 235
Loch nan Leachd 170
Loch nan Uamh 213, 215, 216, 220
Loch Nedd 41, 44
Loch Nevis 191, 201, 202, 203, 204
Loch Papadil 240
Loch Roe 51
Loch Scavaig 169, 170, 176
Loch Scresort 240
Loch Shieldaig 93, 95, 96, 98
Loch Slapin 176
Loch Snizort 146, 147
Loch Sunart 226, 228
Loch Torridon 69, 96, 98
Loch Torridon, Upper 94, 95
Loch Toscaig 104
Longa Island 86, 89, 90, 92
Long Beach 204
Lord Macdonald's Table 134, 140
Lorgill Bay 158, 160
Luinga Bheag 210
Luinga Mhòr 210

M

MacCrimmon pipers 163
MacCrimmon piping school 154
MacDonald, Clan 143, 155, 179, 208, 224, 235
MacDonald, Donald 27
MacDonald, Lord 179
Mackenzie, Clan 91
Maclean's Nose 226

MacLeod, Calum 122
MacLeod, Clan 92, 154, 163, 208, 235
MacLeod, Eric 42
MacLeod, Roderick 151
MacLeod's Maidens 159, 164
MacRae-Gilstrap, Lieutenant Colonel 195
Maid of Kylesku 34
Mallaig 191, 201, 202, 204, 205, 206, 212, 229, 232, 235, 236, 238, 240, 241, 242, 244, 247, 248
Mallaig ferry 183
Manish Point 122
Manx shearwaters 229, 242
Massacre Cave 235
Matheson, Sir Alexander 108
mausoleum, Rum 239
Maxwell, Gavin 114, 171, 172
Maxwell, George 207
McClean, Tom 202
Meall nan Caorach 62
Meall nan Gabhar 62, 63
Meanish 153, 155
Meanish Pier 155, 157, 158
Mellon Charles 82
Mellon Udrigle 64, 79, 80, 84
Melvaig 86, 88
mica mine, Knoydart 203
Midtown 85, 88
Minch, the 134, 136
Mingay island 148
Mingay Island 150
Mol Mòr 58
Moonen Bay 160
Morar 191, 209, 210, 212
Mountain bothies 38
Mountain Bothies Association (MBA) 38
Mountain Coffee Company café 88, 92
Muck 229, 231, 232, 234, 235, 236, 242, 248
MV Pharos 18

N

Nanny's café, Shieldaig 96
Narrows of Raasay 113, 122
Neist Point 111, 156, 157, 158, 160
Neist Point lighthouse 158
Nicolson, Adam 138
North Channel, Eilean Shona 222, 223
North Harbour of Scalpay 137

O

Ob Chuaig 98
Ob na h-Uamha 98
O'Gorgon 141
Oigh-sgeir 248
Oigh-sgeir lighthouse 245
Oldany Island 39, 40, 44, 48
Old Dornie 53, 55, 60
Old Forge, The 204
Old Inn, Charlestown 92

Old Man of Stoer 45, 46, 48
Old Man of Storr 117
Oldshore Beg 16, 20
Oldshoremore 16, 20
Ord 177, 178, 180
Ornsay 186
Ornsay lighthouse 186, 208
Oronsay Island 162
Otter Haven 189
otters 69, 90, 108, 109, 130, 189, 190, 199, 218, 226
Our Lady of Loch Nevis 204
Outer Hebrides 134

P

Pabay 115, 118
Peanmeanach 218
Pig Cliff 55
Piper's Cave 154, 162, 163
Plockton 69, 107, 108, 110
Point of Sleat 181, 182, 184
Point of Stoer 45, 47
Poll nam Partan 232
Poolewe 88
porpoises 162, 234
Port a' Chùil 183
Port an Eilein 26
Port an Luig Mhóir 176
Port Aslaig 186
Port a t-Sluichd 216
Port Bàn 227
Port Duntulm 131, 142
Port Erradale 86
Port Gobhlaig 129, 132, 144
Port Mìn 227
Port Mòr 234, 236
Port na Fagaich 183
Portnalong 161, 162, 164, 165, 168
Port nam Murrach 214
Portree 115, 117, 123, 124, 126
Portuairk 228
Potting Shed café, Applecross 102
Priest Hole 63
Priest Island 61, 62, 64, 84
Prince's Cairn 215, 216
puffins 136, 140, 141, 148, 244, 246

Q

Quinag 34, 40
Quiraing 116

R

Raasay 111, 115, 116, 117, 118, 119, 120, 121, 122
Ranald, Clan 224
Re-Aulay 101
Red Point 92
Red Roof Café, Holmisdale 156, 160
Reiff Bay 55
Reraig 193, 194, 196
Rhue 212, 213, 214, 216, 231, 232, 236
Rigg 125

Ring of Bright Water 114, 207
Rogheadh 148
Rona 111, 118, 119, 120, 121, 122
Rona lighthouse 121
Roshven 219
Rubha Àird Shlignich 226
Rubha an Daraich 199
Rubha an Dùin Bhàin 227
Rubha an Dùnain 244
Rubha Àrd Slisneach 206
Rubha Bàn 86
Rubha Beag 80
Rubh a' Bhàird 136
Rubha Cadail 65, 67
Rubha Cadail lighthouse 67
Rubha Chaolais 218
Rubh' a' Choin 82
Rubha Chuaig 100
Rubha Coigeach 53, 54, 56, 60
Rubha Crion 121, 122
Rubha Cruinn 168
Rubha Duilich 54
Rubha Garbh 164
Rubha Hunish 111, 127, 128, 130, 131, 132, 139
Rubh' Àird an t-Sionnaich 30
Rubha na h-Àirde Glaise 95
Rubha na h-Aiseig 127, 129, 130
Rubha na h-Easgainne 176
Rubha na' Leac 120
Rubha na Mòine 98
Rubha nan Sasan 84, 88
Rubh'an Dùnain 46
Rubha Raonuill 204
Rubha Rèidh 69, 82, 85, 86, 88
Rubha Rèidh lighthouse 86
Rubh Arisaig 214
Rubha Shamhnan Insir 238
Rubha Suisnish 178
Ru Bornesketaig 133, 139, 140, 142
Rudd, Mr C.D. 226
Rum 229, 236, 237, 238, 239, 242, 248

S

Sabhal Mòr Ostaig 208
Salen 225, 226, 228
Saltire 172
Samalaman Island 222
Sand 100, 101
Sandaig Bay 204
Sandaig Islands 186, 188, 190, 206, 208
Sanday 229, 242, 243, 244, 247
Sandwood Bay 17, 20
Scaith Castle 179
Scalpay 111, 115, 116, 118
Scarf Caves 117
Scáthach the Shadow 179
Sconser 118, 119, 120, 122
Scoraig 72
Scott, David 52
Scottish Outdoor Access Code 10
Scottish Wildlife Trust 28

Scott, Sir Walter 174
Scourie 25, 26, 28, 29, 30, 32, 37
sea eagles 75, 76, 86, 95, 98, 116, 146, 162, 165, 226, 229, 238, 239
sea eagles, Rum 242
seal-maidens, the 183
seals 90, 98, 121, 136, 147, 150, 151, 154, 162, 198, 199, 212, 214, 218, 245
Sea Room: An Island Life 138
sea urchins 105
Sgeir Leathan 198
Sgeir na h-Èircann 128
Sgeir nam Biast 151
Sgeir nan Sgarbh 245
Sgeiteadh 166
Sgùrr of Eigg 232
Shark Bay 32
Shiant Islands 133, 134, 136, 137, 138
Shiel Bridge 196
Shieldaig 69, 93, 94, 96, 97, 98, 102
Shieldaig Island 94, 95, 98
singing sands 234
Skye 111, 114, 115, 116, 123, 132, 134, 142, 229, 238, 240, 244
Skye Bridge 106, 109, 115, 118, 185, 187, 190
Skye Diatomite Company 125
Slaggan 82
Slaggan Bay 80, 82, 84
Small Isles, The 229
Smirisary 222
Soay 168, 169, 172
Soay Island 170
Soay Shark Fisheries 170, 171
Soay Sound 170, 172
Sound of Arisaig 213, 214, 215, 216
Sound of Handa 25, 27, 28
Sound of Raasay 124
Sound of Scalpay 133, 137
Sound of Shiant 133, 136, 137
Sound of Sleat 186, 191, 205, 206, 208
Sourlies 203
South Ascrib 147
South Channel, Eilean Shona 223
South Tarbet Bay 204
Soyea Island 50, 52
Spar Cave 173, 174, 176
Split Rock 47
Stac a' Bhothain 147
Stac an Tuill 166
Stac Buidhe 129
Stack Clò Kearvaig 15, 18
Staffin 123, 126, 127, 128, 131, 132, 144
Staffin Island 128
Stattic Point 73
Stein 145, 148, 149, 151, 152
Stevenson, Alun 227
Stevenson, David 86, 208
Stevenson, Robert Louis 227
Stevenson, Thomas 208
St Martin 66
Stoer lighthouse 45

Storr Lochs Power Station 124
Strathaird Peninsula 173
Strome Islands 110
Stuart, Charles Edward 215
Suilven 50
Summer Isles 57, 58, 59, 60, 62, 63, 64, 73, 84
Summer Isles - North 57
Summer Isles - South 61

T

Talisker 111, 165
Talisker Bay 166, 168
Talisker Point 168
Talisker whisky distillery 164, 168
Tanera Beg 58, 59, 60
Tanera Mòr 58, 60
Tarbert 134, 136, 138
Tarbert Bay 245
Tarbet 28, 203
Tarbet Loch Nevis 204
Tarner Island 162
Tarskavaig 180, 181, 184
Tarskavaig Bay 182
The Anchorage 58
Three Chimneys restaurant 154, 156
Tianavaig 116, 118
Tigh an Quay 58
Toll Eilean a' Chlèrich (Priest Hole) 63
Tomb 174
Tormore 183
Torridon 93
Torridonian Sandstone 50, 62
Torridon village 96
Toscaig 103, 104, 105, 106
Totaig 194
Tulm Bay 141, 143
Tulm Island 130, 142

U

Uags bothy 100, 104
Uamh Fhraing 235
Uamh Oir 142
Uig 137, 138, 143
Ullapool 65, 67, 68, 69

V

Van Arman, Dr 63

W

Wade, General George 188
Waternish Point 145, 146, 148
Wester Ross 69
whales 128, 141, 162, 232, 238
Wiay Island 159, 160, 162, 164
William Nicol 186
Wreck Bay 239

X

X-Craft submarine 37

OCEAN

Adventure Suit

Explorer Zip

Explorer Deck

PEAK UK
www.peakuk.com

PERFORMANCE ENHANCING PADDLING EQUIPMENT

Pete Astles. Spurn Head. Image: Paul Ramsdale

SEA KAYAK
PLOCKTON

Sea kayaking for all levels from the beautiful village of Plockton

seakayakplockton.co.uk
Tel: 01599 544422

NORWEST SEA KAYAKING

Guiding | Hire, Drop-off and Pick-up from Gairloch to Durness

Based in Ullapool, Summer Isles & Assynt

T: 07900 641860
E: info@norwestseakayaking.com
www.norwestseakayaking.com

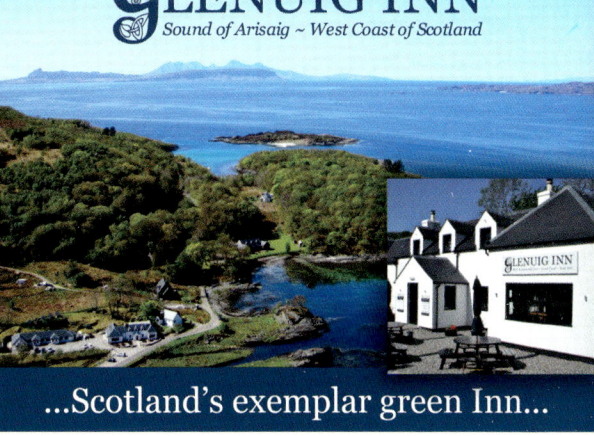

GLENUIG INN
Sound of Arisaig ~ West Coast of Scotland

...Scotland's exemplar green Inn...

Open All Day Every Day All year
Modern Scottish Food & Real Ales
Gluten-free & Vegetarian
In house Smokery
Ensuite Rooms
Bunkhouse
Dog-friendly
Drying Room
Visitor Yacht Moorings
Diver's Air Compressor
Sea-kayaking Guiding & Coaching

Glenuig Inn Glenuig PH38 4NG
01687 470 219 | www.glenuig.com | stay@glenuig.com